Housing in Holland

ISBN 90 5594 252 9 / NUGI 661

Housing in Holland

XPAT MEDIA

Contents

Preface

Home – is it a place of the heart, a residence in mind and memory, or where you are actually occupying space at this moment in time? *Mi casa es tu casa*, 'east west – home is best', home is where the heart is', 'hearth and home', 'a man's home is his castle' ... all expressions concerning the state of being 'at home'; comfortable, safe, warm and dry. In short, a shelter (along with food) is one of life's basic tenants.

So, now you are moving to or already are in the Netherlands and needing a place to stay, to hang your hat, to warm your heart, to relax, to experience family 'quality time', to escape, to LIVE etc.

Finding accommodation is often easier said than done. The dream of the 'Perfect' house may only exist in your own imagination. Standards may be quite different to what you are used to in your home country, as well as the system of rules and regulations to finding your new living quarters in the Netherlands.

This book, *Housing in Holland*, was developed in order to guide the English-speaking foreigner (you) through the process involved in rentals or purchase, to present a list of options, to explain financing, to help in securing legitimate assistance with rental or purchase properties, as well as contracting specialists for home repairs or remodelling. Insurances for the renter or homeowner are explained, as are the extra costs, levies and taxes encountered here in Holland.

We have attempted to include something for everyone, and have included a range of options that varies from rooms for students, studios, maisonettes, apartments, houses – be it rental or purchase and from very inexpensive with government subsidies to super deluxe properties that start with a price tag of over 1 million euros. For good measure we've also included information on living in houseboats, historical monuments, castles and windmills!

Wherever you may feel your 'home' to be, we sincerely hope that *Housing in Holland* will provide you with the assistance you may need and answer your queries regarding finding a place here to live. Likewise, our hope is to encourage you in making your home in Holland, whether on a temporary or more permanent basis. Remember that your commitment to happiness and contentment as stated in 'home is where the heart is' is what you make of your time here. You might even just find yourself losing your heart to the wonderful life you enjoy while living in Holland.

Connie Moser
Editor

1 Understanding the Dutch Property Market: A Historical and current Market review

Holland...

Holland – windmills, tulips, cheese and chocolate, Delft blue, canals ... what's beyond the stereotypes? Is living here really as charming and picturesque as the images would lead one to believe? The country is as flat as a pancake, has a maritime climate where it rains more than 65 cm (30 inches) per year, is a study in contradictions – and you may find, on occasion, that it is frustratingly difficult to deal with bureaucracy, the climate, and the Dutch.

This tiny country – you practically need a magnifying glass to locate it on the map! – is bordered by Belgium, and Germany, and is well-known as a nation with a rich trading history.

Often referred to as the 'gateway to Europe', 'Holland' – or the Netherlands as it is officially known, (Holland refers to the provinces of North and South Holland, and *Hollands* is the 'Dutch' language) – constitutes some 16 million people, 4 million cows and 16 million bicycles! Encompassing some 16,000 square miles, the Netherlands is the 2nd most densely populated country in the world, after Hong Kong, with an average of 2,000 people per square kilometer. More than half of these people live in the provinces of North and South Holland, in what is known as the 'Randstad' area, which includes Amsterdam, The Hague, Utrecht and Rotterdam.

The saying goes that 'God made the world, but the Dutch made Holland'. Indeed, two-fifths of the land is below sea level and, after centuries of fighting against the water, protecting their land with dikes and turning sea into land, the Dutch have managed to reclaim 25% of the land mass. As early as the 7th century, the familiar windmills were in use to drain away the water. A complex system of dikes and pumping stations keeps the land dry today.

In the past, the Dutch were taxed according to how wide the houses were, so there was (and still is today) the tendency to build them narrow and deep, especially in the cities. Additionally there was a glass tax at one point in time, so the windows were also kept small.

So What?

So what does this have to do with finding a house, you may ask? Three important factors are:

- lack of space – too many people live in too small of a country in too little space
- lack of houses – not enough new homes are being built or delivered on time
- lack of money – prices, driven upwards by shortages, are often unaffordable.

Understanding the Dutch Property Market

Small – think small, build small – traditionally Dutch houses have been small. The very wealthy lived in mansions on estates (called *landgoederen*), some in castles; the wealthy merchants divided their time between magnificent canal houses or merchant homes in the city, and their country estates in the summer months. The farmers lived in small farmhouses with a construction whereby the house was usually connected to the barn, providing easy access to the animals and natural heating emanating from the animals. Fishing villages also traditionally had very tiny houses. Small homes were built for the middle to lower working classes, and the urban poor lived in the very smallest of all, or in tiny flats as they still do today.

We can divide the current Dutch housing market into three categories; namely somewhat expensive, really expensive and ridiculously expensive:

- the least expensive housing sector, which falls below € 550, and is mostly controlled by *woningbouwverenigingen* (housing associations) and private landlords
- the *geliberaliseerde huursector*, or liberated rental sector, which has prices from € 550 to € 1,000 and is in the hands of larger real estate firms that manage and/or own the properties, as well as the higher priced rentals of *woningbouwverenigingen*
- the high end of the housing market, which is mostly the expat market, and consists of the privately owned luxury rentals of canal houses, villas, and furnished or unfurnished apartments and homes.

Woningbouwverenigingen – Housing Associations

A large portion of the least expensive houses in the Netherlands are under the control of numerous *woningbouwverenigingen* which are non-governmental associations of housing corporations, individually referred to as a *woningbouwcorporatie*.

Woningbouw Corporations or Housing Associations are private non-profit organizations that manage an enormous amount of the rental properties in the Netherlands, especially in the Randstad region. *Woningbouwverenigingen* were set up at the end of the 19th century for the purpose of providing affordable housing for workers. These homes are often known as *arbeiderswoningen*, or worker's homes. Generally speaking, they are small, unimaginative, built of lesser quality materials, and have aged inelegantly, many having been built prior to WWII. In the post-war period, much needed smaller housing was also built to be affordable, resulting in row after row of *rijtjeshuizen*, or row homes, that were quickly constructed. People were glad to have somewhere to live. These inexpensive houses are so much in demand that waiting lists of a few years are not uncommon.

Occasionally some of the houses from a housing association are offered for sale, usually to a sitting tenant, who is given the option to buy. Due to the fact that the sale of these properties is controlled there is not much movement in this sector – which also has its influence on the real estate market. People who have had to wait a very long time (sometimes years), to become eligible for this inexpensive housing, many of whom enjoy subsidy payments as well, are reluctant (understandably so) to move upwards and onwards to more expensive rentals or to purchase homes of their own. They tend to stay put. This means that those on the waiting list have to wait even longer.

Those people looking for a profit and a move often attempt to *onderverhuur* or sub-let these properties – especially to unsuspecting foreigners and usually at highly inflated prices. Not only is this illegal, you will find your self in serious trouble when you go to register at the *bevolkingsregister* (population register) and discover that you have no right to live there and are an illegal renter. Some people will even attempt to rent out properties that are not even available for rent!

In order to be able to rent from a housing corporation you must meet certain eligibility criteria. You must have a residence permit in order to qualify and there is a certain ceiling placed on the amount of income you may earn. Most expatriates are therefore not eligible for lower income housing, as their salaries tend to be high enough to permit housing choices in other sectors, so that they will find themselves looking in the high end of the market. If you are fortunate enough to have your company pay for your housing this may not concern you too very much, however, for a large percentage of the expatriate population, especially amongst younger people just starting their careers and European Union workers who do not qualify for expatriate status, the choices are rather limited and the search may be difficult.

See chapters 2 *Housing – Rentals* and 3 *Housing in Amsterdam* for more details.

There does seem to be change in recent times towards more home purchases. Given the increase in prices in the property market, and the cost of renting compared with home ownership, many more people are now wanting to purchase rather than rent. Many *woningbouwcorporations* are being pressured to sell off some of their holdings. The lack of available new housing has further added to the problem of a poor selection of rentals (see our paragraph on VINEX-houses further on). In a good economy, fewer people, thankfully appreciative for their good salaries, meet the salary eligibility criteria for the *woningbouwverenigingen* properties, which means that some associations now have an overstock of small properties in a sector which is less in demand. The concentration in many cities of cheap, affordable housing has also caused an imbalance in the market. There just are not enough mid-range priced apartments or houses for rent.

That being said, many people are looking to purchase homes of their own, and the shortages have driven the prices up. All this activity on the housing market has resulted in a property boom in recent years. Over the past ten years prices have more than doubled in some cities, and in the past three years some prices have increased as much as 35% in certain markets. Again, this is the old supply-and-demand story, coupled with the dream of many young people of becoming homeowners.

Liberalized Market

In the liberalized markets very few houses are in the hands of private landlords. Always be cautious of cards hanging up in grocery stores or advertisements in the newspaper. It is best to go through a *makelaar* or housing agency to be certain you are renting legally. They will first check the *bevolkingsregister* and not offer you illegal rentals.

Expat Market

Renting from Private Owners

In the expatriate markets there are no restrictions, basically if you have the money and are willing to pay, you can rent it – *if* it is available. Just because you may have your heart set on a six-bedroom house with a garage, gardens and swimming pool, if no such place is available then no amount of money is going to produce a rental that just does not exist.

More than 25% of the expat housing market is in the hands of private persons who rent out (part) of their property. For these houses the same rules apply as for the houses from the housing associations. Private owners may choose – within the limits of the rules of the city council – whom they will rent their houses out to. The market of private owners who rent out is not transparent at all.

Finding something in this market will probably work through trial and error. There are numerous ways to find private owners, sometimes through the newspapers. Usually the fastest way to find something is through the circle of people around you. Tell everyone that you are looking for a place to live. Sometimes estate agents will be able to assist you fairly quickly, though be prepared for investing some time into your search.

It has been said that corporations that were willing to pay generous housing allowances for their employees have helped to drive up the prices to the level they are today. While this may have contributed in part to the current situation, a vast majority of renters are paying out of pocket.

As the economy has shifted towards recession, Human Resource departments are cutting back, and allowances are not what they were in times past. There was however a lot of speculative building on the part of get-rich-quick homeowners who have built luxury apartments that are overpriced in the current market and remain empty. Tax benefits for landlords of rental properties and for those wishing to rent out second homes have been subject to some changes recently, now making it less interesting from a tax perspective to rent out rooms.

Other Factors

Economic developments, both in Holland and on a global scale, the political situation in the Netherlands, in Europe, and in the rest of the world, the investment climate of business in the Netherlands, the number of new expatriate transfers, the new euro currency... all these factors have some influence on the housing market. What new policies for continued cooperation amongst EU-nations will be implemented? What will the various stock and bond markets do? What is the expected level of unemployment this year? As cost of living increases, what can we look forward to? We live in a complex society. And, as you have read, there are numerous contributing factors, and it is not a simple story to explain why things are as they are – but the problem of housing is being addressed.

The Dutch are attempting to meet the housing demand, and have been studying the problem for some time. New houses have been constructed, and more are in the planning stages.

VINEX Houses

At the end of 1993, plans having been discussed through the 1980s, the government made a report on density and population (*Vierde Nota Ruimtelijke Ordening Extra*, or VINEX) and came up with a ten year-building plan to provide modest housing for the masses. The goal was to provide 700,000 new homes in selected locations throughout the country, which were to be delivered before 2005. These VINEX homes, in VINEX locations, no longer conform to the wishes of the market, and there are wide discrepancies in the quality and types of materials used.

Only half of the proposed houses have been delivered. They appear to be selling well, and even resold at profit, which may indicate that they may be undervalued – however, in a market where more people are demanding the construction of luxury developments with space, gardens and even garages it is hard to say if there will be a shift in the types of projects being offered. Some new housing choices are not even what people want, and some units remain unsold. Also, complaints have been lodged that some of the new VINEX housing developments are located in areas far removed from the city, for instance in the Flevopolder (which is reclaimed land northeast of Amsterdam).

These locations entail long commutes. Additionally, the lack of an infrastructure containing restaurants, schools, shops, churches and sports facilities does not give these developments the same feel and familiarity one has in traditional neighborhoods. It may take many more years for this type of infrastructure to develop, and many argue that these types of facilities should have been planned into the original design to make these new developments more livable. Accessibility to facilities such as grocery stores, banks and hospitals necessitates the use of public transportation or of purchasing an automobile. The government, however, staunchly defends the planning and execution of the projects, and is convinced they will be successful and that the infrastructure that is lacking will be created in time. For info see:

www.vinexonsite.nl – Vinex projects
www.vinex-locaties.nl – locations for proposed Vinex projects

Available Housing: Supply & Demand

In the cities, especially where the demand is the greatest and supply is limited, there tends to be a 'seller's market': you have to make a choice from a limited pool of offerings. If financial limitations further restrict your choice, you will find yourself forced to reevaluate your needs and certainly to adjust your expectations. Dutch houses are small, and what is affordable or available may be much smaller than you are used to.

If you do not see something immediately and have the time to look longer, or come back at a later date on another house hunting trip, by all means do so. The market is in a constant state of flux, and next time around there may be something available that is more in keeping with what you want. Some people will rent for one year and keep their ears open with regard to colleagues or friends moving out. There is always someone who knows someone who is moving.

Traditionally, most properties come on the market towards the end of the school year, with families who know they will be leaving in the summer giving notice to vacate as early as April or May. Posting a notice at the international school asking to be informed of upcoming moves or just 'hearing it through the grapevine' via the school parents network may bring you some good leads for new housing.

The most sage advice that many are given is to look at your temporary stay here in the Netherlands as an adventure as well as a challenge. You may be living differently, perhaps smaller than hoped for, but then again, it's all new and different. You may even decide to choose something entirely different than you are used to, and that is part of the cultural learning as well as the fun of living in another country; making the most of it and of your experiences.

2

2 Housing – Rentals

One of the first things you will want to do is find a place to live. Obviously you will need to consider a few things, such as do you want to rent or do you want to buy? If you are interested in buying property please see Chapter 6 – *Purchasing a House in Holland*.
If you have decided to rent, consider what you want for a rental property. Do you want to rent a room, a studio apartment (which is a very, very small flat) or an apartment? And how large? How about a house? What type of house? Free standing (*vrijstaand*), Semi-detached (*twee onder één kap*), a detached country house or villa, or perhaps even a houseboat (*woonboot*)! You may have even thought about a bungalow park or a camping site with caravans (or even tents) however, you should know that vacation homes cannot be used as a primary residential address. And what's more: do you want furnished, semi-furnished or unfurnished?

House hunting is somewhat time consuming, occasionally nerve wracking and often frustrating, but in the end you get to see a number of great and maybe not so great places to live, so you will most likely be happy to find a place to call your own and have a 'home' here in your home away from home!

A. Where to Begin – Where to Look?

There are a number of possibilities to pursue when looking for a place to live, ranging from housing agencies to word-of-mouth. (For a complete list of Resources refer to our *Looking for Housing – Resource Page*): Rentals come under the heading of *te huur* (to rent or to hire) Houses for sale are *te koop* (to buy or purchase)

- **housing agencies** have multiple listings and often specialize in the expatriate market. They can take care of all negotiations, showing of properties, and contracts

- *makelaars* or **estate agents** are often registered with the NVM or VBO and are licensed professionals. It is no longer required to be professionally licensed to deal in real estate. Those who are licensed have undergone a lengthy study. If you are considering purchasing a house, you will benefit greatly from their expert assistance. They can take care of all aspects of sales and rentals, negotiations, showing of properties, and contracts
- ***woningbouwverenigingen*** handle housing which they own in their association and maintain strict rules on who is eligible to rent. Much of this is so-called social living and there are long waiting lists, in some areas up to seven years
- **student housing organizations** are really not an option, as there is such a shortage for students that they are almost not worth considering unless you are a student yourself
- the **media** might also be worth your while; you will find a reference list of newspapers (including the *Woonkrant*), magazines and Internet sites on our *Looking for Housing – Resource Page*. There is also a TV-program *Woon Magazine* as well as listings on teletext (a feature included on your European television set for local and international networks, whereby you can leaf through hundreds of pages to find information on the weather, traffic, housing, horoscopes, stock markets and more. A sort of TV-WAP option). Keep in mind, that in a competitive and fast-moving market, listings in the newspaper or on the Internet may not be current
- occasionally you will hear about a property by **word-of-mouth**, perhaps through a colleague, but this could be unreliable information or it could be already rented or sold by the time you check into it.

Though the list is extensive, it is advisable, in order to save time and much headache, to register with a housing agency or an estate agent office. These are professionals who know the current housing market and can give you good advice. They often also have computerized lists of available properties.

For information on the Rentals of rooms, see chapter 3 on *Rooms in Amsterdam* and the Resource page websites in chapter 4.

First Steps When Looking For an Agent

You will have to decide whether you want to attempt to find a place on your own (a daunting and time consuming endeavor at best!), or if you want to enlist the assistance of a housing agency representative (see our paragraph on *Housing Agencies*) or an estate agent (*makelaar*). Rental and real estate agencies charge a commission by percentage, or a flat fee equal to one month's rent for their services. In most cases, they require you to pay their fee directly. However, please be advised that you should have this clarified before signing or verbally agreeing to any contract. The contract for the house or flat / apartment you decide to rent (or buy) will be in Dutch – which you may not be able to read, but it will be legally valid nevertheless. You will need to specifically request a copy of the conditions in English, as these are not always provided. If you have questions, ASK!

Advantages

Hiring an agent is a good idea. They can provide valuable information about the various neighborhoods in which you might be considering living, show the shopping areas, conduct negotiations for you, and tell you things about the property that should be disclosed.

Finding an Agent

A listing of estate agents can be found through their professional organizations: You may contact the Netherlands Estate Agents Foundation (*Nederlandse Vereniging van Makelaars in onroerende goederen* or NVM) or the VBO-*makelaars* (*Vereniging Bemiddeling Onroerend Goed*) or MVA-*makelaars* (*Makelaar Vereniging Amsterdam*). They will supply you with a list of members throughout the country, though it might be easier to search via region on the Internet for a listing of local agents, or through www.makelaar.lokaalzoeken.nl.

When choosing an estate agent it is wise to first have a look at their offices and see if everything looks well-documented, and to see what your impressions are. You should also enquire as to the number of estate agents employed by the agency, what kind of services they offer you, and if they are flexible. Will it be possible for instance to view properties in the evening or on the weekend? What is their buy-to-sell ratio, or for rentals, what number of rental properties do they maintain?

Talk to colleagues about their experiences if you want to increase your chances of great service and friendly treatment. Personal recommendations at least give you some idea of how that specific agency works. You may of course check which agencies that are listed in the area where you wish to look by just walking in or making an appointment. That being said, Amsterdam, Rotterdam, Utrecht, Maastricht or any other large city will involve more legwork to cover the distances.
A good map of the area is essential.

Search Instruments

Makelaars have a number of *zoekinstrumenten* (search instruments) to aid them, such as the Internet, connections with other colleagues in the branch (including information exchange programs), notaries and banks. Oftentimes, word-of-mouth recommendations are an excellent form of referral. An estate agent with a well-connected network can operate more efficiently on your behalf.

English-Language Booklet

The NVM publishes a folder entitled 'Your Ten Questions' about viewings, negotiations, purchase agreements, etc. and is in the process of updating their information and adding an English section to their website. For more information call 030 608 51 85 and ask for Consumer information services (*Consumenten Voorlichting*).

Housing Agencies

Most rental agencies do not work weekends or evenings. Therefore, house hunting will most likely have to be done during the week. We suggest you start as soon as you arrive. House hunting in Holland can be different from what you are used to.

Private Listings

An agency will know from their own private listings when one of their tenants is leaving as a consequence of which an apartment will be coming on the market once again. They will generally start showing these apartments as soon as the current renter has indicated plans to vacate. This may mean a wait of one or two months for you, so always ask when the occupancy date will be. Further, you may get lucky and hear about a colleague or some other contact who is moving out.

Fishing in the Same Pool

It is worthwhile knowing that most rental agencies are 'fishing in the same pool' and offer the same listings. Some do have clients of their own, but most agencies have access to one another's portfolios. Therefore it is not of much use to approach all of the agencies. To contact only one or two should be sufficient. You will need to inform them when you have approached and set to work for you other agencies as well. This way you can avoid that the same possibilities are offered to you twice – thereby wasting both your time and theirs. A second viewing of the same house offered to you by another agency cannot be of much use to you.

Newspapers

Aside from a house search through an agency, you could also scan the housing advertisements in the Wednesday edition of the newspaper *De Telegraaf* or the Thursday edition of the advertising paper *Via Via*. Try to buy the *Via Via* at the earliest in the morning so you will be among the first respondents to the ads you are interested in. However, we warn you to be extremely careful with any offers found in this way. You could always come across a less trustworthy broker who may try to take advantage of the fact that you are new to this country and relatively unaware of the rules of the game. Therefore be vigilant and careful. Ask for advice from your relocation company if you are fortunate enough to have assistance with securing housing.

B. Getting Started

The following is a 'Renters Shortlist' of procedures and guidelines for finding your new home: in order to make the best use of your time in a competitive housing market, please read through the following so you will be aware of the process. Generally your house hunting will involve some consistent efforts on your part to remain pro-active in the search. It can take some time, so we would encourage you to be patient, as well as pro-active.

What Are You Looking For?

Make a specific list of all your requirements as well as your preferences for yourself and for the estate agent. Specify which items are absolutes, and which items are negotiable. For example, if you definitely need two bedrooms but do not mind which floor you are located on, or if there is a fireplace in the apartment.
To begin looking for housing based on your requests, you will need to consider things such as the location, size, number of bedrooms, garden, number of family members, will there be pets, is it close to schools, etc. Do you want to live in the city center of downtown Amsterdam, or do you prefer something more suburban? How about the life in a small village? Do you want to live near other colleagues or close to the office?
Also make sure you make note of room dimensions, especially if you are planning to ship large furniture. It may not all fit and you may need to leave some pieces in storage in your home country. Storage spaces here are in great demand and hard to come by.

Costs

A major determining factor is money. You will need to make an informed and valid decision based on your budget / housing allowance coupled with your life-style. Be realistic. There are many additional costs to living in Holland as you will read in section H (see further on: *Extra Costs, Levies and Taxes*). It is therefore advisable not to over-extend yourself. You will most certainly want to enjoy living here and having the means to do so as well.

When Are You Available?

You will be requested to provide the dates on which you are available for house hunting (a minimum of three days in a row). It would be most convenient if you could come up with a first and a second choice of preferred house hunting dates. The restrictions here are housing availability as well as other people house hunting, as a result of which the agents are in demand for viewings and are therefore pretty busy. During your house hunt you are kindly requested not to plan any meetings.

House hunting will take place during weekdays only, since the realtors in the Netherlands (mostly) do not work during the weekends.

Viewing the Properties

Once you have prepared your list of the reputable agencies that you wish to contact, they will then show you available properties. When you are free for house hunting over an extended period, you will generally be able to view a greater number of selections. The more active you are, the better your chances are of success.
Please be advised that the price class you are looking in and the availability of properties in a particular price class are deciding factors. Sometimes it may be necessary to re-adjust your 'wish list' in order to find a suitable dwelling. Some items can be negotiated with the landlord. Just ASK, you may be able to work something out. Landlords may be willing to remove some pieces you do not wish to use (or those that are just too ugly for words!) or possibly include some items that you will need, such as a washer or dryer.
Utilities are almost always your own responsibility. Make sure you ask who pays gas, lights, water, and cable connections (see *Rental Contracts*, section D).

Types of Rental Properties

Different combinations are possible, depending on the landlord.

a. Unfurnished (*Ongemeubileerd*). This is the barest of necessities – namely, empty. Generally nothing much is included here, no carpeting, no curtains, often a minimum of or no appliances and no utilities
b. Semi-furnished (*Gestoffeerd*). Semi-furnished contains some furnishings and carpeting, and possibly a few appliances. Keep in mind to ask for a complete list of what is included. Utility inclusion or exclusion depends on the landlord
c. Furnished (*Gemeubileerd*). Everything has been taken care of and the apartment is ready to be moved into. It may contain any combination of furniture, appliances, curtains, light fixtures, carpets, cutlery and dishes, television, and/or stereo, kitchen appliances such as microwave, dishwasher, refrigerator, and sometimes even bed linens and blankets or down feather beds. Make sure to ask for a complete inventory list before agreeing to anything. If there is anything missing, negotiate it before you sign the lease. Utilities (usually) included.

What to Keep in Mind

When you *do* make the decision to take an apartment or house for rent there are important things for you to be aware of. We will go into more detail on some of these as we go through this chapter:

1. Your word is your bond. If you say you will take the property, it is legally binding. Make certain that you are sure before saying 'yes'.

2. Houses are small in Holland. Space is limited, and apartments and houses will be much smaller than you may have expected. (Next to Hong Kong, the Netherlands is the 2nd most densely populated country in the world, and one of the smallest!) There is a great deal of demand for housing, and a limited supply in the Randstad region. Therefore, if something becomes available that is within your budget, you will not have a lot of time to think about it. If it is suitable and you can live with the setup, our advice is to take it. Your time allotment for living in a hotel is probably limited. You will want to be settled into your new home as soon as possible. You may also decide to rent for one year, allowing yourself the time to look further.

3. Payment. You will not receive the key if you have not paid beforehand. No exceptions.
   Keep in mind that the first month's rental fee, the security deposit and the commission to the estate agent must have been paid before you may move in. Generally an amount equivalent to one or two month's rent is required for the deposit. The commission is either 8% of the yearly rental fee, or one month's rental fee excluding the 19% VAT (BTW).

4. The landlord will want to be paid as soon as possible. Try to open a bank account here so that the funds can be transferred quickly. It is advisable to deposit an amount equivalent to four months rental fee in order to cover your initial start-up costs for housing.

5. The landlord absolutely decides when you can move in, not you.

6. Rental contracts generally are beginning from the 1st of the month or the 15th of the month. If you can't move in yet, or you have a week of training, or your furniture is still in customs, you cannot simply have the rent begin a week or so later. You agree to rent the property for a specified time (contractual agreement) whether you are physically present or not. Sometimes you just need to lose some days of use. If you do not agree to these terms, they will simply rent the property out to someone else.

7. Landlords do not like to sit on empty properties, so the turnover is generally fairly quick. In the odd event that there is a week overlap where you could take possession earlier (if the flat becomes empty earlier) your rental billing will reflect the extra week in addition to the terms of your contract. (Yes, this means the landlord 'double dips' for that week.)

8. Responsibilities of renter and of landlord are spelled out in the conditions of your rental contract. Be sure you read the contract and that you understand

your responsibilities. Please note who you need to call in case of damage (especially leakage), broken windows, or in case the heat is not working. Keep these numbers handy.

9. Should you find something to your liking, please ask the realtor or your relocation service to pre-scan your rental agreement and, after the pre-scan, ask the realtor to draw up the contracts. Do not forget that under Dutch law a verbal agreement is a binding agreement. Thus, if you accept verbally, you cannot get out of the agreement afterwards.

10. Decorating changes *must be approved*! You may not paint walls, wallpaper or make changes to the property without express permission from the landlord. If you are granted permission, you may be asked to return the property to its original state when you move out, which is then an added expense for yourself, plus the time it will require to repaint.

11. Ending your rental contract (*opzegging huur*): always do this in writing and send it by registered mail to the landlord, at least two months ahead of the date you wish to move out. If you do not inform the landlord that you no longer wish to continue renting the property, the rental contract will 'silently continue' just the same (*stilzwijgend doorgaan*). This means you will still have to pay, and lose out on the two months rent (your deposit).

12. IMPORTANT: Sharing: If you decide to share the rental of a property with a colleague, make sure that both of your names appear on the rental contract. This is for your own protection, so that if, for instance, your 'roommate' decides to leave or is transferred, you will still have the right to remain living in the apartment. In order to register at the Town Hall Register (the *bevolkingsregister* of the *gemeentehuis*), you will need to give proof (rental contract) that you are living at that address.

C. Making the Deal

Let the estate agent do the talking for you. Do not act like you like the apartment or house too much (or want it desperately) as this will not work in your favor when negotiating the price. Any obvious flaws could be noted on paper and discussed with your agent outside, not in the presence of the renting agent. Do not say immediately out loud: 'OH YES! I WANT IT!' Verbal contracts are legally binding so it is best to just be quiet at this juncture. Also, do not speak to the renting agent or landlord without having your rental agent present before the deal has been officially concluded.

A Few Details

Before you can 'sign off' on your contract, a few things need to be taken care of. When you have finally found the ideal apartment or house you will need to:

a. negotiate the price on any items you may wish to have included that are not readily apparent
b. ask for a complete inventory list
c. agree on a firm move-in date
d. reach an agreement for the landlord to perform necessary repairs (before you move in!)
e. arrange new painting if necessary or changes to paint color (if possible)
f. arrange professional cleaning services before you take tenancy.

Your agent will take care of these and further negotiations and of the drawing up of the contract. That is what they get paid for.

And, remember, be certain of the definite availability of the property or you could find yourself sitting in a hotel.

Required Documents

You will need to provide documents and funds on some or all of the items listed below:

- a copy of your employment contract, to prove you are gainfully employed and have sufficient income
- one month's rent as a deposit – sometimes two (or even three) months. Sometimes a bank guarantee in lieu of a cash deposit is sufficient
- the first months rent, and possibly the last month's rent
- the fee for your agent, generally equivalent to one month's rent
- a copy of passport and/or your residence permit for identification.

Your agent will take care of most of the paperwork for you.

Inventory Lists

If an inventory list has not been provided, make your own list before you move in, making note of any pre-existing damages to the floors, walls, appliances, bathroom fixtures, cracks, floors, furniture as well as leaky faucets or cracked window glass. If the house or apartment is furnished or semi-furnished, make sure everything has actually been included on the list, noting the present condition of these items. (See chapter 9 on *Inspections*).

D. Rental Contracts

Having everything on paper is your best reference for rights and obligations and all prevailing terms agreed upon by both parties. A property services specialist from your relocation company can screen the contract for you, to make sure that everything is correct and that your best interests are protected. Please do inform the agency beforehand that prior to your signing anything, the rental agreement will first be screened by your relocation advisor. Most will offer to pre-screen contracts for you.

Once again, we repeat: a verbal contract is binding under Dutch law. Therefore, unless you are absolutely sure you will take the property, do not make any written or verbal commitment! Whether you have arranged the contract on your own, or with the help of your estate agent, please make sure you understand the contract before signing anything. Once you have signed, you are legally bound under Dutch law.

Read the following for tips and information.

Arranging Rent Payment

Since a bank usually needs three days to process a rental transfer, please arrange for it to be paid three days in advance of the date that it is due. A phone transfer (*telefonische overboeking*) will guarantee that the funds are deposited on the required day, however, there is an extra charge for this service. Automatic payment (*machtiging voor periodieke overboeking*) is the easiest way to make sure that your rental fee is paid regularly. You can fill in a *machtiging voor periodieke overboeking* at your bank. (This can also be easily discontinued by filling in a cancellation card). Usually the lessee is presented the bill of the connection or hook-up charges for utilities as gas, electricity, water, and telephone, unless otherwise has been agreed upon. It is also possible that a certain amount for gas, water and electricity is included in the rent. Please check carefully if it is a fixed amount, or whether it is an advance payment (*voorschot*) that will be settled at the end of the year based on your actual usage.

Diplomatic Clauses in Rental Contracts

A diplomatic clause in a rental agreement contract is intended to protect the rights of either both or one of the parties mentioned in the agreement. Both the lessor and the lessee may ask for such a clause to be included in the agreement to ensure that, even though the rental agreement may not have expired, the property can be vacated after a notification term mutually agreed upon in advance. Make sure the owner does not include a clause allowing him or her to reoccupy the premises unless this has been negotiated with a sufficient notification period.

As the impact of diplomatic clauses may be quite substantial, you are well advised to first consult with your rental agency and/or have your relocation management services thoroughly screen your rental contract before accepting its conditions. As a transferee you would do well to always negotiate a diplomatic clause to be included in your rental agreement to the benefit of both parties. In the unforeseen event of a serious illness requiring repatriation (or death), without a diplomatic clause you would still be liable for the remaining rental payments.

It is advisable to always negotiate a diplomatic clause into your rental agreement, for the protection of both parties.

Examples of Diplomatic Clauses for the Lessor
If the lessor has been posted abroad, he may agree to let his property for a specified period. In a diplomatic clause it may be stipulated that should the lessor be relocated to the Netherlands during that period and need his property for personal use again, he may terminate the contract before the expiry date – provided the agreed upon notification period is observed. By means of this clause the lessor can legally terminate the agreement before the expiry date and request that his property be vacated within a certain period agreed upon in advance with the lessee.

Diplomatic clauses, especially in favor of the *lessor*, can take various forms and be bound by various conditions, which are subject to negotiation, but must conform with the General Conditions of Dutch Civil Law Art. 2.1 (*Algemene Voorwaarden Burgerlijk Wetboek Art. 2.1*).

Examples of Diplomatic Clauses for the Lessee
Also the lessee may wish to include a cause stipulating that, even though the rental agreement has not yet expired, he can terminate the contract at any time after a mutually agreed notification term.

For instance, the lessee may have accepted and signed a rental agreement for a specified period, but want to take into account the possibility that he could be relocated by his employer – which would entail the need to move house before the expiry date of the contract. There are various scenarios that come to mind – for instance, the parties may agree to this clause if the lessee is transferred to a place more than 50 km. from the actual residence. Or it may be subject to a stricter condition: the lessee must be transferred abroad before the expiry date of the agreement.

Thanks to the diplomatic clause, the lessee will be allowed to terminate the contract, provided a certain notification period is observed, and will not be obliged to honor the agreement of paying the rent to the end of the contractual term. Some lessors are willing to accept a diplomatic clause in favor of the lessee, subject to the restriction that a minimum rental period must have been completed, e.g. one year, before the clause may be invoked.

No Diplomatic Clause Has Been Included
If NO diplomatic clause has been included in the agreement and you have rented a house for a certain period (usually 12 months) you can only terminate your lease at the end of that period.

If, by then, you do not give notice of termination or of your intention to vacate the property, your contract will be automatically renewed for another year. This is known as a *stilzwijgende verlenging* or 'silent renewal'. When a contract has been extended thus, then, after the first year, you may request for a termination of the contract with reference to a notice period (*opzegtermijn*) of one, two or sometimes three months – as specified in your contract thereafter.

If you have rented for a fixed term (*bepaalde tijd*) – for instance a short-term six month-contract – you are liable for the full payment of the rent throughout this term, even if you have to move elsewhere before the end of the specified period. Consequently, you could be held liable for several months' worth of rental fees.

E. Rights and Obligations

In order to avoid confusion while reading the Rights & Obligations here below please note:

'Lessor' refers to the landlord	(OR– the othor is lessor)
'Lessee' refers to the renter	(ME – I am the lessee)

Under most rental agreements the *lessee* is not allowed to deduct the **deposit** stipulated at the conclusion of an agreement from installments of rent or other financial obligations. When you pay a deposit at the beginning of the lease, it will be refunded after you check out, provided your accommodation is found to be in good order. Be prepared to pay a minimum of one month's rent when you move in. Sometimes two months will be required. The *lessor* is not obliged to pay interest over the lessee's deposit and is obliged to return the deposit, or the balance thereof after deducting any amount due to him by the lessee, within three months after the expiration of the agreement.

The **state of the property** at the commencement of the rental period shall be recorded in a dated inspection report drawn up in duplicate and signed by both parties, of which both parties shall obtain a copy. A record shall also be made of any items, which have been taken over by the incoming tenant from the outgoing tenant, and the *lessor* shall be notified of this. If, for whatever reason, an inspection report is not drawn up, the *lessee* shall notify the lessor in writing of any deficiencies he has observed regarding the property within eight days of the commencement of the rental period, in the absence of which the lessee shall be assumed to have taken over the property in good order and without visible deficiencies.

The *Lessee* is **not allowed**, without the *lessor's* prior written consent:

- to sublet the rented property in whole or in part to, or place it at the disposal of, a third party
- to renovate or to make any alterations to the property
- to use the accommodation for any other purpose than living
- to install an aerial or satellite dish for radio and television reception on the premises
- to keep pets in the property
- to alter or remove furnishings or fixtures and other effects belonging to the property.

Maintenance Obligations

Check out your heat and water and all of your appliances when you move in. Make sure that everything works – especially the heating system, the water heater and the radiators (no leaks). If anything is malfunctioning, notify the landlord immediately, preferably in writing.

You might find words to the following effect in your contract: '*The lessee undertakes to use and maintain the property including the garden with due diligence and shall be liable for any damage due to negligence, improper use of the facilities or damage caused by pets, inhabitants or guests. The lessee shall take any necessary steps to prevent or minimize damage to the rented property, the garden and the adjoining premises, including taking measures to prevent damage in extreme weather conditions or possible consequences thereof.*

The lessee should inform lessor forthwith by phone and by written letter of any damage, defect or malfunction occurring or threatening to occur to or on the property. In case of an emergency the lessee should contact the caretaker or lessor immediately. If any defect or malfunction is not duly reported, the lessee shall be liable for any resulting damage or loss and the subsequent costs of repairs or replacements.'

In the event that the caretaker or the lessor cannot be reached, the housing agency should be contacted. If none of these can be reached, you may always contact your relocation company (if you are represented by one) who will see to it that the situation is reported to the lessor as soon as possible. You may also send a fax or registered letter. It is a good idea to ask for emergency phone numbers when you first move in and keep them readily available.
Hopefully you won't need to use them.

Who Is Responsible for What?

Always read the fine print. Make sure you know what is expected of you regarding shared costs. Some landlords will expect you to pay for appliance repairs, shared telephone, shared utilities, garden upkeep or outdoor building upkeep, and even improvements. Have it in writing, be safe.

Make sure the contract clearly states what types of repairs are the responsibility of the owner and which ones you will have to pay yourself. Usually, internal repairs under say, € 200, are the responsibility of the tenant and anything else is at the owner's cost. If a repair is the responsibility of the landlord, do not attempt to fix it or have it fixed on your own initiative unless you have specific written permission to arrange repairs. You could be accused of causing more damage instead of trying to repair it. When in doubt, make a photo, and fax the information to the housing agency or landlord so that you have proof of the damages.

The chart will give you an overview of generally who is deemed the responsible party, unless otherwise agreed upon in writing.

Overview of the responsible party

KIND OF HOUSE MAINTENANCE
Yearly furnace check – *Lessee*
Interior & Exterior cleaning – *Lessee*
Yearly chimney sweep– *Lessee*
Garden Maintenance – *Lessee*
Shut off outside water taps – *Lessee*
Damage by children – *Lessee*
Plumbing up to € 113 – *Lessee*
Damage by pets – *Lessee*
Minor repairs under € 113 to washer, dryer, dishwasher – *Lessee*
Broken window glass – *Lessee*
Broken mirrors – *Lessee*
Handyman services – *Lessee*

Insurance advised:
Liability and glass insurance, Damage due to negligence and improper use

Pest extermination – *Lessee*
Light bulbs – *Lessee*

New alarm system – *Lessee*
Childproof the house – *Lessee*

Theft/burglary, Insurance, Alarm system (new) maintenance – *Lessee*
Installation new satellite dish – *Lessee*

Broken window glass, Insurance New carpet (personal choice) – *Lessee*

Extra phone line – *Lessee*
Interior painting/wallpaper (personal choice) – *Lessee*

Extra sets of keys & locks – *Lessee*
Installation tv/vcr – *Lessee*

Swimming pool maintenance – *Lessee*

Roof gutter cleaning – *Lessee*

Dog/Children's fences – *Lessee*

Pre check-in interior painting – *Lessor*
Existing carpet cleaning – *Lessor*
Pre check-in costs (cleaning) – *Lessor*
Exterior painting – *Lessor*
Equipment belonging to landlord, washer, dryer, dishwasher, all major repairs over € 113, beyond negligence or improper use – *Lessor*
Swimming pool pump – *Lessor*
Touch-up reported leaks – *Lessor*
Pre check-in new carpet – *Lessor*
Existing alarm system – *Lessor*
Alarm system (existing) maintenance – *Lessor*
Maintenance existing satellite dish – *Lessor*
Extra pest extermination costs – *Lessor*
Garden maintenance as per rental contract – *Lessor*

NEGOTIABLE ITEMS
Extra locks/ Dead bolt
isdn Internet connection

Some Other Suggestions

- Safety: Many rental properties, especially private apartments, are not adequately protected against fire. If your landlord will not install fire detectors, then do it yourself. Make sure you are aware of at least one escape route. You or your landlord can also supply a fire ladder or rope in case of emergency. See Chapter 13 on *Safety*
- Unwanted visitors could include mice, rats, cockroaches. Fleas from a former resident with pets could pose problems for you. Pigeons are a big problem in urban areas. Extermination may be required. Make sure your lease covers pest control costs. See chapter 8 on *Pests and Problems*
- Unfurnished apartments will provide you the full protection of the law, which can be quite favorable for tenants. For example, you are entitled to deduct a portion of the rent or to claim repair costs if the temperature cannot be maintained at 20 degrees in the winter
- Radiators may prove to be a somewhat uneven heat source. Central heating like that known in North America is not used here. Exercise caution with apartments where the only source of heat is a metal gas stove (*gas kachel*) or an electric space heater. If you are renting, make sure to have the *kachel* inspected. You would not want to die in your sleep form carbon monoxide poisoning (which you do read about here every year in the winter period in the news...)
- If the owner is paying any utilities, find out in advance. For the expenses that are your responsibility, such as telephone, Internet and cable television, arrange to have the bills mailed to you, and to have your name transferred to the billing. It makes life a bit easier in payment department. In the case of shared utilities or that you are required to pay an advance on utilities, request a copy of the billing charges from the landlord so you can see the actual usage
- Ja/Nee Stickers – *Ja/Nee* refers to Yes, I would like to receive the free local newspaper but No, I do not want leaflets, brochures and advertisements in my mailbox. The *Nee/Nee* sticker indicates that you do not wish to receive any mail that is not personally addressed to you. In placing this sticker on your mailbox you will ensure that you do not receive any leaflets or the free local paper. Many people either do not want to deal with the ever-increasing pile of junk mail or are simply not interested in bargains or local news, especially if they don't read Dutch. Many people place the *Nee/Nee* sticker on their mailbox from an environmental standpoint, hoping that it will save some trees. Stickers are available from the Town Hall (*gemeente*) in your municipality or from the *milieu defensie* (see chapter 14 on *Recycling*).

F. Terminating the Rental Contract

To avoid anxiety and unnecessary costs later, you will need to inform your landlord well in advance at what date the contract for your apartment will expire and that you will be leaving.

Terminating the contract should be done by way of a **registered letter**. Depending on your rental contract, there is a notice period to be given before the expiration of the tenancy of:

- at least one calendar month in case the lessee terminates
- at least three months + one month for every year the property has been rented to the lessee with a maximum of six months in case the lessor terminates the contract
- the period specified in the diplomatic clause of the contract.

When termination of the rental contract has been agreed upon by both parties, and the landlord knows you are leaving, he will try to rent the property to new tenants as soon as possible. Which is only logical, as, if it's empty, he does not make any profit. Upon being given 24 hours' notice the lessee is required to give access to the property for necessary house maintenance and/or house views.
You do not have to stay home for this, though it might be a good idea since strangers will be going through your house.

Checking Out

The lessee shall, at the termination of the rental agreement, hand over all keys to the lessor and deliver up the property, its furnishings, fixtures and other effects in the original condition, normal wear and tear excepted, that is:

- in a state of repair similar to that described in the inventory
- in a state of repair similar to that described in the initial survey report
- clean and in good condition.

G. Important Other Issues

Rent Adjustment

In accordance with official directives as issued by the Central Bureau of Statistics (*Centraal Bureau voor de Statistiek* or CBS), the annual rent stated in the contract can be adjusted once a year. Such an adjustment will be based on the current annual consumer price index as published by the CBS. You will receive a notification of rental adjustment a couple of months before it will be due, together with a form by which you can formally object to the intended rental adjustment. Please contact and consult with your rental agency before accepting any rental adjustment. Website for statistics: www.cbs.nl.

Contract Renewals or Extensions

If you do not specifically stipulate in writing that, after the initial one-year rental period, you will vacate the premises, then the contract receives a *stilzwijgende verlenging* or silent continuance whereby you will be liable for a new year of rental fees. After the initial one-year period, if you wish to continue your lease – but on a month-to-month basis – this can be negotiated after the initial one-year period is over. Month-to-month also works in the favor of the landlord, as either part may give notice (*opzeggen*). You may also choose to continue your rental contract for a longer period.

Subletting (Onderverhuur)

A tricky business at best. Housing under *woningbouwverenigingen* are protected by rent controls through the housing agencies and it is highly illegal to sublet the apartment. You will have problems with registering with the authorities as there could be no evidence of your tenancy so that you could find yourself evicted on short notice.

It is almost certain that if you pay your rent your rights as a tenant are protected, so we advise that you keep it all legal, and that you pay via a bank transfer (*accept-giro*) or via a monthly automatic transfer permission (*automatische overschrijving*). This way you will have records.

Scam Letting

This was in the news and on the Internet so we pass along the warning. Never, ever do a cash deal on a doorstep with the agreement to work out the details and sign the contract later. It would appear that some totally unscrupulous con men (*oplichters*) are showing apartments to prospective renters (*huurders*) and taking a cash deposit (or even the first months rental fee!!) to hold (thus guarantee) the rental. These unconscionable people only have the keys to rooms or flats, and they take your money and run, leaving you out in the cold. As crazy as it may sound and however unlikely you might find it that you would get caught up in such a thing, sometimes desperately seeking living space over an extended period of time can cause people to do crazy things. If it does not look legitimate, keep on looking elsewhere. Be warned.

Sharing an Apartment

Occasionally in order to save costs you may want to team up with a roommate and share a rental property with a friend or colleague or loved one. Make sure that both of your names appear on the lease. Should one of you fall out of love, be transferred out of the county, move out or otherwise disappear, the remaining person occupying the flat will have their rights protected.

Inform your landlord if you are planning to have an additional person in the house. In the case of an advance payment (*voorschot*) on utilities, your costs will most likely have to be re-negotiated due to the inevitable increase in utility usage.

H. Extra Costs, Levies and Taxes

Living in Holland is expensive. When assessing the cost of living in the Netherlands, please refer to the list below with descriptions of additional costs, levies and taxes in addition to your housing expenses, which you either will be obliged to pay or could encounter, based on your living situation. It is very important to be aware of these extra costs, as they will impact your actual living expenses while living here in the Netherlands. Beyond the rent and utilities you knew about, there are a number of 'extras'.

Deposit
In addition to the first month's rent after signing your lease agreement, you will be expected to pay a deposit equal to one or two (very occasionally three) months' rental fee. This serves as a guarantee to the owner that he will be able to recoup the costs against possible damage to the property. It is refundable when you move out if no repairs are necessary.

No interest is paid over the deposit. If there are no damages, your deposit will be refunded to you. This must take place, by law, within three months of your having vacated the property. Make arrangements to have this refunded either to you Dutch bank account (if still open) or by wire transfer to a bank in your new location.

Price Indexing
Rental contracts stipulate the right of the landlord to raise the rent once per calendar year. This is in accordance with the Central Bureau of Statistics (CBS), who review the rent and price index rates annually. Percentages are based on the cost of living index stipulated by the government, and cannot exceed a 6.5% increase.

Commission to the Real Estate Agent
This is compensation to be paid to the real estate agent as payment for intermediary services in securing the property and negotiating and executing the contract.

It is currently set at 8% of the yearly rental price, or an amount equivalent to one month's rent. On your billing, a Value Added Tax (BTW) of 19% is paid on the commission only, not on the deposit or rent.

Sales Tax

You can expect to pay a Value Added Tax (BTW) of 19% on goods and services and 6% for books. Just about everything that can be taxed is. There is even sales tax on your telephone calls and veterinary services for your pets.

Utility Costs

Gas, Water and Electricity costs depend on a number of factors, such as the age and size of the property, its location (town and area), the number of electrical appliances you have in use, the number of persons residing in the residence, and how high you keep the thermostat! Utility costs for a well-insulated two-bedroom apartment in Amsterdam could amount to approximately € 113 per month.

Property Tax

Property tax in the Netherlands is levied on two counts: who owns the property, and who lives in the property. The tax is based on the value of the property, and the rates – which vary per region! – are set by the WOZ (*Wet Onroerende Zaken* or Real Estate Law). As the renter, you are required to pay the resident portion.
If you own the property you live in, you pay both amounts. Your housing agency or landlord should be able to give you an indication of this yearly tax. See chapter 6 on *Purchasing a House*, under WOZ-*Appraisal Value*.

Sufferance Tax

In some places you will be charged a local tax known as *precario rechten* – which is the sufferance tax levied locally on projections over public land. In other words, you pay a contribution for your use of the pavement in front of your house or other public lands such as parks and pathways.

Garbage Tax or Refuse Levy

This is a monthly payment for the collection of your garbage, and amounts to anywhere between € 136 to € 182 per year. Some municipalities send a separate monthly invoice; others include it in the utility charges. Some areas collect organic matter (in a green plastic container) and the general household paper / metal /plastic refuse separately (in a gray plastic container). For large trash, such as furniture, you may telephone the large garbage service (*gemeentelijke reinigingsdienst – grof vuil*) for a special pick-up to discard of it.

For items that could be re-used, re-cycling is also an option. There are special collections for washers and other appliances. Paper and glass are recycled into local containers, called *papierbak* (for paper) or *glasbak* (for glass). Environmental concerns are quite important to the Dutch and almost everyone recycles. There are also special pickup locations for chemicals such as old paint. Many grocery and appliance stores have a red or yellow container for used batteries (*batterijen*). Outdated medical prescriptions can be handed in at your local pharmacy / chemist (*apotheek*). See chapter 14 on *Recycling*.

Environment Tax

Each municipality has its own rates. Costs are based on the number of inhabitants, whereby families and singles are taxed respectively.

Cable TV Connection

You pay a monthly fee for cable connection enabling you to receive all of the available TV and radio stations, beyond the Dutch public stations. Again, the fee may be paid as a separate charge, or through your utilities bill, depending on the town in which you live. In some areas a number of package options are offered such as extra stations or films, which will require an additional cost subscription. Read our special guide **Getting Connected** for additional details and resource information.

Land Draining Rates and Water Purification

You pay an annual tax for water purification, being approximately € 41 for one person and € 136 for families, based on a municipal levy. The land drainage tax is essential for keeping land dry (for instance, by means of the ubiquitous windmills).

Sewer Tax

Property owners have to pay sewer charges for connection to the sewage system and for its regular maintenance. If there are problems, the section from your front door to the street is the financial responsibility of the *gemeente*, any sewage problems behind the door (in the house) are your financial responsibility.

Cleaning of Central Heating Boiler

The cost of cleaning your central heating boiler will amount to approximately € 54 per year. Houses with a fireplace in use must have a chimney sweeper (*schoorsteenveger*) once a year, which will cost approximately € 41. The rental contract states whether the lessor or the lessee is responsible for the arrangements and the costs.

Telephone

To have a telephone connected in your home, KPN Telecom (the Dutch telecom provider) charges clients an initial fee for a fixed installation (equipment and connection) and a (bi-monthly) subscription fee based on use. You will need a fixed line if you want to use the Internet.

Many people choose to have mobile telephones. There are a number of subscription possibilities available, and various types of cell phones – all at competitive rates. GSM phones will give you wider global access. 'Pre-pay' phones, where there are no subscription costs and you pay your telephone calls with a pre-paid chip card inserted in the phone, are very popular. Compare telephone options and costs via the calculation comparisons on the Internet at the websites you will find at the end of the chapter.

Internet Service Providers
You will find a complete listing for the Netherlands at www.thelist.internet.com. Some services are free, such as www.zonnet.nl, www.wanadoo.nl or www.freeler.nl, while www.hotmail.com or www.yahoo.com offer a free e-mail account.

For extensive information and further explanations on (tele)communications please read our special guide **Getting Connected**.

Dog Tax
In many municipalities dog owners must register their dog(s) at the Town Hall (*gemeentehuis*). Most municipalities will provide dog owners with a dog tag (*hondenpenning*). The dog tax varies per municipality, from NO tax to € 59 per animal.

NOTE – You are requested to clean up the droppings from your pet. Failure to do so could result in a fine. If there are no facilities of the sort in your neighborhood, you are expected to train your dog to use the gutter (look out when stepping out of your car!) Many dog owners do carry plastic bags and scoops on walks and clean up after their pets, which is appreciated.

Parking Permits
In Dutch cities such as Amsterdam, Haarlem or Utrecht, it is necessary to apply for a parking permit. Being registered at the Town Hall (*gemeentehuis*) often gives you the right to get a parking permit (at a relatively low price). Keep in mind that there is often a waiting list, especially for the central areas of the cities. In case you are on a waiting list, you could consider renting parking space in a garage (different options are available to you; from renting per week up to per quarter).

Prices of parking permits vary, depending on the area where you live; a parking permit for the center of Amsterdam is double the cost of Amsterdam South. You need to apply in the area of the city you live in (*stadsdeel*). Parking permits do not automatically come with the rented property, especially not in the city center. For instance, in the center of Amsterdam, when someone moves out, the next person on the waiting list gets the permit, not the new tenant. On the other hand, outside the center of Amsterdam parking permits can be tied to an address. Once a tenant vacates a property and de-registers with the parking authorities, the permit becomes available for the next tenant at that property.

CAUTION: Parking fines are hefty – € 41 – for expired meter parking. For illegal parking, yellow wheel clamps are in use in some cities. Finding one of these on your wheel entails your having to go the local authorities (which you have to find and walk to) to pay your fine, after which you have to wait for someone to come and undo the clamp – a lengthy and annoying procedure. Another option for the parking authorities is to have your car towed away. You have to collect you car at the police compound, pay for all costs – up to € 182 – and spend at least half a day attempting to get your car back.

NOTE: www.parkeermakelaar.nl provides information on the rental and sale of parking places and garages (*parkeerplaatsen & garage boxes*).

I. Insurances for Renters

There is:

- Personal Liability Insurance (*WA verzekering particulier*), which costs approximately € 36 annually per family. This insurance is highly recommended since it covers any damage that you (or your children) might cause to other people's belongings or property
- Fire / Household Effects / Burglary Insurance (*brand-, inboedel-en inbraakverzekering*) on your personal goods (furnished apartments are insured by the landlord only on the owner's household contents, not yours). This costs approximately € 45 to € 136 per year. Antiques, artwork, jewelry and expensive photo equipment or stereo installations will require extra coverage.

J. Apartment Hunting Tips

Whether you are looking for a room, an apartment, a studio or a maisonette, being prepared, knowing what you are looking for, and keeping your budget in mind are key factors. In order to make the most of your time, the more prepared you are before you start out on your apartment-hunting trip, the better your search will go.

Before you set out make sure you have the following 'Take Along' items:

1. apartment hunting check list (Xerox enough copies for multiple viewings)
2. notebook with hard surface to write on
3. pens (more than one!)
4. city map
5. small stickers or colored markers (to mark locations on map)
6. digital camera or video camera (helpful to review later)
7. tape measure
8. mobile phone
9. bottled water (it can be a thirsty trip!).

1. **Your wish list** – Make a list of your requirements. Are you looking for a fireplace, hardwood floors, wall-to-wall carpeting, a dishwasher, washer / dryer, etc. Know what you need. You may not be able to find everything you could wish for, but making a plan and setting priorities will help you focus on the essential items.

2. **Apartment Hunting Checklist** – Use the checklist to make notes and to have an overview of each property you have visited. If you are filming your visits, this will be helpful when you are accessing each property in your review.

3. **Relevant information** – Be prepared. The landlord / housing agency may want to see:
   a. your credit history (or a letter from your employer stating your current salary)
   b. your work permit and/or your contract for the expected length of your stay in Holland
   c. your resume or cv
   d. your pay slip or tax return (reference to last address / home country address tax base)
   e. proof of identification – your passport (they will make a copy of this for their records)
   f. your residency permit (*verblijfsvergunning*). You will receive this after you have a rental contract, then you can register with the foreign police and *gemeente* as to where you will reside.

4. **References** – Some landlords will want references from your former landlord, and will want to verify them. Alert the people you have given as your references that they may be expecting a phone call.

5. **Daylight is the best light** – Viewings should be done in the daytime so you can see what available natural light there is. Given the amount of cloudy, gray

and rainy days we have in Holland, you'll most likely want to choose living quarters with the most available light (unless of course you prefer darker habitats!). You can also better judge the condition of the apartment and whether it will need work / paint / etc.

6. **Careful walk-through** – If you are serious about an apartment, do a careful walk-through, ask questions and make notes. Repairs, damages and improvements should be verified BEFORE you commit to the rental contract. Have a note of the existing damages attached to the lease so you will not be held liable at a later date. Remember, a verbal agreement is binding, so don't commit to anything by saying you are interested if you are not certain.

7. **Questions to ask**:
   g. How is the water pressure?
   h. How many electrical outlets are there and where are they located?
   i. Where are the telephone outlets located?
   j. Has Internet service been installed?
   k. Hot water – what is the capacity of the water heater?
   l. Closet space – is there enough, or will you need cupboards?

8. **Meet the neighbors** – Will you be living below someone, or above someone? Do you share (thin) walls? Be bold. Knock on a few doors, introduce yourself, and ask a few questions. (This may not be possible if everyone is at work, but you could try again in the weekend).

9. **Measurements** – Have a list of the measurements / dimensions of your current furniture. Many Dutch apartments are small, and you may not be able to fit all of your belongings. Use your tape measure to measure the room dimensions so you will know for sure if you need to leave some items behind in storage. (Storage facilities in Holland are expensive and few.) Make a note of things you may need to buy here (coat rack, closet, telephone table, etc.).

10. **More is better** – Visit as many places as you are able to. This will give you a good idea of what is on the market, what is available in your budget, and what your money will get you! Use the Apartment Hunting Checklist included at the end of this chapter. You can easily Xerox off a number of copies. Be prepared to act quickly once you have found something you really like.

11. **Read & Know** – Thoroughly read your lease and make sure you understand all of your rights and obligations. ASK – about utilities, pets, cable TV, cohabitating, penalties for breaking the lease, diplomatic clause, etc. If you are uncertain about anything, ask for an explanation.

For detailed information regarding contracts, diplomatic clauses, and your rights and obligations as a renter, please see under *D. Rental Contracts* in this chapter.

K. Apartment Hunting Checklist

APARTMENT CHECKLIST – TERMS AND CONDITIONS
Address of the property
Street
City
Name of Housing Agency/Realtor
Telephone

	YES	NO	COMMENTS
Date available			
Deposit			
Pet rules/deposit			
Late payment charges			
Length of lease			
Penalty for breaking lease			
Physical changes allowed			
Rent amount			
Rent due date			
Subletting (not allowed?)			
Utilities included			
Cost estimate of utilities			
Cost of (renter) tax			
Water			
Heat			
Garbage removal day(s)			
FACILITY			
Air conditioning			
Ample electrical outlets			
Bedroom privacy			
Blinds/shades/curtains			
Cable TV connection			
Carpet			
Hardwood floors			
Closet space			
Fireplace			
Furniture			
Light Fixtures			
Natural light			
Paint/wall conditions			
Patio/balcony			
Pet-friendly			

	YES	NO	COMMENTS
Telephone connection in (which) rooms			
Internet (ISDN) connection			
Storage			
Upstairs/downstairs			
Water pressure			
View			
KITCHEN			
Exhaust fan			
Size and age of refrigerator			
Counter space			
Dishwasher			
Garbage disposal (illegal in Holland)			
Gas/electric stove			
Microwave			
Cupboard space			
Smoothly opening drawers			
COMMUNITY (IN AN APARTMENT BUILDING)			
Mailbox			
Laundry facilities (on site or close by)			
Loud garbage chute nearby			
Noise level			
Parking			
Bike racks			
Elevators/stairs proximity			
Roof access			
Soundproof walls			
SAFETY			
Emergency exits			
Fire extinguishers			
Smoke detectors			
Functioning windows			
Gated entrance			
Intercom			
Lead paint hazards			
Locks on all doors			
Extra security locks			
Outside lighting			
Screens			
NEIGHBORHOOD			
Proximity of grocery, bank, post office, etc.			
Average age residents			
Public transportation proximity			
Distance from school/work			
OVERALL DIMENSIONS			
Living Room			
Dining Room			
Kitchen			
Study			
Bedroom 1			
Bedroom 2			

References

For a complete look at the insurances you will need and those you may choose in Holland, please see chapter 7 *Financial Considerations: Mortgage & Insurances*. A number of helpful websites are listed as well.

References
Nederlandse Vereniging van Makelaars (NVM)
Postbus 2222
3430 DC Nieuwegein
The Netherlands
Tel.: 030 608 5185
Fax: 030 603 4003
www.nvm.nl

For questions or information in English (if available) contact the *Consumenten Voorlichting* (Consumer Information department) at this number.

Vereniging Bemiddeling Onroerend Goed (VBO) Organization of Negotiating Agents for Properties www.vbo.nl

Telephone
Comparing rates:
www.bellen.com – phone rates, discount carriers
www.internetten.nl – Internet providers cost comparisons
www.belwijzewr.nl – mobile & fixed telephone costs
www.vakantiebellen.nl – costs within Europe mobile 'vacation' calls

3

3 Housing in Amsterdam: SWD Stedelijke Woningdienst

This book is of course about 'Housing in Holland' as the title suggests, however, to give you some practical examples and useful background information about how things work, we will use the City of Amsterdam as our 'sample city' for these purposes. Amsterdam is not only Holland's famous capital city, it is also an extremely popular location for expatriates, not to mention all of the tourists! The city's international status also means that a lot of information is available for foreigners, as more than 60% of the population is non-Dutch, comprised of immigrants, expatriates, EU-citizens and some illegal aliens. Amsterdam remains, however, one the most difficult locations for finding housing, especially reasonably priced accommodation. On a world scale, current prices in Amsterdam are comparable to those asked in Paris or New York.

A. Finding a Place to Live....

The information provided here has been extracted from the Amsterdam City Housing Department (*Stedelijke Woningdienst Amsterdam*, SWD) and has been derived from the 1999 Municipal Housing Regulations (*Huisvestingsverordening*). It briefly summarizes your options for seeking housing in Amsterdam, and outlines the municipal regulations you will have to abide by. As rules and regulations are frequently subject to change, we would like to point out that you cannot base any claims on this information in the event of a dispute. Please refer to the English language-section of the website (www.swd.amsterdam.nl) for further information.

Housing Permit (*Huisvestingsvergunning*)

A housing permit can be obtained at the Amsterdam City Housing Department, or SWD, and is required for virtually all rental dwellings and for many dwellings offered for sale. You must be issued a housing permit before you can move in.
No permit is required for dwellings in Amsterdam Zuidoost (Southeast), nor for

any dwelling with a basic monthly rent (*kale huur*) that exceeds € 453. No permit is required to rent non-self-contained accommodation, private lodgings or student accommodation. The requirements for obtaining a housing permit are summarized further on in this chapter (under D. *Housing Permits*).

Renting Lodgings

Information on seeking private lodgings, rooms and student accommodation in Amsterdam can be obtained from the English web page of www.steunpuntwonen.nl or by phoning Amsterdams Steunpunt Wonen at 020 523 0130.

B. Renting through Housing Associations and *WoningNet*

To be eligible to rent a dwelling from a housing association in the Amsterdam Region you must first register at WoningNet. You can do this via the Internet, www.woningnet.nl or by contacting one of the housing associations (see listings under *Woningbouwverenigingen* in the Yellow Pages). You can also request a registration form by telephone, or by sending in the coupon from Woningnet-Magazine (available in many public places such as libraries and post offices and some municipal offices).

Upon receipt of the registration fee of € 43.11, WoningNet will issue you a client number and an Internet password. From that moment on, you can apply for advertised dwellings. Whether you are eligible for a WoningNet-dwelling, depends on your status as 'transferee' or 'starter', which you will read about further on.

Available Dwellings

Dwellings that become vacant in the Amsterdam Region are announced weekly in Woningnet-Magazine, on the WoningNet website and on page 888 of the AT5 and TV Noord-Holland Teletext.

Transferees and Starters

The sequence of candidates in the allocation of dwellings is based on their duration of occupancy or duration of registration. 'Transferees' (*doorstromers*) are ranked in the order of their duration of occupancy and 'starters' by the length of their registration.

What Qualifies You as a Transferee?

You are classified as a transferee if you are the principal tenant or owner occupant of a self-contained dwelling in the Amsterdam Region. Owner-occupants or principal tenants of house-boats with permanent moorings also qualify as transferees, as do caravan dwellers with recognized permanent pitches. 'Duration of occupancy' (*woonduur*) is the amount of time that you have been the principal tenant or owner-occupant of your current dwelling in the Amsterdam Region.

You do not need to register until you are ready to seek other accommodation.

What Qualifies You As A Starter?

You are a starter if you are not the principal tenant or owner-occupant of a self-contained dwelling in the Amsterdam Region. Starters accumulate 'duration of registration' (*inschrijfduur*). The longer you are registered and on the waiting list the better your chances become. It is good advice for you to register at WoningNet promptly in order to build up the longest possible duration of registration.

Waiting Times

How long you will have to wait for a dwelling depends on the type of accommodation you are looking for. You should allow for a wait of at least five years (some people say it is now closer to seven years). Your chances of obtaining a dwelling (from a housing association) increase to the extent that you:

- make fewer demands
- have a longer duration of occupancy if you are a transferee
- have a longer duration of registration if you are a starter.

Waiting times are somewhat shorter for most dwellings in the Bijlmermeer high-rise blocks in Amsterdam Zuidoost.

C. Rental Dwellings through Private Landlords

To find rental accommodation through a private landlord you can consult the *Makelaars* (estate agents) section of the Yellow Pages. You can also apply to a housing agency (*woningbemiddelingsbureau*, see under *Woningbureaus*). All such firms are required to have municipal permits and to abide by municipal regulations. They deal mainly in more expensive accommodation. You can read more about both of these in chapter 2 *Housing – Rentals*.

D. Housing Permits

Dwellings For Owner-Occupation

If you want to buy a dwelling in Amsterdam to live in yourself, you should first know whether you need a housing permit to do so and, if so, what requirements you must satisfy for obtaining one.

Owner-Occupied Dwellings – No Permit Required
No permit is required for:

- former rental dwellings with a monthly rental value higher than € 453
- dwellings for owner-occupation with a purchase price higher than € 87,130
- dwellings in Amsterdam Zuidoost (Southeast)
- your present rental dwelling (of which you are the legal tenant), if you buy it from the present landlord.

Owner-Occupied Dwellings – Permit Required
A permit is required for:

- dwellings for owner-occupation with a purchase price below € 87.130, buyer's costs (also known as 'k.k.' or *kosten koper*, see chapter 6 *Purchasing a House*) excluded
- former rental dwellings with a monthly rental value below € 453.

Requirements for Permits

- you must be 18 years of age or older
- you must hold Dutch nationality or a valid residence permit.

No restrictions apply with regard to income, ties to the Amsterdam Region or size of household.

Newly-Built Dwellings for Owner-Occupation
Separate rules, sometimes varying by building project, may apply to dwellings sold at completion for owner occupation. The city district in which the dwellings are being built can provide further information.

Rental Dwelling

In order to qualify for a housing permit for a rental dwelling, you must:

1. be 18 or older
2. have Dutch nationality or a valid residence permit
3. have ties to the Amsterdam Region or to Almere.

These include any of the following:

- economic ties (employment or study in the Amsterdam Region or Almere)
- social ties (two years current residence in the Amsterdam Region or Almere, or at least six consecutive years of residence there in the past ten years).
- equivalent status to persons with ties. This is accorded to individuals resident in the Netherlands who are long-term unemployed (2 ½ consecutive years), retired, fully incapacitated for work, recognized refugees, returning emigrants lacking housing, or divorced with resulting lack of housing.

4. Your annual taxable household income must not be greater than € 28,840 for dwellings with monthly rents up to € 341, or greater than € 40,390 for more expensive dwellings up to € 453). (For dwellings of five or more rooms with a monthly rent up to € 341,income limits apply of € 22,711.70 for persons under age 65 and € 19,625.99 for persons 65 and older).
5. The dwelling must not be too large for your household, in accordance with the table below:

HOUSEHOLD CONSISTING OF:	BASIC MONTHLY RENT UP TO € 341	BASIC MONTHLY RENT FROM € 341 TO € 453
one adult	3-room dwelling maximum	3-room dwelling maximum
two adults	3-room dwelling maximum	4-room dwelling maximum
household with 1 child	4-room dwelling maximum	4-room dwelling maximum
household with 2 children	4-room dwelling maximum	5-room dwelling maximum
household with 3 – 5 children	5-room dwelling maximum	6-room dwelling maximum
with 6 or more children	6-room dwelling maximum	no limitation

NOTE: Rent and income limits are valid until July 1, 2002
Purchase price limit is valid until January 1, 2002
For further information contact any woningbouw vereniging.

Applying for a Housing Permit for an Owner-Occupied or Rental Dwelling

To apply for a housing permit for an owner-occupied dwelling, you must complete a form obtainable from De Zuiderkerk Housing Information Center of the SWD (see opening times at the end of the chapter).

Tip: If a dwelling you are about to buy requires a housing permit, include a contingency clause in the contract of sale that will nullify the purchase if the local authority does not issue you a housing permit. Housing permits for rental dwellings are applied for by the landlord or estate agent that manages the premises.

E. Financial Assistance

There are various types of financial assistance available. The City of Amsterdam Housing Department (website www.swd.amsterdam.nl) can give you more information on financial assistance for renters or for those people who wish to purchase. Here are a few examples.

Rent Allowance (*Huursubsidie*)

Nearly 100,000 people in Amsterdam are eligible for rent allowance. Not everyone who qualifies takes advantage of the scheme. That is unfortunate. Rent allowance can be a welcome supplement to help cover your monthly expenses.

Landlease Holders' Compensation Scheme (*Subsidieregeling erfpacht*)

Financial support is available for landlease holders who, after a rent increase on expiry of their lease term, may be unable to meet the payment obligations for retaining their security of tenure. See also www.erfpacht.amsterdam.nl.

Supplementary Grants for Energy Conservation and Sustainability

The *Energie Prestatie Plus*-scheme provides grants to owner-occupiers, landlords and tenants who make sustainable or energy-saving improvements to Amsterdam dwellings. It also covers alterations that promote a more healthy environment.

Amsterdam Middle-Segment Mortgage

The Amsterdam Middle-Segment Mortgage (*Amsterdamse Middensegment Hypotheek*) was developed to bring newly built market-sector housing within the reach of households with incomes from € 20,425. to € 38,575.

Purchase Subsidy

A new scheme has been introduced known as 'purchase subsidy' (*koopsubsidie*). This is an allowance to help repay the mortgage of a home. The subsidy is paid monthly to the owner-occupant and is comparable to a rent rebate. You can download the brochure P*urchase Subsidy (Koopsubsidie) Means Freedom Of Choice* or request a copy from the following website:
www.koopsubsidie.nl, tel.: 0800 566 77 82,
or e-mail: koopsubsidie@ibs.dghv.minvrom.nl

F. Rooms for Rent

Renting rooms in the city is usually the domain of students. For information on private lodgings, rooms and student accommodations in Amsterdam you can go to the English section web page of: www.steunpuntwonen.nl, which is Amsterdam's support site for rooms or by phoning 020 523 0130.

The information provided in this chapter is extracted from *Amsterdams Steunpunt Wonen*, or ASW. You can approach the ASW for any additional information, such as on contracts, the so-called 'point system', and more. Their website offers a great deal of relevant information.

Accommodation is Scarce

In Amsterdam there is a great housing shortage for people who want to live in the city. This is why people who are looking for a reasonably priced house have to comply with the rules set by the City of Amsterdam Housing Department (SWD).

For a self-contained house with a rent of under € 453 you need residence permission from the City of Amsterdam Housing Department, except for Amsterdam Zuidoost (Southeast). To get a residence permit you have to work or study in the Amsterdam area or you have to have lived there for at least two years. If that is not the case, you will probably have to accept a room in someone else's house or in the attic. Usually you can use your landlord's kitchen, toilet and bathroom.

House Hunting Costs Time and Effort

The search for a room in Amsterdam takes a lot of time. It is impossible to look for a room in the city without going there yourself. Moreover, landlords or landladies want to meet the person they are going to accept as a tenant. This means that the search is up to you, and that you cannot leave it to relatives or friends.

Before going to look at a room, be sure of what you consider important. Once you're there, have a good look around the place to see if it meets your needs and wishes.

The best rooms you will find through relatives, friends, and acquaintances. Therefore, tell everybody that you're looking for a room and ask them to be on the look-out for you. You can also consult the papers (don't forget the Amsterdam papers, such as *Het Parool*, the *Amsterdams Stadsblad* and the *Echo*) or consider the advertisements in the supermarket or in the *Via-Via* (a region-bound newspaper containing only classifieds).

Untrustworthy Landlords

Unfortunately, it is not uncommon to run into untrustworthy landlords. Therefore, you had better not go alone, and you had better not pay anything before you have made clear agreements. Ask for a receipt saying how much you have paid and for what. Better yet, arrange for all payments to be made through your bank so you have proof of payment.

Rent Prices

In the Netherlands the rental prices of houses and rooms are determined by a 'point counting' system (*puntensysteem*): the quality of the room or house is expressed in 'points'. The landlord may not ask more than the rent according to this system.

This 'point counting' system does not apply to houses with a rent higher than € 521. When renting a house for more than € 521 per month, make sure that the rent is still somewhat in keeping with the 'point counting' system. If you feel that it is not, you have six months in which to object officially.

Often landlords ask 'all-in' rent. NB: try to find out what you pay for the basic rent and what for service. In furnished properties, the rental fee may be split three ways, for the *kale huur*, or basic apartment fee, for the furnishings, and for the utilities. Ask to have this specified into which portion is rent, and which is furniture. For tax purposes, there is a differentiation between the cost of a house rental and the additional (extra – non-deductible) furnishings.

(Non)Commercial Room Agencies

In Amsterdam there are three room agencies run on a non-commercial basis: ASW, ASVA, and SRVU. All the other room agencies in the city are run on a commercial basis, which means that they profit financially due to the great housing shortage. All commercial agencies offering houses or rooms must be registered with the Amsterdam authorities. They are allowed to ask only a reasonable registration fee. They have to offer you a house or room within four months, if not, you can get your money back. If they find you a room, you have to pay for their services. This amount also has to be reasonable. We advise you to be very careful when you register with such a room agency. Often it will only cost you a lot of money. What follows is an example of the services of one of above non-commercial room agencies: the ASW (Amsterdam Steunpunt Wonen).

ASW *Room Agency*
ASW mediates in finding rooms for individual persons. Lots are drawn to decide who gets a chance to view a room. You cannot enroll in advance as there is no waiting list, but you may participate in each 'draw'. The draws take place on Mondays, Tuesdays and Wednesdays, at ten o'clock in the morning and on Thursdays at seven o'clock in the evening.

Two persons may view the available accommodation. If you are drawn to be one of the viewers you pay a mediation fee of € 12.

Living in a Group
The ASW mediates candidates for co-housing groups. If you are interested in living in a group, let them know.

Temporary Housing
The ASW sometimes also mediates in the case of temporary housing offered by housing associations. To get this kind of housing you have to bring a valid means of identity paper (passport or driver's license) and sometimes proof of your earnings. The allocation of these houses usually takes place on Thursdays at seven o'clock in the evening.

Information Room Availability
General information about the rooms that will be mediated can be heard on the recorded message (tel.: 020 623 50 37). You can phone daily, preferably after 4 o'clock in the afternoon.

Visiting Addresses
Once you are at an address, it is both you and the landlord who decide if you are going to live there. The ASW stays out of this and cannot be held responsible for agreements made privately between you and the landlord. They would, however, like to know as soon as possible if you accept the room or, if you don't, the reason why not. In that case, you can have your money back.

ASW *'Office Hour'*
If you are During the ASW 'office hour' you can get all the information that you may need to help you find a house or room in Amsterdam. The ASW office-hour team supports anyone who has been confronted with, for instance, too high a rent, illegal letting, breach of contract or discrimination when dealing with commercial housing or room agencies or landlords.

G. Elementary Questions and Huurteams

In the Netherlands there is a legal maximum rent for all houses and rooms. *Huurteams* (rent teams) can help you to calculate what your rent should be. If your rent is possibly too high, you can start a procedure. The *huurteam* will assist you during this procedure. They can also advise you when the landlord does not carry out necessary repairs. There are *huurteams* in almost every local council (*stadsdeel*) within the city of Amsterdam and there is a special phone number for the other areas. The *huurteams* visit all houses, but you can also call to make an appointment.

Here are a few elementary questions they have helped us answer:

What Does a *Huurteam* Do?

A *huurteam* helps you to calculate the number of 'points' your home has and to work out the maximum amount of rent you have to pay. A *huurteam* also informs and assists you with the procedures needed to adjust your rent. The services of a *huurteam* are completely free of charge and your details are kept confidential.

If you have not personally phoned to make an appointment, then you could be included in the routine visiting schedule of housing blocks by the *huurteams*. These visits are always announced in advance in writing.

When Should I Contact a *Huurteam*?

1. If you are paying too much rent according to the 'point' system
2. if your landlord neglects to carry out necessary maintenance work
3. if, faithfully, you always pay the rent increase but you don't know if that's right or not
4. if you are paying a so called 'all inclusive rent'.

Is There Such a Thing as Minimum Rent?

No! There is no such thing as rent that is 'too cheap'.

What Is the Maximum Allowed Rent?

Every home has a certain number of 'points'. The number of 'points' a home is awarded depends mainly on its size, age and the number of facilities it has. These 'points' are defined by the house valuing system in the so-called Rent Pricing Act. Relating to each point score there is a maximum allowed rent! Each year your landlord can propose to increase your rent. You can object to this, for instance if the landlord has done nothing about your maintenance complaints.

What Is Lack of Maintenance?

Your landlord is obliged to properly maintain your home. If he/she has neglected this for a long time, this is considered lack of maintenance, or either maintenance that should have been done a long time ago.

Mind you: Small repairs are the renter's duty.

How Do I Report a Lack of Maintenance?

The best way to alert your landlord to a lack of maintenance is to send him/her a letter, in which you list all your complaints. If necessary do this a number of times. If you would like help with drafting a letter or you want to take other action, you can enlist the help of a *huurteam*.

Can a *Huurteam* Also Help Me to Ask for Rent Subsidy?

No, for this you should go to the Amsterdam City Housing Department (*Stedelijke Woningdienst*), tel.: 020 552 75 52, or go to your neighborhood council adviser. Neighborhood Council Advisors are representatives of the sector you live in (*deelraad* of the city) and can be contacted through the local neighborhood center (*buurthuis*). They hold a regular *woonspreekuur* where you can come to discuss your housing problems.

In order to determine your *stadsdeel* location, search on:
www.amsterdam.nl/stadsdelen
www.amsterdam.nl/e_neighbourhoods – information on neighborhoods in Amsterdam.

How Does it Work if I Rent a Room?

In principal the same rules apply for renting a room, only the method for calculating the maximum rent is different.

Can a *Huurteam* Also Help Me if I Sub-Rent?

Yes, above all the *huurteams* look at the price and quality of the accommodation, regardless of who lives there. So in this way the *huurteams* also helps sub-renters.

What if There Is No *Huurteam* in My Area?

Huurteams can still help you. There are members of staff that advise and support renters from all the other areas in Amsterdam.

H. Housing and Rental Agencies

In addition to *makelaars*, realtors or estate agents, you may engage the services of an intermediary association, such as a housing (rental) agency. These agencies have various properties to rent, however they do not need to have a certified real estate license such as the certified NVM brokers. When looking for a reputable Housing or Rental Agency, it is important to know that it is forbidden by law for agencies (*bemiddelingsbureaus*) to negotiate for, or offer to let properties with out a special license (*vergunning*). This *vergunning* must be readily visible in the establishment as legal proof for all to see that it is a 'bona fide' agency. The 'Bewoners' net for Amsterdam publishes a list of housing agencies that have been issued a permit (*vergunning*) on www.bewoners.net.

You may also check with the Chamber of Commerce (Kamer van Koophandel) for a list of licensed housing agencies at www.kvk.nl under 'kies regio' (choose region) for addresses.

Although it is essential to have received permission to conduct business from the city government and to have been issued a *vergunning*, this in no way guarantees that a commercial agency (*commercieel bemiddelingsbureau*) will all abide by the rules. It is, sadly enough, always possible that you may have dealings with a housing or rental agency that is guilty of disreputable practices. This can happen in any country, and is most unfortunate. Human greed is a universal problem – be forewarned in your search!

Please check the list of registered agencies to be sure. There are currently circa 49 agencies in operation in addition to the three official bureaus for students rooms mentioned above.

A bureau that does not operate within the rules, will receive a warning that they must better the situation within 14 days, or be punished. This can range from being subject to having their license revoked and no longer being able to do business legally. They may also be subject to a hefty fine (€ 2,270) or, in a worst-case scenario a prison sentence of three months! So as you see, legitimate business practices and the rights of the renter are taken quite seriously.

You are strongly advised NOT to negotiate with an illegal bureau. The clandestine practice of illegal subletting (*illegale onderverhuur*) could find you at risk of renting something that you have no permission to live in. Not only will you be evicted, the fact that you are an illegal renter makes you guilty of illegal activity along with the illegal agency.

The three most important points to watch for are:

1. Does the housing agency have a valid license to operate and negotiate for rental properties? (should be on display)
2. What rules do housing agencies need to abide by?
3. What about the status of temporary contracts?

After you have checked the list to make sure the agency is bona fide, the following are the rules that they need to adhere to:

1. The agency needs to calculate for each property offered what the maximum rental is, and they may not offer the property at a higher rate.
   What often happens is that an apartment, according to the official rules should be offered for € 400 and it is actually offered for € 1,135 (obviously quite a difference in price!). This a lucrative business for the housing agencies, as the service fees (*bemiddelingskosten*) are usually equivalent to one month's rental fee. The higher the rent, of course, the bigger the fee! Unfortunately, the city (*gemeente*) does not regulate the agency service fees – these are left open.

2. For all of the housing with the official rent of € 442 the renter will need a rental contract as well as permission (*toestemming*) to live there, which is known as a *huisvestingsvergunning*. The city of Amsterdam checks to see if you have a connection or binding to the region (via work or school) and that you are not living too large (one person in a 3-bedroom flat) or that you are living too cheaply (economic check – salary above social housing eligibility norms).

Unfortunately it does happen that agencies will sublet properties without the necessary housing permits and insist that everything is in order and that no *vergunning* is necessary! There are also agencies that ask for a registration fee (*inschrijfgeld*) to assist you in finding properties, and then do not offer you any pro-perties to see.

Temporary contracts (*Tijdelijke Contracten*)

Another fair warning – the issuance of 'temporary contracts' is often not legally binding under law (*rechtsgeldig*). The Dutch law is fairly strict as to when a dwelling can be rented on a temporary basis. This is only allowed in clearly stipulated cases. Your contract may state that the time frame is temporary or *tijdelijk* or *voor bepaalde tijd* for a specific period in writing. If a temporary contract is not drawn up in compliance to theses rules, it will not be considered legal. This is to protect the rights of renters so that they may not be evicted or that agencies would attempt to circumvent the rent protection (*huurbescherming*) statutes.

All-In

Many bureaus will offer a dwelling with 'all-in' rent (*huur*) – or everything included. For one price, everything is included such as (for instance) furniture, curtains, energy costs. This is not allowed by law. The rental fee for the apartment or room must be stipulated separately from the *kale huur* (bare dwelling price). Therefore, a simple procedure to complain to the *huurcommissie* can substantially lower your rent!

Unreasonable Demands

An agency may also not insist on unreasonable demands (*onredelijk beding*) such as asking you to pay extra for the keys or pay costs to take over a dwelling from another party, or that you would be asked to sign on to agree to carry the costs of upkeep that are actually the responsibility of the landlord.

Refund Registration Fee – *Inschrijfgeld*

Agencies must also return your registration fee (*inschrijfgeld*) if they have not produced any suitable offering within four months. Specifically, something you could have rented that met your criteria. If you have indicated in writing a maximum rental allowance and a specific neighborhood and you were continually offered more expensive housing in other sectors of the city, you may request the refund.

Additional information and/or Problems Living in Amsterdam Housing

If you should have a complaint about the practices of an agency you have dealt with, you can report this to the city government (*gemeente*) or lodge a complaint via email to either the www.steunpuntwonen.nl (info@steunpuntwonen.nl) or www.bewoners.net sites.

On the support website of steunpuntwonen.nl you will also find links to a number of interest groups in the city representing residents, renters groups, neighborhood groups, as well as the *woningbouw* corporations, city government and data bank. Further, city statistics, a list of all empty dwellings from WoningNet, information on taxes, fees, the point system and how to calculate the maximum rentals are also provided. Although much of the information is in Dutch, most agencies will have someone who can explain things to you in English, or possibly other languages as well. There is an excellent English-language section on the site which provides a great deal of information, however, the entire site has not as yet been translated. This site gives invaluable information to those seeking and living in Amsterdam. If you have complaints, they can be lodged on line through their complaint form or *klachtenmeldingsformulier*.

Squatters

A phenomenon that you may come across is squatters – otherwise known as *krakers* – who live in squatted buildings (*kraakpanden*). A combination of factors including the short supply of inexpensive housing in both the rental and purchase sectors combined with the number of empty houses and buildings purchased for profit speculation has lead to a Squatters' Movement (*Kraakbeweging*).

While we do not advocate going this route when looking for housing, it is well worth mentioning it, as every Dutch person you speak with knows about the *krakers* and *kraakpanden*. The law is such, since 1993, that if a building has been empty for a year, you can claim it as a squatter and move in with your 'squatter's set' of a chair, a table and a bed, along with a new lock and tools. Indeed, on day number 366 squatters will take over an uninhabited dwelling.

Of course the owners of the buildings generally are not at all pleased to have squatters occupying the premises, as now they are unable to either rent or sell the property. There will be a lengthy judicial process to ask for *opruiming* – whereby the police will come and forcibly evict the squatters. Sometimes battles ensue with the squatters dumping things out the windows onto the police below, and the police in riot gear using the water canon to attempt to really 'clean out' the place.

References

SWD, (Stichting Woning Dienst) Zuiderkerkhof 72, 1011 WB Amsterdam,
tel.: 020 680 68 06, fax: 020 552 76 11. Mon 11.00 – 16.00
Tue – Fri 9.00 – 16.00 (Thu till 20.00). www.swd.amsterdam.nl.

More information: order *A Question of Housing*: Looking for Accommodation in Amsterdam. This guide is for everyone who is looking for accommodation in Amsterdam and wishes to know about the rules and regulations, the risks to avoid and the best way to find a place to live. Price: € 3.40 (plus € 0.90 for postage in the Netherlands).

Non-Commercial Room Agencies

ASW Room Agency / Zuiderkerk Housing Information Center, Nieuwezijds Voorburgwal 32, 1012 RZ Amsterdam, tel.: 020 523 01 30, fax: 020 638 29 76. Information room availability, tel.: 020 623 50 37.
Office-hours: Mon. – Wed.: 10.00 – 12.30, 19.00 – 21.00

ASVA Studentenunie Kamerbureau, Binnengasthuisstraat 9, 1012 ZA Amsterdam, tel.: 020 525 31 36, e-mail: kamerbureau@stuc.uva.nl
Costs: € 15 (including membership of the students' union) and a deposit of € 5.00 if you take an address with you.
Open Mon. – Fri. 12.30 – 18.00
(in August till 16.00).
Drawing of lots: Mon., Tue. Wed. and Fri. 16.00 – 18.00

SRVU Kamerbureau, De Boelelaan 1083 A, room N-096, 1081 HV Amsterdam, tel.: 020 444 94 24, e-mail: kamerburo@ext.vu.nl, fax: 020 444 94 23.
Costs: € 10 (per college year including membership of the students' union).
Mon. – Fri. 12.30 – 15.30

Studentflats

Woonstichting De Key (from 18 to 27 years), Hoogte Kadijk 179-189, 1018 BK Amsterdam and Jan Tooropstraat 29, Amsterdam, tel.: 020 621 43 33 or 020 621 44 44
Entrance fee: € 11. Mon. – Thu. 8.30 – 16.30; Fri. 8.30 – 12.30
You may phone for information and a registration form. www.dekey.nl

Intermezzo (from 18 to 29 years), Uilenstede 108, 1183 AM Amstelveen, tel.: 020 543 11 00 or 543 11 23.
You may phone for information and a registration form. Entrance fee: € 15.88.
Mon. – Thu. 9.00 – 16.30, Tue. 9.00 – 17.00, Fri. 9.00 – 12.00

Huurteams

Back Office Huurteams, NZ Voorburgwal 32, 1012 RZ Amsterdam, tel.: 020 428 38 65, fax: 020 638 2976, e-mail: bo.ht@wxs.nl

Other Addresses

Casa Academica, J. Wattstraat 75, 1097 DK Amsterdam, tel.: 020 665 71 81. Only rooms from October 1 until May 31.

Foreign Student Service, Oranje Nassaulaan 5, 1075 AH Amsterdam, tel.: 020 671 59 15. Only for students and for short periods.

Youth hotels
Vondelpark City Hostel, Zandpad 5, 1054 GA Amsterdam, tel.: 020 589 89 99.
Arena, 's Gravesandestraat 51, 1092 AA Amsterdam, tel.: 020 694 74 44.
Studentenhotel, Keizersgracht 15, 1015 CC Amsterdam, tel.: 020 625 13 64.
Stadsdoelen, Kloveniersburgwal 97, 1011 KB Amsterdam, tel.: 020 624 68 32.

The Woonbond publishes a useful booklet entitled 'Op Kamers' or Living in Rooms. See www.woonbond.nl

4

4 Looking for Housing – Resource Pages

There are a number of places you can look for housing. Looking, reading and asking will take up a good deal of your time. You can orient yourself on the current market and see what types of housing are available by visiting the offices of Estate agents or housing agencies. Though most expatriates are not eligible for this, if you are, registering with a *woningbouwverenigingen* or housing association is also an option. Try to have a look at 'reading' the advertisements in the local newspapers, or buying the *Woningkrant*. The Internet offers more information, so consider checking websites via the Internet.

This chapter is about possibilities and resources. Where to look:

Newspapers

The largest daily newspapers available in the Netherlands are:
www.detelegraaf.nl – De Telegraaf
www.volkskrant.nl – De Volkskrant
www.ad.nl – Algemeen dagblad
www.nrc.nl – NRC Handelsblad
www.trouw.nl – Trouw
www.parool.nl – Het Parool

There are also local weekly newspapers in many regions with a small offering of properties.
See http://kranten.nl for a list of all newspapers in the country.

Abbreviations

When reading newspaper advertisements, a number of abbreviations are used in order to save space, and to reduce the cost of the advertisement. Translations of some of the most common abbreviations found in advertisements are:

c.v.	*centrale verwarming* – central heating
t.k.	*te koop* – for sale
kmr.	*kamer* – room
v.o.n.	*vrij op naam* – vendor pays transfer cost
kkn.	*keuken* – kitchen
k.k.	*kosten koper* – costs to be borne by buyer
beg.gr.	*begane grond* – ground floor
vr.p	*vraagprijs* – asking price
verd.	*verdieping* – floor
e.w.	*eensgezinswoning* – single-family dwelling
v.v.	*voorzien van* – equipped with
h.h.	*herenhuis* – mansion
geren.	*gerenoveerd* – renovated
e.g.	*eigen grond* – own ground
ged.	*gedeeltelijk* – partial
app.	*appartement* – apartment
roy.	*royale* – spacious
bijdr.	*bijdrage* – contribution
bj.	*bouwjaar* – building year
vve	*vereniging van eigenaren* – association of owners
karakt.	*karakteristiek* – characteristic
uitz.	*uitzicht* – view
aanv.	*aanvaarding* – acceptance
ben.w.	*benedenwoning* – ground floor living accommodation
i.o.	*in overleg* – to be agreed upon
bov.w.	*bovenwoning* – upper floor accommodation
evt.	*eventueel* – possibly
wk.	*woonkamer* – living room
opp.	*oppervlak* – surface
slp.	*slaapkamer* – bedroom
o.v.	*openbaar vervoer* – public transport
ind.	*indeling* – floor plan

House-Hunting Vocabulary

Also helpful in your search is familiarity with several Dutch terms and phrases that you will see repeatedly during your house-hunting. The most important ones are listed below.

Kosten koper, k.k.	Notaris and registration fees are paid by the buyer.
Vraagprijs	Asking price (negotiable)

Badkamer	Bathroom; usually without a toilet
Bijkeuken	Room off kitchen (pantry or laundry)
Bungalow	Bungalow, a free-standing house with one floor
Centrale verwarming	Central heating
Dakkapel	Dormer
Dakraam	Skylight
Douche	Shower
Eetkamer	Dining room
Eetkeuken	Kitchen with space for eating
Garage	Garage
Gemeentelijk energiebedrijf	Regional or municipal power company
Gemeubileerd	Including furniture
Gestoffeerd	Including drapes, carpeting, ceiling lights
Half vrijstaand/Twee onder een kap	Half of a duplex
Hoekhuis	Corner row house
Hypotheek	Mortgage
Inbouwapparatuur	Built-in appliances
Kamer	Room
Keuken	Kitchen
Ligbad	Bathtub
Makelaar – onroerend goed	Real estate agent
Notaris	Attorney of real estate and wills
NVM	Dutch Association of Real Estate Agents
(Goed) onderhouden	Well-maintained: in good condition
Open haard	Fireplace
Serre	Sun room
Slaapkamer	Bedroom
Taxateur	Appraiser
Te huur	For rent
Te koop	For sale
Trap	Stairs
Tuin	Yard, garden
Verhuurd	Rented
Verkocht	Sold
Villa	Large free-standing house with grounds
Voorlopig koopcontract	Offer to buy (binding)
Vrijstaand	Completely detached or free-standing
Wastafel	Washbasin; sink
Woonkamer	Living room

Websites and resources

There are a number of 'start pages' available where search engines have provided lists of resources. If you go to www.startpagina.nl you can see alphabetical category listings or *rubrieken*. Some subject matter has so much information available that they have made up offshoot pages or *dochters* under a stand-alone heading, and then new sub category listings to take you further into the subject matter.

Dutch Search Engines

You may also go to the favorite search engines or *zoekmachines* to look for more information:
www.ilse.nl
www.google.com
www.vindex.nl
www.altavista.nl

Here are a few listings of sites to get you started:
Rentals
www.steunpuntwonen.nl – support for renters
www.bewoners.net – network for renters, agencies, even a manual for squatters
http://kamers.pagina.nl – rooms throughout the country, student associations, commercial and non-commercial bureaus
http://bewoners.pagina.nl – more info on 'living' somewhere

Housing Start Pages
http://makelaars.pagina.nl – (in Dutch) lists all estate agents in the country
http://woning.pagina.nl – 'living' numerous resources for homes
www.makelaar.lokaalzoeken.nl – search for a listing of local agents

Housing Websites
www.eigenhuis.nl – Vereniging Eigen Huis – Homeowners 'own house'
www.huisnl.com – houses, building lots, company sites in the Netherlands
www.inform.nl/woningbv/index.htm – list of all *Woningbouwverenigingen* or Housing Associations
www.funda.nl – site of the NVM Dutch *Makelaars vereniging* – Professional Association of Dutch Estate Agents. This is the largest site online covering 60% of the housing market
http://www.mva-makelaars.nl – see members listing (*leden*) for MVA estate agents
www.vbo.nl – *Vereniging Bemiddeling Onroerendgoed* – professional association of estate agents who negotiate for real estate transactions.
www.woningcourant.com – news of houses for sale and rent and developments – data bank for National Woning Instituut (NWI) Housing Institute also for *kavels* building sites
www.housingonline.nl – website in English covering housing, cities, pathfinders, registrations, etc.
www.huislijn.nl – site from the LMV
www.huisplein.nl – site from the VBO
www.woninggids.nl – site from the ERA estate agents

www.woonkrant.nl – Living/housing newspaper on line
www.digimmo.nl – you can check on the price developments in respective areas, all transactions that are listed in the *kadaster* (city registry)
www.huistekoop.nl – house for sale site
www.wonenplein.nl – also English section
www.vveplaza.nl – purchase of apartments
www.123huren.nl – For those who would rather rent than buy
www.kadaster.nl – the cadastre register information in English
www.tvnsite.nl – temporary rentals for residential accommodation and housing management
www.perfecthousing.nl – website in English covering housing
www.ikzoekeenhuis.nl – house for sale site

Architecture
www.archistart.nl
www.house-of-design.nl
www.bna.nl – the bond of Dutch architects (*Bond Nederlandse Architecten*)

Interior Architecture & Remodeling
www.interieurplein.nl – decorating your interior
www.bouwen.nl – looking for contractors, plumbers and other skilled building trade
www.bouwnet.com – info on building and remodeling

Legalities
www.wetwegwijzer.nl – everything you ever wanted to know about Dutch laws
www.notaris.nl – notary (*notaris*) info
www.nvm.nl – estate agents
www.bestemmingsplan.nl – if you have building plans this is the site you need
www.vrom.nl – Housing and environmental agency
www.minjus.nl – The Ministry of Justice has listed under 'Boetebak' (Fines) a listing of all the penalties or fines for breaking the law, speeding, parking, etc.
www.fiscaal.nl – starting point for fiscal questions
www.belastingdienst.nl – the national tax inspection (folders available in English)

Exchanging Dwellings
www.woningruil.nl

Around the House
www.repairclinic.com – how to fix things:
www.karwei.nl/klussen- tips to do things your self
www.tuinen.nl – garden information
www.klusplein.nl – information on domestic house projects (*klussen*)

Safety / Prevention

www.politie.nl/home/preventie/default.htm – preventing break-ins
www.veiligheid.pagina.nl – everything having to do with safety (*veiligheid*).
www.ncpreventie.nl – national center for prevention

Costs & Finances

www.nibud.nl – The Netherlands Institute for Budget planning – costs of kids, study, house
www.hypotheker.nl – mortgage calculator
www.fx.nl – info on insurance, pension and investments
www.verzekeraars.org – consumer information about insurance/insurers
www.delaagsterente.nl – lowest interest rates
www.independer.nl – comparisons of banking products
www.huis-hypotheek.nl – information from independent professional mortgage advisors

Newspapers and Magazines

The *Woningkrant* is published by the municipality (*gemeente*) and lists available housing in that area. This newspaper-version, which appears each week, has often been surpassed by the online version. Those people having access to the Internet have been able to respond more quickly to apply for accommodations than those waiting for the paper version. www.woningkrant.nl

When searching, often if you type in the name of the city you wish to live in followed by '.nl' you will most likely find the municipality (*gemeente*) information, for instance www.amsterdam.nl or www.rotterdam.nl or www.utrecht.nl. Sometimes there will be an 'online' added to the name such as in www.haarlemonline.nl

Municipalities

You may also check www.nvg.nl *Nederlanse Vereniging van Gemeentes* which is the organization of the Association of Dutch Municipalities. This site will provide connections to all available *gemeentes* online. This will give you access to a great deal of local information from all municipal departments and names of the relevant contact persons.

Television

There are listings of houses available through the local TV *Woningkrant* or *Woon*TV and Woonmagazine on the local television station, again, it's all in Dutch so it may not help you other than to look at the photos and see the prices. Additionally, there is information in Dutch provided on the *Teletext* system of your television. Programs on decorating and home improvements have also become very popular, and a good way to come up with new ideas, or to see firsthand how to do some projects yourself. For more ideas on remodeling jobs (*klussen*) see http://klus.pagina.nl

Looking for Rooms

Rooms (*kamers*) are hard to find, you may have more luck finding a hotel! Studio apartments are extremely small apartments, but a step up from *kamers*. A *Maisonette* is a small apartment on two floors, or levels.

www.opkamers.nl – rooms general
www.studentenkamers.nl – rooms for students
www.kamernet.nl – network for looking for rooms
www.kamers.nl – more rooms

New Housing Projects

http://architectuur.pagina.nl – start page for architecture
www.archistart.com – architects
www.archinned.nl – architects in the Netherlands
www.vastgoedsites.nl – property for sale in Holland
http://nieuwbouw.pagina.nl – startpage for new construction homes
www.nieuwbouwwoningen.nl – new construction
www.vinexonsite.nl – Vinex projects
www.vinex-locaties.nl – locations for proposed Vinex projects
http://ro-projecten.pagina.nl – start page for building projects

International Housing

There are of course hundreds of websites to look at from most countries. A few suggestions that contain some good articles about moving, searching, remodeling etc. in English are:

www.owners.com – Online housing market with supporting services
www.realtor.com – The largest Internet site for properties (also international)
www.rent.net – Over 6.5 million rentals in 6,000 cities
www.vivenda.nl – Publishes Vivenda Exclusive magazine, a quarterly in English offering spectacular up-market properties. Vivenda is a member of EEP, the European Estate Publishers, an international media concept for real estate agents in Europe, the USA and internationally, offering access to the top of the market supply. Prices begin at 1 million euros and continue upwards.
www.droomhuis.nu – dream houses
www.landerije.nl – estates (*landgoederen*) and *woonboerderijen* (gentleman's farms).
www.europropertise.com – properties in Europe

Other Dutch Housing

If you are thinking about some rather non-traditional housing options here are some ideas.

Houseboats
Houseboats can be found throughout the country in waterways, on lakes or right alongside the canals such as in Amsterdam. One benefit is that you do not pay any property tax when you live on a houseboat. You will need to have access to utilities for which you will pay a hook-up fee and your use.

http://woonboot.pagina.nl – the start page for houseboats
www.bootwoningen.nl – living on boats – houseboats for sale
www.awn.nl – advice bureau for info over a *woonboot* or *woonark*

Monuments
The Dutch are proud of their architectural heritage and many of the old buildings come under the protection of *Monumentenzorg* or Protection of Monuments. If you purchase a house that is protected by the *Monumentenzorg* you are bound by strict regulations and cannot just remodel or change anything in the house without express permission. This is to ensure that beautiful old homes will not be modernized beyond recognition and lose much of their characteristic charm.

www.monumentenzorg.nl – Care and Protection of Monuments site
http://monumenten.pagina.nl – Start page for information on all listed monuments
www.bmz.amsterdam.nl – The Amsterdam monuments have pages in English
www.monumenten.nl – Dutch monuments site

Castles
Remainders from a rich past and colorful history, a good deal of castles can still be found throughout the country. Some have been converted into restaurants and hotels, conference centers and even a health spa. A weekend get-away might be an enchanting option if you are not looking to buy. If you are in the market however to become 'lord of the castle' they are offered for sale.

http://kastelen.pagina.nl – This page has listings for every castle in the Netherlands. You might like to visit them, some are open to the public, or at least have a look on a drive by. Some castles are for sale!

Windmills
Although people like to fantasize about living in a windmill, the truth of the matter is that only millers (*molenaars*) have permission to live in them if the mill is a working windmill, since they need to be maintained. If they are no longer in use, the inhabitant will still be a miller as the association or guild keeps the care and upkeep of the mills within their own group of knowledgeable millers.

See the start page: http://molen.pagina.nl for more info (a *molen* is a windmill!)

Eco-Houses

The Dutch have also built ecologically friendly houses, usually in special eco-developments where everyone is *milieubewust*, or environmentally conscious. These homes are fabricated using special energy saving techniques such as having a portion of the building underground or built into an embankment for insulation purposes. Some houses even have sod with grass growing on the roof.

Eco houses also use environmentally friendly energy sources such as solar panels and have water saving devices installed. For all information regarding environmental issues see: http://milieu.pagina.nl

Other Resources

Events – Decorating Art/Furnishings/Antiques

www.huishoudbeurs.nl – The Household Fair (*Huishoudbeurs*) is held at the RAI (Convention Center) in Amsterdam in March featuring the latest trends in furniture, accessories, kitchens, bathrooms, food kitchen gadgets, cosmetics and fashion

www.tfo.nl – Home and Lifestyle Fair – an exclusive fair with inspirational and new decorating ideas

www.hollandartfair.nl – Holland Art Fair in The Hague featuring old and modern art

www.tefaf.com – The prestigious European Fine Art Fair in Maastricht

www.artrotterdam.com – Art & Antiques fair in Rotterdam

For a listing each month of arts and events, check the information in Roundabout magazine: www.roundabout.nl

Free Gifts

When you are moving, be sure to contact the following organizations for free gifts:

www.felicitas.nl – Felicitas means, 'to congratulate' – Order online the new house package for the 'newly moved' Felicitas also has 'congratulations' packages for babies & newly-weds

www.rejoice.nl – Rejoice company – order online – free box of gift products from a Christian organization for new homes (*nieuwe woningen*) also for newly-weds, anniversaries, and babies

www.vt-wonen.nl – *Het Nieuwe Huisplan* – book full of ideas in Dutch for moving and one for remodelling. Order online under moving (*verhuizen*)

Helpful Tip

For more information to help you understand the lingo in your search for housing please refer to Chapter 6A for the translation of vocabulary terms having to do with housing.

A list of useful organizations with their contact information and websites is included in the back of this book. Both should prove helpful.

5

5 Buying a House in the Netherlands – An Overview

For many residents in the Netherlands, Dutch or foreign, there comes a time when they take a critical look at their housing situation. Renting a house or apartment may give more freedom of movement, less hassle with maintenance and yearly upkeep, and lower taxes. But on the downside, a rented place will never be your own, rents rise yearly and getting your landlord to do the necessary maintenance and repair works may prove an exercise in frustration.

Buying a house, on the other hand, gives a feeling of stability, investing in something that will ultimately become your property. With mortgages that can be set at fixed interest rates from 1 up to 30 years, you can plan your housing costs as far ahead as you chose. Obviously there are also less charming sides to owning a house: higher taxes and the costs of repairs and maintenance which are your sole responsibility. Nevertheless, when weighing the pros and cons, and with affordable rental properties in short supply, many people take the step towards buying a house.

Especially for expatriates, as attractive as the idea may be, in practice this may seem a daunting prospect. When you are not fully aware of the legal ins and outs and the common practices in the Dutch real estate market, the process may easily become overwhelming.

NOTE: This overview will give you a 'basic guideline' in the steps to take when you are considering buying a house. ***For full information*** **refer to the next chapters listed where we will go into more detail.**

A. Location

One of the most important decisions to make is where to buy. If you have lived in a town or city for some time and like it there, the choice may be easy. But if you are looking at other cities and are not familiar with the area, it may be a good idea to drive around and see if they match your requirements (e.g. in the vicinity of schools, shops in the neighborhood, commuting time to work, etc.). Location is also a very decisive factor in setting price levels. In order to get a general idea of what is available in the market and at what prices, the following two websites may prove helpful: www.funda.nl (in Dutch) and www.era.nl (also in English). Please note that there may be a delay in the updates of the listings on these web pages, so properties advertised may already have been sold.

B. Mortgage Advice

(See chapter 7 *Financial Considerations – Mortgages and Insurances* for more details)

Before you actively start looking around and approaching real estate agents, it is useful to know how far you are able (and willing) to go financially. There are various ways of getting advice and information on mortgages:

1. **From your bank**: the advantage here is that they know you as a customer and have your financial 'history'. The disadvantage is that they only offer one product: their own, and this may not always be the most tailor-made solution for you.

2. **From an 'independent' mortgage adviser** (shops such as 'De Hypotheker', 'Huis en Hypotheek'): the advantage of these shops is that they offer a wider portfolio of mortgages from various sources and will advise you on the product that best meets your needs. A disadvantage is that some of these shops are known to steer you in the direction of the mortgage provider that offers the best commission. Whilst the outcome may still be a good deal for you, it begs the question how independent these shops really are.

3. **From a financial advisor** (often found in-house with many real estate agents): the advantage here is that these finance consultants can offer advice on more than just mortgages. Taxes and insurances are mostly also part of their services, so you can get a complete picture. However, as they will be working in close co-operation with the realtor, they may not be completely impartial in their advice.

One word of warning: all providers tend to offer mortgages to the top of your financial limits. As tempting as these amounts may seem, it is wise not to go over the top. With current interest rates on the low side, monthly payments may seem reasonable. But will you still be able to afford this in ten years time, if the interest rate should have doubled? Also, there are rumors that the tax benefit on mortgage interests (see *Taxes*) will be reduced by the government in line with European harmonization. This will substantially increase the financial burden of many house owners. A general rule of thumb is that housing costs should be roughly one-third of your monthly income.

C. Real Estate Agent

(See chapter 6 *Purchasing a House*, under The *Makelaar, or Estate Agent*)

The next step is finding a real estate agent. For over a year now, the position of estate agent (realtorship or *makelaardij*) has been a 'free occupation', meaning that it is no longer necessary to study and do exams to become a realtor. Whilst there are undoubtedly a number of knowledgeable and trustworthy free agents in the market, there is a safeguard in using a real estate agent who is a member of the nationwide association NVM (*Nederlandse Vereniging van Makelaars*), simply because they have years of experience and a whole organization behind them. Another well-established realtors organization is ERA, which only allows NVM realtors to become members.

Local Agent

It is advisable to contact a real estate agent in the city you want to buy in. Although some realtors work across a wider area, they may not always be aware of the specific ins and outs of a city, if they do not work there regularly. Things such as bidding systems, advice on building plans in a certain area (*bestemmingsplan*), soil contamination and city council regulations are items that are specific for each city. A local realtor is best equipped to advise you on this.

Assistance from Beginning to End

In principle a real estate agent can assist you from beginning to end: from searching for and viewing houses to the taxation, technical inspection, negotiations and the administrative work that comes with this. You can opt to look for houses yourself (driving around or via the Internet) and only use the realtor for viewings and negotiations, or you can place a so-called 'search order' (*zoekopdracht*). During an intake meeting the realtor will take down all your requirements and you will automatically be informed when a property becomes available that matches your requirements. There is a one-off cost involved in placing a search order, but this will mostly be deducted from the brokerage fee once a house has been found.

New House

If you are considering buying a house that is to be / being built, with a set price, the role of the realtor is somewhat more limited. Nevertheless, a realtor can assist by assessing the construction drawings and mediate if any problems should occur afterwards.

In general, the work of a realtor does not stop once you have moved into your house. If there should be any constructional or other problems that the previous owner should have told you about (and that were not noted during the viewings and inspections), the realtor is the person to deal with these problems.

Brokerage Fee

Real estate agents charge a brokerage fee (*courtage*) for their services. This is usually between 1.5 to 2% of the purchase price of the house, but with some realtors the percentage is negotiable. On a house of € 500,000. a 2% *courtage* amounts to only € 10,000. Considering that the estate agent negotiates from a business perspective and not an emotional one as you may be inclined to do, and has handled all the details for you, the chances are he was able to negotiate some discount on the house or other extra savings for you. Money well spent for service and professional advice.

D. Costs Involved in Buying a House

(See chapter 2 *Housing – Rentals* under *Extra Costs and Levies*)

For an existing house, on top of the purchase price, you pay the so-called 'buyer's costs' (*kosten koper* or *k.k.*), which consist of the costs for the notary public, appraisal costs, costs for concluding the mortgage, conveyance tax and the realtor's brokerage fee. In total these buyer's costs amount to approximately 10 % to 12% of the purchase price. The costs related to financing are tax-deductible.

Newly built houses are sold 'free on name' (*vrij op naam*), meaning that no conveyance tax is due. In total the costs then amount to between 7 to 8% on the (fixed) purchase price. However, during the building period interest is due on that part of the house that has been finished.

It is also a good idea to find out what the current costs (*lasten*) are for the utilities and taxes on the house. The current owner can provide you with this information.

These are additional costs you need to be aware of when deciding what you can afford to pay out each month.

E. Buying an Existing House vs. One That Is to Be Built

(See chapter 6 *Purchasing a House*, under *Nieuwbouw*)

Apart from your personal preferences for older or new houses, the following aspects are to be borne in mind.

The extra costs of buying a newly built house are a few percentages lower than those for existing houses and for the first couple of years there is less maintenance to be expected. Sometimes it is possible to adapt the construction drawings to your own requirements, although additional costs may be involved in this. Frequently the house has already risen in value by the time it is finished. On the down side, a new house will cost you more on interior finishings (floor and wall coverings) and garden architecture, as it is delivered completely bare. Plus you will never be completely sure what the house and the neighborhood will look like once finished. Also, some cities have restrictions on selling a newly built house for the first couple of years, to prevent housing speculation.

With existing houses what you see is what you get and the only additional costs, if any, to be budgeted for are those of renovating (parts of the) house to meet your special requirements. Older houses, depending on their state of upkeep, may require more maintenance right from the start.

F. Once You Have Found a House

(See chapter 6 *Purchasing a House*, under *Procedures*)

When you have found the house that matches your requirements, things start firming up. If, after inspection by your real estate agent, you are not 100% convinced of the technical details, it is wise to have an architectural report made up. Costs of such a report depend on the size of the house but on average you should count on € 272. Your realtor should be able to assist you with this, or otherwise you can request an impartial report from a specialized building consultant or from the Dutch House Owners' Association (*Vereniging Eigen Huis*). If you subscribe to the latter association you will receive their bi-monthly magazine and can always fall back on their expertise and assistance against reduced rates. Annual subscription is € 16.

Act Quickly

In a market where demand is far greater than supply, it may be necessary to act very quickly if you really want to secure a property. For your realtor to be able to negotiate successfully on your behalf, (s)he needs a full briefing as to how far you are willing to go. Whereas previously the asking price was the maximum the seller was hoping to receive for a house, with so many bidders in the market, it is not uncommon for houses to be sold well above asking price. Bidding on houses varies from city to city; in some cities no second bidder is accepted until the first one is definitely out, in other cities a second bidder can make one offer over the first and then it is up to the seller to decide. Your realtor will be able to advise you on this and on the best way to proceed.

Taxes, Costs & woz-Appraisal Value

Do check with the seller of the property what the most recent woz-appraisal value (see below and chapter 6 – *Purchasing a House*) of the house was. This value of the house is essential for establishing the rental value in relation to the tax benefits on owning a house (see Taxes below). Also check what the last known local property taxes were, to get an idea of the yearly costs involved here. It may be helpful to inquire as to what kind of utility costs the current owners have been paying.

Provisional Purchase Deed

Once your bid is accepted, the property is technically yours. Verbal agreements are legally binding in the Netherlands; so do not say 'aye' unless you're really willing to buy. When the deal is concluded, a provisional purchase deed will be made up by a notary public selected by the seller. An important clause in this deed is the one that makes the purchase conditional upon your being able to obtain the necessary financing. If you cannot obtain the financing, the contract is dissolved, but you have to be able to prove that you have indeed made all reasonable attempts to secure the financing. Other articles in the purchase deed include any taxes and levies attached to the property and the ground rent (land lease, *erfpacht*), if the house is built on ground belonging to the city council. With the provisional purchase deed you will need to make a deposit, usually in the form of a bank guarantee, of 10% of the purchase price. This refundable deposit or bank guarantee can be arranged through your mortgage provider.

Appraisal for Mortgage

Between the provisional and the final purchase deed, which is usually on the day you accept the key to the house, all details regarding the mortgage are finalized. Your mortgage provider will request an appraisal report (by an independent realtor) to assess the height of the mortgage in relation to the value of the property. The appraisal value is not based on the free market value of the house, but on what it would raise if it were sold of necessity. Hence it is always less than the purchase price, but the closer it approaches the purchase price, the better it is, as the mortgage provider will finance up to 125% of the appraisal value. The mortgage provider will also require proof that you have concluded an adequate building insurance (*opstalverzekering*). As the house is their security, they want to be sure that, should it be destroyed through e.g. fire or weather, it is insured for re-building.

Walk-Through

On the day of conveyance, it is common to do a walk-through of the property together with your realtor, the seller and the seller's realtor. This is the time for a last inspection of any hidden defects and the utilities are transferred to your name. After the inspection all documents are signed at the notary public and you are now the legal owner of your house. It sometimes happens that you can receive the key to the house prior to the conveyance date, in which case so-called 'key money' (*sleutelgeld*) is required as an insurance to the seller should anything go wrong in the house while (s)he is still technically the owner.

G. Monthly Housing Costs

Depending on the type of mortgage chosen, you will have to pay the monthly interest on the amount loaned plus a monthly installment to redeem the loan, or a monthly premium if you have chosen for a savings or investment scheme. For apartments and depending whether there is an Association of Owners (*Vereniging van Eigenaren* or VVE), monthly service costs are due for the cleaning and maintenance of communal areas. If you are considering buying an apartment, do check if there is an active Association of Owners and check whether its financial position is solid. This to avoid unpleasant surprises and high costs when essential repairs need to be done and there are no sufficient funds so the individual owners need to pay for the repairs out of pocket in addition to the monthly service costs.

H. Taxes

(See chapter 6 *Purchasing a House*, under The WOZ-Waarde, or WOZ-Appraisal Value and chapter 7 *Financial Considerations* – Mortgages and Insurances, under Interest Rates)
The most common taxes for house owners are: property tax (owner's and user's part), waste disposal tax, sewage tax, land tax, pollution and inhabitants tax, and ground rent (*erfpacht*, or land lease) if your house is on land owned by the city.

woz-Appraisal Value

The height of most of these taxes is in percentages of the city's appraisal value of your house. Once every four years, the city council does this appraisal in the context of the Law on Real Estate Taxation (*Wet Onroerende Zaakbelasting* or woz). The result will be communicated to you in a letter from the city council, together with an explanation on how to object. As the resulting amount is not only relevant for local taxes, but also determines the height of your tax reimbursement (see below), it is advisable to seek advice on the effects this appraisal has on your financial situation.

Reimbursement

If you are on Dutch payroll and all taxes are paid to the Dutch government, you are entitled to the same benefits Dutch citizens have. Apart from social welfare, this also includes a tax reimbursement for owning a house. Basically, the calculation works as follows: take the yearly interest paid on the mortgage minus a fictitious rental value of the property you own (*eigenwoningforfait* – or deemed rental income – which is determined on the basis of the woz-appraisal value and is explained in the folder that goes with the tax reimbursement request). The resulting amount, divided by twelve, gives the gross monthly amount to be reimbursed. From this deduct the percentage in taxes related to the tax bracket you are in and this gives you the net amount that will monthly be reimbursed to you by automatic payment.

In general, the tax reimbursement request forms are sent out at the end of October and should be in before December 1 in order to be handled and come into effect as of January 1 the next year. If you have bought a house in the course of the year, you can pro-rate the amounts to the corresponding period.

You can also opt not to apply for a monthly reimbursement, but settle this via your yearly statement for income tax statement to be submitted before April 1 each year. Depending on your personal situation and the tax bracket you are in, the advantage in this can be that you receive one lump sum instead of monthly installments.

If you need any further detailed information on taxes and tax reimbursements, we suggest you visit a specialized financial consultant.

I. Insurances

The following insurances are advisable, if not mandatory, if you own a house: building insurance (required by the mortgage provider), glass insurance, third party liability insurance and household goods insurance. Optional are insurances such as personal belongings and valuables, sports equipment and additional coverage on your household goods if you take them outside the house, for instance a camera or skis when traveling. We explain each type in some detail in chapter 7 *Financial Considerations: Mortgages & Insurances.*

Obviously there are a great number of things to take into consideration when renting or purchasing property in the Netherlands. Each of the following chapters in *Housing in Holland* will go into much further detail on these and a variety of other subjects, so ... read on!

6

6 Purchasing a House

Owning your own home can be a benefit to you not only from a sense of 'homeowner's security', it can have positive financial implications as well. As it is a big decision, we recommend that you should first rent for at least one year and then decide whether you would like to purchase a house or not. This will give you time to decide on where you would like to live and if you would like to live in the Netherlands for a longer period of time. The following is a brief overview of the subject matter this book will go into in greater detail throughout subsequent chapters.

A. Financial Aspects

Given the high costs of rentals in the Netherlands, many expatriates are looking at home purchase as an option. Prices have risen steadily some 8 to 12% per year over the last few years. In the well-populated Randstad area (Amsterdam, Haarlem, The Hague, Utrecht, Leiden, Rotterdam) prices have practically doubled since 1992.

Still, investing in property is highly speculative at best. Although housing prices have been on the increase over the past few years, there are indications of stabilization in the Dutch market.
Appreciation of property values has slowed to a more moderate pace and there is no guarantee of selling with a hefty profit.

If you move elsewhere and decide to rent the property, it will be considered a second home for tax purposes, and any deductions will be lost. Should you decide to rent out the property here, there are agencies who will manage properties for you for a fee. However, there is no guarantee that they will maintain the property as regularly as you would like, especially if they manage a large number of properties. You also never know if you will incur extra expenses for the upkeep or repairs to the property due to neglect, storm, fire, flooding, bad tenants or other maintenance problems. It may often be easier to re-sell the Dutch property (hopefully with a profit) and just purchase a new home in your next location.

Costs

As a general rule, the costs of purchasing a house in the Netherlands amount to approximately 10% of the price of the house. These tax-deductible expenses cover:

- appraisal costs (expense for having the house officially appraised in order to secure mortgage)
- notary costs mortgage deed (*hypotheekakte*) (VAT/BTW)
- cadastral registration fee mortgage law
- cadastral investigation cost (mortgage including VAT/BTW)
- administration costs mortgage deed
- closing costs
- National Mortgage Insurance – *Nationale Hypotheek garantie*.

If you take out a mortgage to finance your house in the Netherlands, you may deduct the full amount of interest and specific mortgage-related expenses from your taxable income. On a house of € 350,000 your approximate cost would be an additional € 35,000 over and above the € 350,000 asking price.

Asking Price

When bidding on properties, the asking price (*vraagprijs*) can probably be negotiated down by 5 to 10%, so you can consider it the ceiling price, unless of course there is someone biding against you on the property.

Extra Costs

On top of this there are the additional costs of property taxes, environmental levies, water purification taxes, and the land draining rate, (typically Dutch since we are below sea level). Include as well in your financial picture the costs of refuse collection, utilities, telephone, Internet service provider, cable rates, radio and television license fee, (dog tax) and of course your home maintenance and your property and liability insurances. For the complete list refer to the end of the chapter on Rentals.

In the Netherlands property is taxed based on both ownership and tenancy. Thus, as a homeowner living in your own home you are taxed on a 1/3 percentage for the rental/living in portion and 2/3 for the ownership portion. Bear in mind the extra costs as well of redecorating, painting, curtains, hardware, carpet, lighting fixtures, etc. When purchasing a home here be sure you have an exact inventory made up of what items are specified to remain in the house to avoid surprises. Oftentimes anything that is not specified will be removed from the property. (This may include overhead lighting, stained glass, bathroom accessories, even if deemed 'bolted down' items.)

Kosten Koper – Buyer's Costs

Often, in an advertisement of flyer, you will see the abbreviation 'k.k.' or the words *kosten koper*. This means 'the costs to the buyer' and is comprised of the following (some of which you will already have seen above):

- purchase price (*koopsom*)
- transfer tax of 6% (*overdrachtsbelasting*)
- notary cost of deed conveyance (including VAT/BTW)
- cadastral investigation costs (proprietary act)
- cadastral registration fee (proprietary act).

Of interest to know is that the following costs listed below are tax-deductible and can be declared (one-time) on your income tax return:

- notary costs mortgage deed (hypotheekakte) (VAT/BTW)
- cadastral registration fee mortgage law
- cadastral investigation cost (mortgage including VAT/BTW)
- administration costs mortgage deed
- closing costs
- National Mortgage Insurance – *Nationale Hypotheek Garantie.*

Financing

Since as an expatriate or new arrival you will have no credit rating in the Netherlands, you will need to supply some references to the Dutch bank when applying for a loan, showing your good credit history in your home country or last place of residence as a homeowner. You will need to open an account with a Dutch bank, where your salary will be deposited each month, and provide a copy of your employment contract. A reasonable amount in deposit for a down payment is advisable (10% or more). It is a good idea to find out beforehand what your limit for financing will be, what the current rates of interest are, what types of mortgages are available – in other words, how much credit the bank is willing to extend to you. It will also save time in the negotiating phase if you can already show that securing your financing poses no problem. Very often a real estate deal will fall through due to the buyer being unable to finance the mortgage.

The bank will also require a certified report (*taxatierapport*) on the condition and value of the house before granting the loan. An Inspection and report made by a professional estate agent – the cost is a percentage (*promillage*) rated to the value of the property in the taxation report. The percentage is 1.85 for properties up to € 123,536 with a minimum of *taxatie* costs of € 123.50, for houses above this minimum yet under € 490,894 the *promillage* is 1.65, and above this rate, higher than € 834.52 the promillage is 1.5 Please note, these rates are a guideline, as the rate may be negotiated with your *taxateur*). Read more in this chapter under *Taxaties* in section E. You may be asked to carry extra life insurance (secured loan) to meet the banks repayment criteria (arranged by the bank in conjunction with the duration of the loan).

There are many forms of financing a house. The mortgage (*hypotheek*) interest rates vary based on the term and conditions of the loan. On new construction homes, some mortgages are currently offered at a much lower rate, however these homes are in high demand and there are long waiting lists for the purchase of new construction homes.

The housing market in the Netherlands is quite competitive, and given the scarcity in some areas and price classes, you may find it a very time-consuming and often frustrating affair to search for a house. Many people currently are bidding well over the asking price, further driving up the prices. This adds to the tension due to frequently having your bids rejected. Set a limit for yourself.

Residency

Most often it is easier to secure the bank loan once you have already established your residence here and all your registrations with the Foreign Police (*vreemdelingenpolitie*) and Town Hall are in order. Once you decide to 'make the move' you will need to arrange to speak with an estate agent who can give you detailed professional advice, as well as arrange an appointment with a Dutch financial institution to discuss the various constructions available for loans. European Union (EU)-residents may have fewer problems than other foreigners in terms of residency – nonetheless, when it comes to finances, the banks remain strict.

Many expatriates who are considering purchasing a home here opt to rent for a few months and get a 'feel' for different areas and lifestyles in Holland before making the commitment to purchase in a particular area. This gives them time as well to research the market, to allow the estate agent (*makelaar*) to work effectively on their behalf and to establish their residency.

Tax Benefits

As an expatriate, it is always advisable to secure good tax advice from your company's tax experts, taking into consideration the terms of your employment contract, the duration of your stay abroad, your housing allowance in the Netherlands (paid by employer or self), and where you claim your principal place of residence, should you be maintaining a property in your home country, or if you have a vacation home. Please be aware that buying a house can be financially attractive, since the interest paid for your mortgage is still tax-deductible.

Generally, it is not advisable to purchase if you will be re-selling within two years, as you will not recoup your initial investment due to all of the costs incurred. Should you rent the 'Dutch house' out when leaving the Netherlands – for tax purposes – it will be regarded as a second home and a higher rate of tax will be applicable since this will no longer be your principal place of residence.

For expatriates who are taxed under the 30%-ruling, real estate investment could provide some good deductions on your taxable income. For Dutch tax purposes, the local authorities allocate one percent tax to the book value of properties, which will again add costs to your taxable income. Granted, in the first year of purchase a number of deductions can be taken for income tax purposes, but thereafter, the appreciation needs to be fairly substantial in order to recoup your investment.

B. Things to Be Aware Of Before Purchasing

As with most things, the better informed you are beforehand, the more informed your decision will be when purchasing property. When you are out looking, keep in mind the following:

1. **Sitting tenants** – Watch out; it can be a lengthy and costly process to remove tenants from a residence if they are unwilling to vacate the premises. If the building is currently rented out to 'sitting tenants' make sure that the rental contract in effect explicitly states that the house will be *leeg opgeleverd* (delivered empty). The responsibility thereby remains with the seller.

2. **Quick Fix Renovations** – A newly renovated house that is being sold immediately is generally cause for suspicion. Carefully examine the condition of the building inside and out. A building in poor condition may have received a quick plaster and paint job to camouflage defects such as cracks in the walls, putty and paint over rotting windowsills or to hide asbestos. If there are obvious cracks on the outside these will also show up on the inside. Always look carefully at the general condition of the house to spare yourself unpleasant and

expensive structural surprises. Keep in mind that a speedy renovation for a quick sale will most likely not have been carried out with the care and quality of materials you yourself would have chosen.

3. **Aanschrijvingen** – Occasionally the *gemeente* will issue compulsory work orders. If you are willing to commit to carrying out the required repairs, an apartment building with an empty floor can provide an inexpensive way to purchase. However, generally the repairs must be carried out with in a specified period of time. If the building is listed as a monument strict adherence to the provisions is absolutely essential. Monuments must be restored in the 'original' style with a minimum of 'modernizing' which restricts your redecorating choices. It is also a good idea too check with the *gemeente* for proposed development projects in the area.

4. **Floors** – Inspect the condition of the floors, especially if the premises are located on the ground level, for soft spots, which indicate rotting underneath. Rising damp in the walls is another sure sign of rotting floors. If in doubt, bringing in an expert for advice could save you the cost and inconvenience of installing an entirely new floor.

5. **Plumbing and Fixtures** – Many old houses in city centers still have lead water pipes. Old pipes have furred up over the years with chalk and lime deposits, so this does not pose a health risk, as many people believe. The government has ruled that all lead pipes must be replaced by 2002, the expense of which will be incurred by the OWNER of the property. Consider this cost when deciding what to bid for the property.

6. **Old Electricity** – Watch out for old wiring in steel conduit, and old wiring in cloth covered cable; these will need to be replaced with new cable in PVC conduits. If you are planning to add large appliances such as a dishwasher, clothes dryer, or large oven you may need to add another 'group' in your electric service *meterkast* to handle the additional load.

7. **Old Central Heating** – How old is the system? Given Holland's damp and chilly climate the last thing you want to discover is that the central heating is not working. Most central heating boilers or CV *Ketels* are written off after about ten years. They become too costly to repair or the parts are discontinued. New systems such as a *hoge rendement ketel* (high performance system) provide energy-efficient savings and efficient output.

8. **Funderingsrapport (Foundation Report)** – Many older Dutch houses are built on wooden piles and some parts of the country affected by higher water levels are slowly sinking. A good portion of the Netherlands lies below sea level. The *funderingsrapport* is a survey conducted by the local municipality (*gemeente*) to determine the quality of the building's foundations. Not every house needs this inspection; generally only buildings dating before 1920 or in areas where problems have been found. A poor foundation or sinking soil bed could cause structural damage to the building, the least of which is cracks in the walls (which could, however, lead to collapsing floors). Newer buildings have steel or concrete piles, which are not susceptible to wood rot. Ratings will be 1 through 4, with 1 passing inspection and 4 indicating that serious repairs will need to be made. In some *gemeentes* you may be eligible for a subsidy for repairs. The seller is legally under obligation to mention the *funderingsrapport* findings to a potential buyer and failure to do so will result in the seller being held liable for the repairs. The seller is expected to negotiate in good faith. If you have doubts, check with the *gemeente* to see if an inspection has been carried out and if indeed a foundation report exists.

9. **Bewonersvereniging** – The Dutch equivalent of an Apartment Building Cooperative (owners' association) or a Body Corporation which needs to be taken into consideration when purchasing an apartment that constitutes part of a block of units. There will usually be a yearly maintenance fee for the use of shared or common areas of the building and exterior upkeep. Enquire as to what the exact costs and responsibilities are when calculating the total cost of the mortgage.

10. **Erfpacht (Land Lease or Leasehold Property)** – In some situations a house is sold under *erfpacht* which means you do not purchase a building situated on your own land, or *eigen grond*, but rather that the ground is rented to you for a certain amount per annum, which is paid to the *gemeente*. The house is yours, but not the property. This cost should be calculated into your mortgage payments, as the costs can be quite high. *Erfpacht* contracts are usually renegotiated every 50 years or so. Check to see when the contract is up for renewal. With the *herindexering* or reevaluation of property values in some cases *erfpacht* rates have increased substantially – up to 1000% in some cases! Avoid an expensive and long-term obligation.

11. **Monument Status** – Houses that are protected under *Monumentenzorg* are subject to strict regulations and restrictions regarding maintenance, and any changes have to be approved by a commission from the Association for the Preservation of Monuments. Even seemingly straightforward matters such as the color of paint used often needs approval. It can take months of waiting for approvals, and in the meantime you are prohibited from making any changes.

12. **Recht van Overpad** (the 'Right of Way') – When there is *recht van overpad* on a property, the owner must allow access over the property to others, usually to a neighboring property though sometimes it is allowing walking access to a footpath. This *recht* or right is sold with the property.

13. **Recht van Overpacht (Leasehold Tenancy)** – The right of the tenant to lease the property (*pacht*) is sold with the property, often used with farmlands.

14. **Oil Tanks** – Due to leaks and environmental damage, it is highly illegal to have a buried oil tank in the garden, empty or not. Oil soaking into the ground is destructive, pollutes the soil, and could also seep into drinking water. If an old tank is present, you may have to pay to remove the tank and for the clean up (*reiniging*) of the ground. You can be held responsible (*aansprakelijk*) for the ground pollution (*bodemverontreiniging*) and have to pay for the cleanup. When looking at country homes make sure to ask beforehand about oil tanks.

15. **Asbestos** – In older buildings were asbestos (*asbest*) has been used, you will have the added costs of removing this health hazard, and thoroughly cleaning the premises. If you discover beforehand that asbestos is present, you may demand to have the owner pay for the removal and clean up before the purchase can take place. If you are a renter and discover asbestos in your building, you also have the right to have the owner or *woningbouwvereiniging* remove the asbestos and provide you with a clean, safe living space.

16. **Professional Advice** – Benefit from the good advice of a *hypotheekadviseur* (mortgage advisor); this is an excellent service, free of charge. The banks pay their commissions. You will be well advised on the various aspects of your purchase and on what are currently the best rates.

Certainly it is advisable to first familiarize yourself with the housing market in the area you wish to live in by physically driving around the types of neighborhoods, bearing in mind the proximity to schools, shopping facilities, public transportation, proximity to highways, distance to the office, local taxes, etc. Searches on the Internet or visits to an estate agent's office (*makelaarskantoor*) will also give you an idea of the types of housing available and an indication of the price ranges.

C. The Makelaar or Estate Agent

If you are looking to purchase a house, it is advisable to seek professional assistance. The *Makelaar*, or estate agent, can provide a range of services. *Makelaars* who are professionally licensed have undergone a rigorous and extensive study before receiving accreditation to be licensed. However, the position of *makelaars* has changed in that recently it has been decided that it is no longer necessary to have the professional certification to handle in real estate. The profession (*beroep*) has been freed of this requirement (*vrijgegeven*). This is not to say anything one way or the other as to the qualifications of an agent without a diploma. Your agent should be able to answer many questions ranging from the neighborhood background, housing construction, types of building materials used, accurate pricing, advice on monumental buildings, repairs, financing, etc. He/she should also be aware of any proposed building plans in the town.

A list of estate agents can be found in the Yellow Pages (*Gouden Gids*) or in the regular phone book in the Pink Pages (*roze pagina's*) under *Makelaars*. A listing of estate agents can also be found through their professional organizations: you may contact the Netherlands Estate Agents Foundation (Nederlandse Vereniging van Makelaars in Onroerende Goederen or NVM) or the VBO-*makelaars* (Vereniging Bemiddeling Onroerend Goed) or MVA-*makelaars* (Makelaar Vereniging Amsterdam). They will supply you with a list of members throughout the country. For regional searches of *makelaars* on the Internet 'look local' under: www.makelaar.lokaalzoeken.nl

The NVM is working on an English section for their website. They also have a computerized lists of all available properties throughout the NVM system on NVM-Net® which makes searching so much easier. They offer approximately 60% of the houses on the market.

Our Resources Section also provides a number of websites for national associations on housing, as well as housing related topics. There are also a number of housing websites listed at the end of this chapter. (See chapter 4 and *Important Housing Addresses* at the back of this book.)

House Styles

Housing in the Netherlands may range from city apartments in a variety of sizes and price classes, to re-converted merchant warehouses on canals, houseboats to duplexes, and quaint single-family dwellings to grand estates in the country. Most estate agents have photo-flyers with specifications available, and many list the properties on their Internet sites. Occasionally you will find video previewing. Some regions also have a selection of offerings on the local television station. There are a number of websites with photos and specifications of properties as well.

It is also handy to have a visual perception of the real life dimensions (*woonoppervlakte* or *vloeroppervlakte* – square meters of living space) especially if you are thinking in square feet, not calculating in square meters! Keep in mind the size of your furniture as well, otherwise you may wind up putting things in storage. A metric conversion chart is provided in the back of this book.

Process

The process is as follows: you register with a *makelaar* and give him/her a *zoekopdracht*, or the 'orientation search requirements' regarding your *woonwensen*, or 'wishes for living' space. For an agreed upon period, you will receive regular mailings of available properties in the requested region based upon your selection criteria. Your *makelaar* will then make appointments for you to view the properties with potential. This is known as a *bezichtiging* or 'viewing'. Walking around with him to view the premises is called a *rondleiding*.

The person selling the house will have enlisted the services of an estate agent. Those commission and fees will be settled upon closure with the transfer (*overdracht*) of the property. The seller must pay his/her estate agent's brokerage fee. In the sales procedure the agent serves the interest of the seller, not that of the buyer. Therefore it may be wise for the buyer to employ an estate agent of their own. See the beginning of the chapter for more information on the so-called buyer's costs (*kosten koper*).

Key Phrases

There are a few key phrases you will want to know the meaning of:

- *Zoek een koopwoning* – is to look for a house to purchase
- *Zoek een huurwoning* – is to look for a rental property
- *Zoek een makelaar* – is to look for a broker.

The determination of the condition of the property ranges from *matig* (poor), *redelijk* (below average) *goed* (good) and *uitstekend* (very good). Whereas condition is a relative observation, generally speaking the Dutch idea of *goed* will most likely need work, and *uitstekend* would be comparable to 'move-in condition' although painting and personalizing are advised. Anything that is *matig* should probably be gutted and you can start again from scratch – a definite handyman's special.
Also worth noting is the term *in originele staat* (in original condition), which *can* be translated as 'nothing has been changed since it was built in 1926' or 'there is no central heating, only heaters (*kachels*)'. Further, *originele details behouden* (original details present) can refer to anything from stained glass windows to wood paneling, carved banisters or marble fireplaces that have been 'kept' in their original state.

Specifics

Some *makelaars* have a system of *bewaren van gegevens* (a system of 'saving specifics') of interesting objects (properties) containing neighborhood information, notes, and contact addresses in the area. It is a good idea for you to always make notes and keep your own notebook with your observations, as you are busy with your housing search.

Camera

TIP: Some people take along a video camera or a (digital) camera in order to record their impressions and to assist them later on in the decision making process. Your memory for specific details may not be as clearly useful days later if you have viewed a great number of properties. This is very helpful to have another look as it were.

Making an Offer

Houses are often listed higher than the price the owner actually expects to get, so generally there is some room for negotiation. The range is usually 10 to 15% higher.

Sometimes there are furious bidding wars on a property and it will sell for much more than the actual worth to someone who absolutely is passionate about owning the property. When making an offer (or *bod*), try not to make a bid too low, especially if you are not the first bidder. Do not criticize the condition of the property in an attempt to lower the price.

Taking an *Optie*

An *optie* is the right to place a bid on a property; this does not mean you will definitely decide to purchase, but that you have indicated your willingness to take an option or *optie* to do so.
If you make an offer (place a *bod*) the property is *onder bod*, which is an agreement between the *makelaar* of the seller and yourself that this offer (or bid) is being considered, and no other bids are being taken, until the owner decides whether or not to accept your bid, or to continue further. The *makelaar* may still show the property to others during this stage. If your offer is accepted, then you will be required to pay a minimum of 10% of the purchase price as a deposit or *waarborgsom*. You may also use a bank guarantee (*bankgarantie*) for this purpose. You will have about three weeks to have this money paid into the account of the notary (*notaris*), but first, some paperwork will need to be done.

Approval

Depending on the *gemeente* you are in you may need to get approval from the local housing authority before you can purchase a house. Sometimes it is necessary to show you have economic ties (you are *economisch verbonden*) in the area such as your work. (see chapter 3 on *Housing in Amsterdam* – SWD). Check with your estate agent.

Purchase Assignment

Once you have found something you are interested in, you will enter into a *koopopdracht* or 'purchase assignment' and your estate agent will negotiate on your behalf with the placement of bids. You will be assisted throughout the entire process, from the search to the signing, and any items open for further negotiation such as what will be included in the inventory will be discussed and agreed upon by both parties. Contracts will be drawn up and screened. Your agent will be working on your behalf to secure the best possible terms and purchase price.

By a *koopopdracht* or 'purchase request' your *makelaar* will perform the following services:

- inspection of the property – what is the overall condition, walls, roof, electrical and plumbing facilities, age of the central heating, type of neighborhood, and is the asking price a realistic one
- if you decide to go ahead with the purchase, the real agent will present your opening bid and conduct o*nderhandelingen*, or handling negotiations. The *vraagprijs* is the 'asking price'. Generally if more parties are interested, more than one bid will be necessary. The counter-bidding will be controlled though the agent. If you are fortunate enough to be the first bidder, you have the 'right of first acceptance / refusal' which stipulates that any bids will always come back to you first before the sale can be completed. You may make a counter bid, or refuse to continue with the bidding and forfeit the purchase
- when a price has been agreed upon, you will be advised to enter into the agreement under *ontbindende voorwaarden* or 'dissolving conditions' – for instance based on the financial conditions such as the securement of the mortgage financing (*hypotheek*). Contingent upon the outcome, if for any reason the funds should not become available, the purchase agreement will become null and void, and you will no longer be 'bound' to the agreement
- *taxatie* – the official taxation inspection to determine the actual worth of the property is done by a professional *taxateur* and is obligatory for the bank in order to secure financing. Location, size and general condition of the property, as well as current market prices are all taken into account in the taxation process
- *overdracht*, or handover. Shortly before you take possession of the property, the real estate agent will do a walk through the property with you, in order to

make sure that everything is in the agreed upon state of good repair, and that everything is present in the building (nothing missing) as agreed upon
- assistance with the 'notary' (*notaris*) with the completion of the contracts and the land registration (*kadastrale registratie*) in the registry of the town hall.

Guarantee

When purchasing a property, the *waarborgsom* or guarantee will be forfeited if for any reason you do not go through with the purchase of the property, once the *koopakte* has been drawn up and the deposit has been paid, unless you have included the contingency that you must be also to arrange financing and this indeed falls through. Make sure these *ontbindende voorwaarden* (dissolving conditions) are clearly stipulated.

Fee

The *courtage* is the fee you pay for the services of the *makelaar* are generally 1.5 to 2% of the purchase price (*koopsom*) of the property. Be sure you discuss this *before* signing an agreement to search for property.

If You Are Not in the Country

You may also give your makelaar a *gerichte aankoopopdracht* or 'specific purchase order' which will give him the right to negotiate for a specific property on your behalf, especially useful if you are not in the country.

NVM Website – Other Services

With the NVM official website, www.funda.nl you can use their Dutch online services to do the following:

- *Zoek een huis* – Search for a house
- *Stap-voor-stap* – Step for step information only in Dutch, but we have covered it all here in this book
- *Bewaren van gegevens* – Saving data – The registry of 'finds' to record your list of potential choices and wishes
- *Alles over de buurt* – Everything about the neighborhood – Local information.
- *Vind een huis en meer* – Find a house and more, such as maps (*plattegrond*) and local news (*regionale nieuws*)
- *Handige adressen* – Handy addresses, such as a neighborhood estate agent (*makelaar in de buurt*)

- *Klustips* and *wooninfo* – Household repairs and decorating information with step-by-step information for do-it-self plans
- *Het aankleden* – Adding the finishing touches; a shopping section.

Of course if your Dutch language skills are less than adequate, you can always just start out by visiting an estate office in person.

Can You Do This Without a Makelaar?

Purchasing a house is a fairly complicated process. From finding the right house, through all of the negotiations, financial aspects, legalities, taxations, and registries, the real estate agent is an invaluable help. Of course, you may well decide to go it on your own, which is your good right, as the Dutch would say. However, looking around and finding something is one thing – the legalities, technicalities and negotiations are another matter entirely.

There are a number of matters to take into consideration, not the least of which is what risks you may be undertaking:

- Have you searched out all possible material or structural defects, or technical problems in the inspection of the building?
- Is the contract drawn up properly and are the dissolving conditions (*ontbindende voorwaarden*) listed?
- Will you pay too much for the property through lack of knowledge of market value?

Knowledge, means and experience are the keys held by the professional you hire to successfully negotiate the purchase (or sale) of the property. And if you are not good at arranging financial and legal transactions it may be wise to weigh the cost savings against the cost of your time and efforts. The real estate agent:

- knows the housing market in the region
- knows what 'proposed building plans' (*bestemmingsplannen*) the municipality (*gemeente*) plans to carry out and in what time frame
- can inform you about important legal matters such as *erfpacht* or *recht van overpad*
- has the technical skills to ascertain the condition and possible defects of buildings
- is a skilled and experienced negotiator which works to your benefit
- can inform you about negative aspects of the house that could influence your decision or the price – such as poor upkeep (*achterstallig onderhoud*) or foundation defects (*defecten in de fundering*)
- can advise you on the responsibilities of the seller to reveal defects (*gebreken*) to the buyer. Failure to do so by the seller before the sale can result in later

legal problems or claims. These 'hidden problems' are known as *verborgen gebreken*
- can arrange a *bouwkundig rapport* – a building report commissioned to ascertain the building defects which will contain recommendations of costs and potential solutions to building problems. Not to be confused with the *taxatierapport* which is used to determine the economic or cash value.

Do-It-Yourself Estate Agent

Still, you might decide that you can do this all without the help of a *makelaar*. Here are a few tips, for when you decide to go it on your own:
- take the time to become very well informed as to all the ramifications and legal obligations
- make sure that you know your market, do a lot of research beforehand. Visit properties to compare quality and prices. Check the newspapers and the Internet
- talk to friends or colleagues about their experiences with buying or selling properties
- you can pay for a three-month *oriëntatieopdracht* from an estate agent to provide you with initial research
- read brochures from *makelaar's* offices on buying and selling properties
- know what houses in a particular area are selling for. You can check with the *kadastertelefoon* and ask how much houses on the same street have sold for
- know the neighborhood, have a look around, talk to people
- if selling, make sure the house is as open and light as possible. Get rid of excess furniture
- be honest about any shortcomings the property has, make a list of strong and weak points to comply with the *mededelingsplicht* (See chapter 8 under A for details '*Responsibilities on Purchased Property*').

D. The Notaris – Notary

In the cast of characters involved in the purchase of your new home, in addition to the makelaar you will also come in contact with the *notaris* and the *taxateur* (see under E).

The Notaris

The *notaris* is a special real estate lawyer who draws up the contracts surrounding the real estate transaction. This is a specialist with a great deal of experience regarding the sale of *onroerende zaken*, or property sales. Without the intervention of a *notaris*, it is impossible for property to change hands. The offer should include all the items that you think you will be getting with the house – such as stained glass windows, lighting fixtures, curtains, cabinets, bathroom fixtures, kitchen appliances and other fixtures. It should include as well a number of contingency clauses. Your *notaris* will advise you on these.

Agreement of Sale

Once the deal has been made, the *notaris* will draw up a *koopakte*, or agreement of sale. He can supply you with legal advice on judicial questions and terms of sale, etc. After making sure that the information contained in the *koopakte* is correct, he will then draw up de *akte van levering*, or the 'terms of delivery', for the *overdracht*, or 'handover'. Further, he will draw up the *hypotheekakte*, or 'mortgage terms and conditions'.

Registration

After all is said and done, the *notaris* will arrange for the *inschrijving in de openbare registers* (or the entering or 'writing in of the sale and transfer of property title into the public registry'). This includes the *leveringsakte* and the *hypothecaire akte* (property transfer and outstanding mortgage on the property).

Deposit

A deposit or prepayment or a *waarborgsom* is required before the purchase can take place. An amount of 'good faith', generally some 10% of the price, or more if possible, is paid by the seller to the account of the *notaris* to indicate intention to complete the transaction with payment in full at the closing.

Fee

The fee for the *notaris* is based upon 'tariffs' (rates) referred to as *minimum-en-maximum tarieven*. These are based upon the sale price of the property and upon the amount of the financial loan. It is possible within a broad context to negotiate the fee of the *notaris* based on these reference points and the percentage charged by the *notaris*. It is a good idea to contact more than one *notaris* beforehand in order to ascertain who has the best fee structure. Most *makelaar* offices have a *notaris* they use, but this may not be the least expensive one.

Payment

The *notaris* is also responsible for the portion of the financial transaction from buyer to seller and he makes sure that this transaction proceeds without problems.

On the day of the contract signing and transfer (*overdracht*), the money will be transferred by telephone to the *notaris* who will then make sure his own fees for services rendered are paid as well as the transfer of funds into the bank account of the selling party (unless of course you plan to pay the full amount in cash!!).

Keep in mind that there are a number of fees to be paid: the commission to your estate agent, the *notaris* fees, the 6% transfer tax, a land registration fee, a mortgage fee, the fees for cadastral investigation, and administrative costs.

Transfer

The *transport* is the judicial handing over or transfer of title (*levering*) of the property by the *notaris*. The actual 'delivery' of the property (*levering*) occurs after the legal or judicial portion, when the keys will be handed over.

Sleutelverklaring – Key Declaration

Keys are usually given at the time of the transfer (*overdracht*) of the property when the final papers have all been signed, and all funds transferred. If the keys are to be handed over earlier than the time when the legal transport is to take place a *sleutelverklaring* will have to be signed. This indicates that you, the buyer, will now be responsible for the property. You (the buyer) need to arrange to be insured in this period, as you are not yet officially the owner, however, should any damage occur you are now liable.

E. The Taxateur – Surveyor

The *taxatie* has more than one purpose and a property has more than one type of value. The seller of a house will want to know a different determination of property value than will the bank. The *taxateur* is a *makelaar* who is experienced in this aspect of the business and who will inspect the property keeping in mind different aspects of inspection. All his/her findings will be presented in a *taxatierapport*. Some of the aspects that are inspected are:

- the condition of the property and maintenance
- the interior measurements and overall dimensions of living space plus number of stories
- the 'functionality of the layout' (*functionaliteit van de indeling*) of the floor planning (rooms / bath / kitchen)
- the construction and quality of the materials used to construct the building
- the degree of materials used for insulation (*isolatie*) and energy savings (*energiezuinigheid*)

- any obligatory restrictions, rights and responsibilities pertaining to the property (*verplichtingen en rechten die op de grond rusten*) such as *erfpacht, recht van overpacht and recht van overpad*
- the 'lay of the land' (*ligging en omgeving*); how the house is situated on the property and the location of the neighborhood, facilities, roads, etc., in the area where the house is located.

The *taxateur* will also take into consideration any 'price developments' (*prijsontwikkelingen*) in the current market for similar properties and will know if any major construction projects are scheduled to begin building in that particular area. Likewise, he can perform a *kadastraal onderzoek* to determine if the information provided in the cadastral registry is actually true based on his physical inspection of the property in question.

The Purpose of the Taxation

As mentioned earlier, a *taxatie* can have different purposes and a property has different values; each party has their own criteria for determination:

- the seller is interested in a good sale price (*verkoopprijs*); he will want to know the *onderhandse verkoopwaarde* (the price on the open market between buyer and seller 'under hands', that is to say, without the assistance of a *makelaar*)
- if you, the buyer, need a mortgage (*hypotheek*), the bank will want to know the *executiewaarde*. This is the worth of the property if you are 'forced to sell' (called a *gedwongen verkoop*), for instance if you fail to pay the interest or the monthly amounts of your mortgage
- you may wish to determine the real value of the property in order to secure financing for your mortgage – called a *taxatie voor de financiering*
- the insurance company (*verzekeringsmaatschappij*) will be concerned with the *herbouwwaarde*; the cost to rebuild the house in the event of serious damage. This value will be included in your insurance policy and be used to determine your yearly insurance costs (*jaarpremie*)
- the tax office (*belastingdienst*) will want to know the market value (*waarde in het economische verkeer*) of your house. This will be used to determine your tax in box III (*vermogensbelasting*) and the deemed rental income (*eigenwoningforfait*), which is the amount that you as the house owner must report on your income tax. The *eigenwoningforfait* is a 'set amount' (*vaste percentage*) determined by the municipality (*gemeente*) times the woz-worth of your house (see further on). It has been created to compensate the government (!) for the tax they would have collected on the rental income the property would have generated on the open market had you rented it out
- the tax office is also interested in the worth of the property, as they wish to determine inheritance taxes (*successierechten*) in the case of death of the

property owner and subsequent inheritance bequests of the property to inheritors, whether family or friends – and the inheritance taxes are steep!
- if you plan to temporarily rent out the property, you will want to know the 'rental value' (*economische huurwaarde*) in order to assess the rent (*huurprijs*) based on the current rental market.

F. The woz-Waarde – woz-Appraisal Value

Every four years the municipality (*gemeente*) has each house inspected / reviewed in order to determine its worth to be used for taxation under the *Waardebepaling Onroerende Zaken* (woz). All homeowners are subject to this inspection for taxation purposes. The woz makes sure that the determination takes place with equivalency; in other words that similar houses on a street are taxed at an equivalent rate, without one being taxed higher than the one standing next to it.

Who Wants to Know?

The *gemeente* is the party requesting the determination of the worth (*opdrachtgever*). However, also the government (*overheid*) wants to know the worth of your property to in order to determine the following taxes:
- the *onroerendezaak belasting* – property tax
- the *eigenwoningforfait* (homeowner's deduction) for income tax purposes
- the *waterschapsbelasting* – to determine the 'water tax' for the water control authorities (*waterschap*) that supplies water to your home or business.

Decision

After the *taxatie* has been carried out you will receive a *beschikking*, or official decision, whereby the economic worth that has been determined is given. Your future taxes will be calculated from this base amount for the next four years. The tax office (*belastingdienst*) and the water control authorities (*waterschappen*) will also receive a copy of the *beschikking*. Other than this, the report is not a matter of public record and its contents are deemed 'secret'. Generally speaking, neighbors on a common street will compare notes just to make sure the tax office is not being 'equivocal' in its taxation.

Notice of Objection

In the event of any discrepancies or if you do not agree with the amount of the assessment, you may submit a notice of objection (*bezwaarschrift*) within six weeks to your *gemeente*. You may request that your own *makelaar* carry out a *taxatie*, which you may use to substantiate your claims with your disagreement with the findings (*bezwaar*).

G. Old Houses – Monuments & Rijksmonumenten

Monument status is given to objects that have a specific cultural or historical significance. Monuments that have a national unique worth are given the status of *Rijksmonument*. The RMDZ or *Rijksdienst voor Monumentenzorg* can provide more information on these monuments that make up part of our national heritage.
Website: www.monumentenzorg.nl

Two Categories

There are two categories of monuments: the architectural / archeological monuments and the city or village landscape monuments. Monuments fall under *onroerende goederen* (immovable property) and could be bridges or houses, archeological or architectural objects, of more than 50 years of age that are important due to their beauty, scientific or cultural value. Portions of a village or city may also fall under a protected status, referred to as a *beschermd stads- of dorpsgezicht*, often in an attempt to prevent destruction and new building construction in old city or village centers, which would destroy the characteristic charm of the area. Roads, trees and parks as well as village squares can also be included under this protection.

Permission

Buildings that are protected under *Monumentenzorg* are subject to strict regulations and restrictions regarding maintenance and any changes have to be approved by a commission from the Association for the Preservation of Monuments. Even seemingly straightforward matters such as the color of paint or types of materials used often needs approval. Structural changes for safety may be carried out, but thereafter you are obliged to restore the building to its original glory. Often great attempts will be made to secure antique or salvage material from old homes. It can take months of back and forth and endless negotiations with the commission of the *Monumentenzorg* before you will be issued permits (*vergunningen*) to begin the required work. While you are patiently waiting for permission, you are prohibited from making any changes. Changes made are subject to inspection by the commission.

Passion for History

Aside from the limitations to your freedom to change the building if you are living in a monument, the thrill is in the uniqueness of the monuments. People who choose to purchase monuments generally have a special passion for history and delight in living in a historical monument, even if the floor layout may be inconvenient – such as in the front and back houses in Amsterdam canal houses – or in navigating the ridiculously steep and narrow stairways. There is something incredibly special about living in a house that is hundreds of years old. One's imagination is peaked thinking about all the people who have crossed the floors before when living in a building so steeped in history and containing many stories ...

Special Tax Regulations

Owning a monument can provide some financial relief in special regulations for tax deductions. This applies only to a monument you own outright, not a city monument or one that is on municipal ground. There are also subsidies available for renovation construction costs from many *gemeentes* that are worth enquiring about. Additionally, before you begin with the restoration, the Tax Office (*Belastingdienst*) can help calculate your deductions. To this purpose, you can ask for a special form from:

Belastingdienst/Particulieren Amersfoort
Postbus 4050
3800 EB Amersfoort
tel.: 033 450 52 22

For additional information on monuments see: start page: http://monumenten.pagina.nl. The Amsterdam monuments have pages in English www.bmz.amsterdam.nl Also of interest is www.monumenten.nl.

H. New Houses – Nieuwbouw

Most home purchases are of already existing properties in the Netherlands. However, given the extreme housing shortage, a number of new homes are built each year – though not nearly enough to meet the rising demand. This controlled shortage of course keeps the housing market in a continued state of tension and guarantees that prices will remain high.

New Project Developments

These new communities of houses are known as a *nieuwbouwprojekt* or a new building project. If you are interested in becoming the owner of a brand new house, you will need to inquire at the *gemeente* or with an estate agent as to what types of building projects are scheduled to begin. This information is also posted in the newspapers. You will be able to ask for a prospectus on the project and will receive brochures showing the different types / sizes of houses to be built, the floor plan layout, lot location in the development, and the costs of the ground and property. Most projects have a mix of price ranges included in the building development. In a large project of say 100 houses or more, a few homes will be very deluxe and in the best location, possibly free standing, the majority of homes will be middle range – priced based on size and located throughout the development – and a smaller number will be of lower priced and smaller homes.

Drawing Lots

Due to the overwhelming demand for housing, especially for new houses, a system of drawing lots, or het *verloten van huizen*, has been established. You will need to take your chances along with everyone else who is vying for a new home to have the opportunity to buy. If you are interested in a house, you will need to register (*laten inschrijven*) for the drawing. If your name is drawn in the house lottery you will receive permission to further negotiate the possible purchase of one of these hopefully soon to be built new homes.

Which Parts Are Standard?

In many *nieuwbouwprojekten* the project has been developed to have identical houses and the materials used are standard design, so that you will purchase the standard package. The building prices can be kept lower by using *pre-fab* or pre fabrication techniques. Sometimes you will have a choice between a few selections of tile or kitchen units, though not when it comes to roofing, doors or windows, which are purchased in bulk for the project. Sometimes it is possible to adapt the construction drawings to your own requirements, although additional costs may be involved in this. Changing walls in the floor plans or having built-in closets or fireplaces put in or other tiles or parquet floors are often done at a later date by the homeowner.

Financial Pros and Cons

The extra costs of buying a newly built house are a few percentages lower than those for existing houses and for the first couple of years there is less maintenance to be expected. Frequently the house has already risen in value by the time it is finished. On the down side, a new house will cost you more on interior finishing's (floor and wall coverings) and garden architecture, as it is delivered completely bare. Plus you will never be completely sure what the house and the neighborhood will look like once finished. Some cities have restrictions on selling a newly built house for the first couple of years, to prevent housing speculation. You may have to agree to live in the house for a certain number of years before it can be resold, or risk a penalty payment should you be forced to sell before the term of the agreement.

Finances

Financially, you will be issued a building fund loan (*bouwfondslening*) which is a type of mortgage for the duration of the building, since you cannot have the official transfer of the property (*overdracht*) until there is actually a house to take possession of. Payments are done in installments to the builder, and after completion, the official mortgage will begin. Often it is possible to secure very attractive financial arrangements for new homes, as the bank and the developers are anxious to have each unit sold before they will begin building. Mortgages of 100% are not uncommon. Lower interest rates and special financing may be offered as further enticements. If you are between houses, having not yet sold your present home, you may be issued a ' bridging loan' (*overbruggingslening*) to help defray the costs of maintaining two properties.

Estate Agent

Again, the services of a professional estate agent are most helpful in organizing all of the paperwork for you. Once the sale has been completed, the building can begin.

Building Methods

There are a number of building methods to choose from:

Traditional Building

This centuries old-method makes use of *stapelbouw*, or 'stacking', building which consists of laying bricks one upon the next to build walls that are held together with mortar. The floors, window, doorsills and roof construction are of wood and the roof covering consists of clay roof tiles or *dakpannen* (often orange in color, sometimes black).

Modern Version

The interior walls and weight supporting walls are made of blocks of concrete – some weighing 300 kilos. The ground floor is also made of concrete. The roof construction is wood, with wood plates, the window sills and doors can be wood, aluminum or of a type of weather resistant plastic (*kunststof*). In this modern construction there are few to no cracks in the walls, and the moisture regulation and warmth insulation is optimal.

Logbouw – Log Building

This method comes from Finland and consists of wood. The exterior construction and the interior walls are built of stacked beams of massive wood, which are slotted and grooved to connect each log with the next. The foundation is generally of wood although cement could be used. The floors are of wood. The most popular sort of log building is pine wood or *grenen*. These homes require more maintenance of the wood, as with the high moisture content, the wood expands and contracts. This *grenen* wood does however become harder over a period of time.

Houtskeletbouw – Wood Skeleton Building

In America and Scandinavia *houtskeletbouw* is a popular manner of building. The wood skeleton construction is filled up with insulation material for optimum warmth. Floors are of wood or cement. To avoid condensation, special foil (*folie*) is placed on the exterior walls. The ventilation is excellent as the walls cannot take up any moisture. The thermal properties of the wood make it an ideal building material. Building materials are all imported, as Holland has a limited amount of trees and they are protected plus there is no lumber industry.

Prefab – Prefabrication

This house is a 'building packet' and is a combination of traditional and prefabricated construction. The units are put together in a factory or workplace precisely to size, and then brought out to the building site. A combination of wood and cement is used. Some companies also deliver complete kitchens and bathrooms, others only a shell or basic house that you can finish off with other contractors.

Waterbouw or Water Building

The water house is known in Canada and the U.S. but is relatively new to Holland. This is not a houseboat, but rather a house that is built on a barge-like base construction that the house floats upon. Constructed of wood and prefab units, the water house can easily be moved to a new location over the water, where it can be moored in a place of your choosing as a permanent address. There are a number of experimental projects in progress in the Flevopolder in Almere-Buiten. Some 200 floating residences are planned for the IJburg area. In Middelburg unique houses are being built on triangular floating platforms. *Waterwonen* or living on water may be the next 'environmentally friendly' trend for the new millennium.

Delivery

The building developers of the project will give you an indication as to when your home will be completed and ready for delivery (*oplevering*). A word of caution: you never can be absolutely sure that the target date will actually be met, due to adverse weather conditions, delays in material delivery, shortage of builders, etc. You may find yourself in temporary living quarters if your new house has not been finished on time.

Bouwfondsgarantie – Building Fund Guarantee

Make sure you have secured a *bouwfondsgarantie* or building fund guarantee. This will ensure that the contractor pays the costs of damages to the house or non-delivery as stipulated. Most contractors are members of either GIW or *Bouwgarant*. These organizations ensure that you do not run into problems if the contractor does not complete his work.

Landscaping

The site landscaping and gardening is one of the last items to be completed in a new development, so be forewarned, the first year may be a bit of a muddy mess, especially if you take possession of your home while the construction of other homes is still in progress. The noise factor may be considered here as well. Rest assured, within a year or two, everything will have been established and the plants and flowers will be blooming. Other than trees or grass in the public areas of the development you will be responsible for the costs of all the landscaping and plants in your front and back gardens.

Small Projects

Some projects are small and consist of only a few units, often in cities where old buildings have been torn down. As this is usually between existing buildings and in a good center city location, the price of this real estate is generally high. Often it is possible with this type of project to arrange for changes to the interior design since the scale of the project is much smaller, and the architect and building contractor are willing to work with you regarding changes reflecting your personal taste.

I. Do-It-Yourself Building Project

Buying a piece of land and hiring an architect to design your dream house on a specific location is without a doubt the most difficult way to go about having a new house in Holland. The availability of ground for sale coupled with the housing shortage and lack of available space in this crowded little country do not make this an easy undertaking.

Purchasing Ground

Ground that is offered for construction is scarce, and since the government strictly controls the use and building growth in the Netherlands, generally the municipality or province (*gemeente* or *provincie*) are the purchasers of land. Some private property is handled through an estate agent. You will generally not see listings of private advertisements for a piece of land in a newspaper. Most land that is sold is offered for sale from the municipal or provincial governing agencies.

Costs of Land Vary

The cost of ground varies widely. A square meter of land in a farming community such as Oldenzaal last year costs € 61 while a square meter of land in Amsterdam costs € 1,470 and in Utrecht € 1,248 (figures CBS 2001).

Building-Ripe Land

When you purchase ground you want *bouwrijpe grond* – or building-ripe land. This is ground that has been approved for building and for which a building permit has been issued containing also the permission for connections of electricity, gas, water, telephone and sewage. Roads and utility connections are already in place. It is not advisable to purchase ground that you will have to make *bouwrijp* yourself. You could run into a good deal of expense doing this, and it is possible that, in the end, you are not given permission to build. The department of *Bouw-en Woningtoezicht* of the *gemeente* can inform you if any parcels of land (*kavels*) are for sale.

J. Architects

If you go with a project developer of course you are restricted to the plans of the project that have already been approved. With your own architect, you can design a house to your specific wishes.

When choosing an architect, it is not only a question of finances, it is also a question of taste. You will want at look at the work and different styles of a number of architects. Do not just look at photographs, it can be helpful to take the time to visiting buildings they have designed. Working with an architect will take more time, but the result is that you will have something unique built to your specific wishes. The architect will first make a sketch plan which will be submitted to the *gemeente* for approval before the drawings are fully worked out. The fee (*honorarium*) of the architect needs to be discussed upfront. Further, once the drawings are completed the architect will meet with everyone involved, contractors, subcontractors, and those delivering the materials to make sure that there are not all kinds of changes made to the actual building plans and the quoted materials. This is also to control the costs. It is also frustrating (not to mention expensive) to keep changing the drawings once the building has begun!

For information on finding an architect check the Yellow Pages under *architect* or contact the Registry of Architects or Het Bureau Architectenregister (tel.: 070 346 70 20). You may also visit the websites www.archistart.nl, www.house-of-design.nl, or www.bna.nl (the Bond of Dutch Architects – Bond Nederlandse Architecten).

Approval Building Commission

As mentioned earlier, very occasionally a *gemeente* will sell land, but usually this land will only be offered in the form of a proposed development project, or offered *in erfpacht* whereby you do not own the property but merely lease it and own the building constructed upon it. If you are able to secure a piece of property, the *gemeente* or township will want to know what type of building you are planning to construct. The plans of the architect will need to be approved by the local building commission (*woningbouwcommissie*) and in some areas there is also a 'beauty commission' (*schoonheidscommissie*) who will determine if the proposed structure will be aesthetically pleasing in the intended location. This is intended to keep really ugly architecture from being built, or something way too modern in an old historic section of the city.

It may take quite some time for the building commission to review and approve your plans, and don't be surprised if they ask you to change a few details. A list of technical specifications must be submitted along with the architect's drawings in order to comply with current building codes.

Permits

You will also need to request a building permit, water connection and sewage permits, new cable and telephone installation permits. Your building contractor (*aannemer*) can take care of these details for you, and make sure that the project proceeds in the proper order with the necessary specialists. See chapter 10 on *Tradesmen – Vakmensen: Getting the Help You Need.*

Inspections

During the construction you will undoubtedly receive a few visits from the local building inspector just to make sure that you are really building what you said you were and using the proper materials. Once the building has been completed, he will come again so that the final approval can be given and the cadastral registration can be completed.

Worth It

Having designed and built your own home you will of course have had exactly everything done to your own personal tastes and specifications – a real dream come true. Perhaps this will be a long and tedious process, frustrating at times and occasionally overwhelming. However, the results and pleasure that you will enjoy living in your new home will be well worth the effort.

Other considerations

Find out if you are eligible for the national *hypotheek garantie* when arranging your financing. Explanations on NHG and financing can be found in the *Financial Considerations: Mortgages & Insurances.* (chapter 7)

K. House-Hunting Tips

If you are moving to the Netherlands, your house-hunting may not be a fun, leisure-time activity. When you are relocating to a new city, you may have to complete your research and come to a decision in the space of one orientation trip or within a matter of a few weeks. The secret to a successful house-hunting trip is to be as informed and organized as possible before you go.

1. Decide before hand what your needs are. Make a list of the critical requirements for your new neighborhood. These include:

- commuting time to your employer
- school requirements
- community demographics (age, education, lifestyle)
- population density (urban, suburban, or rural)
- community institutions that are important to you (being close to entertainment, places of worship, or other amenities)
- safety.

2. Obtain a map of your new city, and try to become as familiar with it as you can. If possible, do research via the Internet. During your house-hunting it

may be helpful to place small stickers on the map to mark the locations of properties you are viewing.

3. Get an idea of which neighborhoods are likely to meet your requirements. Try to talk with other employees who already live in your new city to gain their perspective. Your colleagues can offer first-hand information based on their experiences. Don't re-invent the wheel – take advantage of any tips they may have.

4. Determine a price range to look for a home in your new city. It is important to arrive on your house-hunting trip with a realistic expectation of what you will need to spend in order to afford a home in a neighborhood that meets your requirements. Do not be lured into looking at properties that are not in your budget. Don't forget, the cost of living here also needs to be considered in your budget.

5. If at all possible, try to interview estate agents by phone before you make your trip. Decide on a realtor and work with that person to plan your trip. Ask if they have properties online that you may view, or if they can e-mail information prior to your trip.

6. Be clear – Make sure that the realtor understands your neighborhood requirements and your price range, and that the realtor believes that your price range is realistic for the type of property you expect to find. Do not let yourself be swayed by 'sales talk' – stick to your plan and your budget. Read the section on *Financial Aspects* in this chapter, where you will find extra costs.

7. Do tell your realtor that you only want to look at houses that are priced to sell, (or, if renting, properties that fall within your budget). Some home-sellers overprice their listings. You do not want to waste time or confuse yourself by looking at houses with unrealistic asking prices.

8. When you go on your house-hunting trip, take along your city map, your notes on your research concerning communities (schools, amenities, etc.) and a house-hunting checklist. Make sure to make good notes. The checklist included under *Apartment-Hunting Tips* may prove useful. This checklist is a list of key features of houses, so that you can take organized notes on every house that you visit. You can use your city map to mark locations of houses for easy reference. Photos or video can also be helpful in reviewing properties seen.

   Make sure you have the following:
   - house-hunting check list
   - notebook with hard surface to write on

- pens (more than one!)
- city map
- small stickers or colored markers (to mark locations on map)
- digital camera or video camera
- tape measure
- mobile phone
- bottled water (it can be a thirsty trip!).

9. Read the sections on Finances and Insurances so that you are aware of what is involved in purchasing property in the Netherlands, and what insurances you will need.

10. Availability – always let the realtor know where you can be reached for on going negotiations, when you will be at your hotel, mobile phone, and e-mail.

With good planning and a helpful realtor, you can accomplish a good deal on your house-hunting trip!

For additional tips on 'home hunting' please refer to the suggestions given under *Apartment Hunting Tips* and *Apartment Checklist* at the end of chapter 2.

References

Information (in English) from **tax authorities** on mortgage interest tax-deductibles: 070 330 42 39. Form for a monthly refund: 070 330 42 46.

Dutch Housing Association (Vereniging Eigen Huis)
Tel: 033 450 7752
Fax: 033-450 7432
Email: veh@veh.nl
www.eigenhuis.nl

Books in Dutch
Hoe (ver)koop je een huis zonder makelaar
(How to buy or sell a house without an estate agent)
By Rene Bouwmans
ISBN: 9055017442

Zo verkoop ik zelf mijn huis – (How to sell my house myself)
J.A. Koster van Voorhout
ISBN: 9039509360

Websites for Housing
www.woningcourant.com – news of houses for sale and rent and developments
www.eigenhuis.nl – site from the Vereniging Eigen Huis (Dutch Homeowners Association)
www.kadaster.nl – the cadastral registry of properties, also a helpline to inquire about prices
www.funda.nl – site from the NVM offering 60% of the available houses
www.huislijn.nl – site from the LMV
www.huisplein.nl – site from the VBO
www.woninggids.nl – site from the Era *makelaars*
www.woonkrant.nl – Living/housing newspaper on line
www.digimmo.nl – you can check on the price developments in respective areas
www.huistekoop.nl – house for sale site
http://verhuis.pagina.nl – 'start page' on moving
www.verhuis.net – information on moving or *verhuizen*

Estate Agents Organizations
www.funda.nl – the official site of NVM Makelaars
www.vbo.nl – Vereniging Bemiddeling Onroerend Goed
www.lvm.nl – Landelijke Makelaarsvereniging
www.erkend-makelaars.nl – Recognized (certification) estate agents
www.online-makelaars.nl – Estate agents online
www.era.nl – ERA group of estate agents
www.koophuis.nl – home purchase
www.garantiemakelaars.nl – Guarantee estate agents

Search
http://makelaar.lokaalzoeken.nl – looking for local estate agents
http://makelaars-bedrijf.pagina.nl – estate agent companies search

Consumer Issues
For any Consumer issues regarding any purchased 'products' or items in the Netherlands, whether your house, furniture, garden supplies, etc. you may want to check with the Consumentenbond (Consumers Bond). They publish a monthly magazine, and www.consumentenbond.nl

Extraordinary Dream Houses
If you are looking for an estate, a castle, a villa, or something absolutely extraordinary and are willing to spend a few million, or if the price is no object at all, check out the following sites:
www.vivenda.nl – Publishes Vivenda Exclusive magazine, a quarterly in english offering spectacular up-market properties. Vivenda is a member of EEP, the

European Estate Publishers, an international media concept for real estate agents in Europe, the USA and internationally, offering access to the top of the market supply. Prices begin at 1 million euros.
www.droomhuis.nu – dream houses

www.landerije.nl – estates (*landgoederen*) and *woonboerderijen* (gentleman's farms).
www.europropertise.com – properties in Europe

Free Items
When you move into a new home you may want to request any of the following free items:

Verhuismand or Moving Basket
The *verhuismand* is intended for persons who are moving. It contains tips on preparing for your move, special offers and coupons and a magazine *Verhuizen* (Moving) with ideas and contact addresses for a variety of products and services.

Contact them for a request form (*aanvraagkaart*):
De Verhuismand
Antwoordnummer 4000
1380 VL Weesp

Nieuwhuisplan van VT Wonen
(New houseplan from VT Wonen, a magazine about leisure time and living)
This free package filled with inspiration and new ideas, as well as practical information and special offers and coupons can be requested through:
www.vtwonen.nl – request form online
www.gamma.com – request form online, or fill in a card at the Gamma building market.
www.karwei.nl/klussen – tips for projects
www.praxis.nl – building market.

Felicitas
This organization (aptly named 'Congratulations') offers welcome packages not only for you in your new home, but also for newlyweds and new babies. The *Felicitas Nieuwe Woning* package also contains useful information and sample products. www.felicitas.nl.

Moving
Don't forget to go to the Post Office and pick up the *verhuispakket* with information on sending out change of address cards and changing over your utilities. You can also order online: www.verhuisservice.nl.

Translations of Housing Terms

A

aanv. aanvaarding (*acceptance*).
aflossingsvrije hypotheek (*no pay-off mortgage*) in principle with this mortgage form there are no repayments, which keeps the monthly costs low. Only the monthly interest is paid, without a separate premium to build up capital. The disadvantage is that this mortgage is not secured by repayments and/or an insurance. A (part) no pay-off mortgage can be interesting when buying a house at a later age.
annuïteiten hypotheek (*annuity mortgage*) with this mortgage, payments in the first few years consist mostly of interest and a small amount in repayment. This gives the maximum tax benefit, as interest payments are tax-deductible. This tax benefit decreases with the years, as interest payments go down and repayment rates go up. This will result in higher monthly costs.
app. appartement (*apartment*)

B

b.g. begane grond (*ground floor, American: first floor*)
bankgarantie (*bank guarantee*)a guarantee statement issued by a Dutch bank. By means of this statement, the bank guarantees that the buyer will be able to meet the financial obligations resulting from the purchase contract up to the amount specified in the guarantee.
beg.gr. begane grond (*ground floor, American: first floor*)
beleggingshypotheek (*investment mortgage*) with this mortgage there is no separate life insurance; the money is invested directly in stocks. This means there will be no adverse fiscal consequences if the mortgage is ended within 20 years (requirement for fiscal benefits). It is advisable to also conclude an additional 'death risk' insurance.
ben.w. benedenwoning (*ground floor apartment*)
beroepsaansprakelijkheidsverzekering (*professional liability insurance*) an insurance concluded by real estate agencies to cover liability resulting from mistakes or omissions in the carrying out of their profession.
bestemmingsplan (*zoning plan*) This plan, developed by the city council, is binding for the citizens. It consists of a planning map, building instructions, a further explanation and a development scheme. On the planning map a buyer can see what the intended use is of the parcel for sale. The building instructions further outline building possibilities and purposes in the area, such as gutter heights, building contents, green areas and clearing lines, building intensity etc.
bijdr. bijdrage (*contribution*)
bj. bouwjaar (*date of building*)

bod (*bid*) An offer on a house by a serious candidate, including the amount offered, any annulment clause(s), date of acceptance and a list of moveable and immoveables.
bov.w. bovenwoning (*upstairs apartment*)
bungalow (*bungalow*) a house with all rooms on the ground floor.

C

c.v. centrale verwarming (*central heating*)
courtage (*commission*) an agreed amount, paid to a real estate agent, for services rendered. The height of the amount is negotiable and is put in writing upon contracting. VAT is charged on top of the commission (19%).

E

e.g. eigen grond (*private property*)
eengezinswoning (*single-family dwelling*) with this type of house there are no floors above or below in use by other occupants. The entire house is intended for occupation by one family.
effectenhypotheek (*stocks mortgage*) this form of mortgage is similar to an investment mortgage. The major difference is that investment is not done by means of a capital insurance. At the start of the mortgage and agreed one-off amount in stocks (shares, government securities, etc.) is bought or brought in. The increase in value of these stocks is intended to raise the necessary capital.
eigenwoningforfait (*deemed rental income*) (formerly known as *huurwaardeforfait*) the amount that the owner of a house needs to add to income before taxes. The rental value is a fixed percentage of the Real Estate Tax (WOZ)-value of the house as determined by the city council. Current relevant percentage levels for each city can be obtained from the tax office.
erfpacht (*ground rent*) the right to use a real estate object, a piece of land owned by others (e.g. the city council) against a fixed monthly or yearly payment (canon).

G

ged. gedeeltelijk (*partly*)
geh.gemod. geheel gemoderniseerd (*fully modernized*)
geren. gerenoveerd (*renovated*)

H

helft van dubbel (*semi-detached house*)
herenhuis (*mansion*) originally a stately house, nowadays also used for a spacious row house.

hoekwoning (*corner house/end house*) house on the corner of a street or at the end of a row.
huurwaardeforfait (*deemed rental income*) see *eigenwoningforfait*.
hypotheekakte (*mortgage deed*) this document reflects the agreement between the buyer and a financial institution in relation to the mortgage. After signing the deed at the notary public it is entered in the land register.

I

i.o. in overleg (*in consultation with*)
ind. indeling (*lay-out*)

K

k. kamer (*room*)
kadaster (*land register*) the land register records the division of parcels in the Netherlands and to which these parcels belong. In addition it holds information on the size of the parcels, whether there is an order for soil clean-up, whether a property a listed as a monument and which numbers the parcels (or properties) are registered under.
karakt. karakteristiek (*characteristic*)
kkn. keuken (*kitchen*)
kmr. kamer (*room*)
koopakte (*purchase deed*) this document confirms a verbal purchase agreement for a property in writing.
kosten koper (*buyer's costs*) these consist of the costs for the notary public, appraisal costs, costs for concluding the mortgage, costs for registering the mortgage deed, conveyance tax and the realtor's brokerage fee.

L

landhuis (*country house*) a spacious house (smaller than a villa) located outside of the city center.
levenshypotheek (*life insurance mortgage*) with this form of mortgage there are no repayments: only the fiscally deductible interest is paid. Linked to the mortgage is a life insurance, for which a premium is paid. At the end of the mortgage term, the life insurance is paid out and used to repay the original mortgage amount. In case of death before the end of the mortgage, the insured amount will nevertheless be paid in full. There is a slight risk to this form of mortgage as the insurance pay-out is not guaranteed at 100%.
levering (*delivery*) delivery of a property consists of two parts. At the legal delivery, the property is transferred on paper to the buyer. This is done by signing

the delivery deed, also called a conveyance deed, at a notary public. The factual delivery will be at the time of accepting the key to the property.

lineaire hypotheek (*level repayment mortgage*) monthly costs consist of an equal part in repayment and rent. As the debt decreases due to the repayment, the rent will decrease as well. This means the monthly costs will get lower, but they are fairly high at the start.

N

Nationale Hypotheek Garantie (NHG) (*National Mortgage Guarantee*) a national fund that provides a surety in case the borrowing party is not meeting the repayment and interest requirements resulting from the mortgage. A mortgage can be requested with this national guarantee, with the advantage that mortgage providers will give a better interest rate. However, there is a restriction on the maximum purchase price. Above this maximum limit it is not possible to take out a mortgage with this guarantee.

Nederlandse Vereniging van Makelaars in onroerende goederen en vastgoeddeskundigen (NVM) (*Dutch Association of Real Estate Agents and property specialists*).

NVM-Erecode (NVM *code of honor*) rules of conduct as laid down by the NVM for its members. The rules of conduct are the basis for everyday practices.

NVM-Huisgarantie (NVM *house guarantee*) based on a technical inspection a buyer can take out an insurance against any hidden defects. The seller of the property can also have a technical inspection performed and offer the report at sale. A potential buyer can then take out the required insurance.

NVM-net® (NVM-net®) this is a computerized database in which all houses offered for sale through the NVM realtors are registered and which is available only to them.

O

o.g. onroerend goed (*real estate/property*)

o.v. openbaar vervoer (*public transportation*)

onder bod zijn (*being under bid*) a commitment by the realtor of the seller to a potential buyer not to undertake any definite transactions with other potential candidates. Viewings of the property are still possible, but bidding is restricted to the first candidate.

ontbindende voorwaarden (*annulment clause(s)*) conditions that can be included in a (provisional) deed of purchase, based on which the buyer can cancel further negotiations free of charge. Annulment clauses include the obtaining of the necessary permits, the obtaining of the necessary financing, the obtaining of a National Mortgage Guarantee or the results of a technical inspections.

opp. oppervlak (*surface area*)

optie (*option*) a right to enter into a purchase contract by means of a unilaterally expressed intention. The person holding this right is not obliged to use it.

overdrachtsbelasting (*conveyance tax*) a tax levied on the buyer of a property. Presently at 6%, the tax is based on the purchase price, minus the moveable objects that are included in this purchase price. The division between moveable and immoveable objects is recorded in the deed of purchase.

R

recht van overpad (*right of way*) the right that the owner of a property/land has to cross the property/land of another person. The other party is obliged to allow this and maintain the right of way.

roerende goederen (*moveable objects*) objects that are not joined to/fitted in the property and can be sold by the seller to the buyer.

roy. royale (*spacious*)

rvs. roestvrijstaal (*stainless steel*)

S

sk. slaapkamer (*bedroom*)

sleutelverklaring (*key acceptance report*) this report is made is the factual acceptance of the property (the hading over of the keys) takes place before the legal conveyance at the notary public. From the time of key acceptance, the buyer is responsible to make sure the property is insured.

slp. slaapkamer (*bedroom*)

spaarbeleggingshypotheek (*savings-investment mortgage*) this form of mortgage is a combination of a savings mortgage and an investment mortgage. The person taking out the mortgage can decide which part of the insurance premium goes to a savings account and which part is invested.

spaarhypotheek (*savings mortgage*) with this form of mortgage there are no repayments: only the fiscally deductible interest is paid. Linked to the mortgage is a life insurance, for which a premium is paid into a savings account. At the end of the mortgage term, the life insurance is paid out and used to repay the original mortgage amount. In case of death before the end of the mortgage, the insured amount will nevertheless be paid in full. This amount is fixed and therefore secure. On the other hand, because of the savings aspect, the amount will never exceed the preagreed fixed sum, as is sometimes the case with life insurance mortgages if the insurer has made a profit with the moneys invested.

T

taxatie (*appraisal*) the issue of a valuation report by an authorized person and for a specific purpose, e.g. obtaining a mortgage, to determine the real value of a property before bidding, to determine the death duty in case a natural person dies.
transport (*conveyance*) the legal transfer of ownership of a property at a notary public.
tussenwoning (*terraced house/row house*) a house that is bordered on both sides by other houses.

U

uitz. uitzicht (*view*)

V

v.v. voorzien van (*equipped with/furnished with*)
verd. verdieping (*floor*)
Vereniging van Eigenaren (VVE) (*Association of Owners*) as owner of an apartment or flat, by law you are a member of the Association of Owners. Together with the other owners, the association looks after the common interests of the occupants in the building, such as cleaning of communal spaces, staircases and elevators, maintenance of outside walls and roofs, etc. For apartment blocks, there will be a 'division deed' which specifies each owner's part in the whole building.
verspringende tussenwoning (*staggered terraced house/row house*) this type of property only borders on another building through a secondary room (e.g. garage, scullery etc.).
villa (*villa*) a large detached or semi-detached house.
vraagprijs (*asking price*) the price a seller would like to receive for a property. The price is usually negoatiable and intended to invite a bid.
vrij op naam (v.o.n.) (*free on name*) in this sale transaction the costs involved in the conveyance of a house are for the seller, not for the buyer.
vrijstaande woning (*detached house*) a house that is not bordering on another property.
vve. Vereniging van Eigenaren (*Association of Owners*)

W

waarborgsom (*deposit*) an amount paid up front by a buyer (or issued in the form of a bank guarantee) as surety that the buyer will honor the commitments made.
waardebepaling (*appraisal*) the valuation of a property by a surveyor, based on a number of criteria. These include location, size, age, lay-out and the state of maintenance.

wk. woonkamer (*living room*)
wma. wasmachineaansluiting (*connection point for washing machine*)
woz Wet Onroerende Zaakbelasting (*Law on Real Estate Taxation*). This law regulates the appraisal of real estate, such as houses. The result of the appraisal is used as the basis for various taxes.

Z

zoekopdracht (*search order*) formal order by a buyer to a real estate agent to assist with the search for and purchase of a house. The real estate agent is entitled to a commission fee for these services. The exact contents of the search order (which services are included) depends on the agreement between real estate agent and buyer.

IEDEREEN EEN
WATERMETER!

Centru

MODELWONIN
geopend op
ZATERDAG EN ZONDA

7

7 Financial Considerations: Mortgages and Insurances

In this chapter we will explain about securing financing for your mortgage, and discuss the differences in the various financial constructions. We also take a look at insurances, both mandatory and optional.

A. Finding Financing

As the saying goes 'you got to have the money, honey'. Finding the financing for your home purchase is essential! If you are a foreigner you most likely will not have established a line of credit, unless you have rented for sometime and have a credit card history built up. This could make it more difficult for you to secure financing. Banks, however, are in the business of making money, so if you can show that you are not a great risk, you should be able to 'get the money'.

Establishing Credit

Establishing credit can be done by providing the Dutch bank with records from the bank in your last location as well as copies of your foreign outstanding loans to give them some idea of your banking history. You will also need to supply a copy of your employment contract and payroll slip with deductions. If you are benefitting from the 30%-facility it is advisable to mention this, as your world income will be taken into consideration. If you have an investment portfolio, do let the bank know.

If you take a letter from your employer stating your length of employment with the company and the expectation as to the length of your stay in Holland, this will certainly help. The banks are generally not too difficult about giving loans for purchasing housing. With the current shortages and inflated real estate market, if you default, they will have no problem recouping their money if forced to sell.

It is a good idea to gather information before you begin your house hunting so you will know just how much financing you will be able to secure.

Additional Costs and Their Financing

When you purchase an existing house, you will see K.K. or *Kosten Koper*. These are the costs the *koper*, or buyer, pays such as the cadastral registration of the new owner in the mortgage register of the cadastre, the tax on the conveyance fees, and the notary costs for the transfer (see chapter 6, under A).

A newly built house (*nieuwbouwwoning*) is sold as V.O.N. (*vrij op naam*) – literally translated as 'free of name', which means that all of the costs involved with the transfer of the ownership of the property are included in the purchase price (*koopsom*).

You can of course include these costs in your loan when you arrange for financing. It is worth mentioning that if you have previously sold an existing property you will first need to pay off the current mortgage, and to take care of splitting the remaining real estate taxes (*onroerende zaakbelasting*) with the new owner as well as paying the fees of the estate agent. The balance of the purchase price will then be deposited into the account of the seller, and the transfer written into the cadastral registry. You will then go through this same process with your new house.

Do Not Over-Extend

Do keep in mind you want to LIVE here and to enjoy it as well. Do not over-extend yourself to the extent that you have a loan beyond your means to comfortably repay it. Some people opt for a lower rate of interest on a short-term mortgage of five years, with refinancing after the fifth year. If the rates stay low, this could work to your advantage. However, you could find yourself locked into high rates for the next financing period. Most people choose a construction whereby they are certain of what the costs will be each month for a fixed period. Most mortgages are for a period of 20 to 30 years.

Professional Advice

The best advice is to get good advice from a professional. They are knowledgeable, and well informed as to changes in the property or financial tax law, and will be able to explain the various forms of financing in greater detail and to advise you what would best suit your situation both financially and with consideration taken for long term planning of future needs, as well as your spending or investment limitations. It is their job to help you arrange for the most advantageous construction.

As we mentioned before, your bank knows you and your financial history, the drawback is they will want to offer their own products, whereby an independent financial advisor has a variety of products to choose from. Many estate agents have financial consultants who can provide advice on mortgages and insurances.

English-Language Advice
There are many, many good websites with a wealth of information, online tools available such as cost calculators, comparison studies, online mortgage advice, monthly payment calculator, excess worth calculator, etc. all of course in Dutch. Occasionally some companies will provide a portion of their online information in English, you will have to take a look. So, unless your Dutch language skills are adequate, they will be of little use to you. You are well advised to make an appointment with your bank or with an agency specializing in mortgage advice. You may always call to talk to someone, and they do speak English and a number of other European languages. They want to do business and will be able to help you further. Meeting in person at some juncture is ultimately preferable to attempting to get all the information you need over the phone.

B. Types of Mortgages – Hypotheekvormen

There are any numbers of creative forms of financing (mortgage loans, or *hypothecaire leningen*) available to pay for your new home. Explanations of some of the most popular forms are:

1. **Levenshypotheek (Endowment (Life) Mortgage)**
   The *levenhypotheek* is the most familiar sort of insurance in the Netherlands; a life insurance or *levensverzekering* that is coupled with the mortgage loan. You do not need to pay off the capital lent to you; you only need meet your requirement of paying the monthly interest (*maandelijks rentebedrag*) and to have a life insurance that you pay a monthly premium for. The endowment policy is used to generate capital. When the term of the loan / insurance has been fulfilled, the insurance provider will pay out the amount saved plus interest (*gespaard bedrag + rente*) and this amount must be used to pay off the mortgage in full. Usually a portion of the capital is guaranteed at the end of the term and the remainder is made dependent on the investment return. The amount guaranteed is often less than the mortgage loan, however, with investment return it usually covers the mortgage. If the policy underperforms you may opt to extend the mortgage until such time as the capital saved does

cover the loan. If however it outperforms, the borrower makes a profit. If you should die before the loan has been repaid, the life insurance will pay off the outstanding mortgage.

The tax deduction is the maximum, since you are only paying interest. Another benefit is that the monthly payments are stable. The *spaarhypotheek* (see further on) has originated from the structure of the *levenhypotheek*.

2. **Lineaire Hypotheek (Linear Mortgage)**
   In a linear mortgage (*lineaire hypotheek*) you pay an equal amount each month against the capital as well as the interest. The total amount you pay in interest each month become less as time goes on. That is because the interest you pay each month is based on the outstanding capital loan, which slowly but surely decreases. A benefit of this form of financing is that you can deduct the monthly payments, however, the initial costs are high as the 'line' goes from more to less, as a consequence of which you start with large payments which gradually decrease.

3. **Aflossingsvrije Hypotheek (Redemption-Free Mortgage)**
   The *aflossingsvrije hypotheek* has the lowest monthly payments, because you do not repay, or 'redeem', it (*aflossen*). The only thing you pay is the (partial) tax-deductible interest on the entire sum of the loan. In this construction you do not build up any capital, and your mortgage debt remains constant. You only pay the interest. The assumption here is that when you sell the property, you will have the funds to repay the capital loan. The insurance that best matches this loan is a life insurance policy for an insured amount that decreases annually (i.e. linear). This is calculated in such a way that the insured amount is always sufficient to cover the unredeemed part of the mortgage loan.

   The *aflossingsvrije hypotheek* may not be higher than 65% of the 'fire resale' value (*executiewaarde*) of your house. The remaining 35% you pay out of your own pocket. You can also choose for a combination of *aflossingsvrije hypotheek* with another form to cover the 35%, such as by means of a *spaarhypotheek* (savings or special endowment mortgage). According to the current tax laws you may not deduct interest on this form of a mortgage for a period exceeding 30 years.

4. **Beleggingshypotheek (Investment Mortgage)**
   The investment mortgage or *beleggingshypotheek* is derived from the *aflossingsvrije hypotheek*. Here you build up your capital through investing in stocks. This gives you the guarantee that later you will have less to repay. You can choose for a less risky or very risky investment form, this is up to you.

The riskier the investment, the greater the chance of profit – but also the greater the chance of loss in a poor investment climate. The market fluctuates. If you choose for this form, it is wise to purchase a level term insurance (*overlijdensverzekering*) to cover costs in the event of your death during the loan period.

5. **Annuïteitenhypotheek (Annuity Mortgage)**
The *annuïteitenhypotheek* has been around for a long time in the world of mortgages. The attraction here is that this form has nothing to do with fiscal rules and limitations. The total monthly payments remain the same as long as the interest rate does not change, and you repay a small portion each month against the capital. Your debt gets smaller every month, so your rent decreases monthly as well. The downside of this is that each month you have a lower tax deduction. In the beginning your costs comprise a larger portion of interest and a smaller repayment of capital. As time passes and you have repaid a good portion of the loan, you also have less interest to pay over the outstanding loan, which leaves you more room to repay a greater portion of the debt. The insurance is a life policy with a non-proportional decrease in the amount insured, which is in line with the redemptions made.

6. **Spaarhypotheek (Special Endowment (Savings) Mortgage)**
With the *spaarhypotheek* (savings mortgage) you do not repay the loan. You pay ONLY interest over the entire outstanding loan. The tax deduction remains constant – as it does for the *levenhypotheek*.

With the *spaarhypotheek* you purchase a 'savings insurance' or *spaarverzekering*. The premium (*premie*) that you pay consists of a risk portion and a savings portion (*risicodeel en spaardeel*). Thanks to the *risicodeel* the loan is repaid when you die, depending on the ratio of the risk and savings portions. The savings portion is deposited on a bank account.

The tax-free interest compensation (*belastingvrije rentevergoeding*) that you receive over the savings portion (*spaarsaldo*), is equal to the interest percentage that you pay for your mortgage loan. At the end of the term of the loan (*looptijd*) you know for certain that the necessary capital to repay the loan has accumulated. At the end, the capital saved exactly matches the principal of the mortgage loan.

The Special Endowment Mortgage is therefore no risk and ideally suited for people with limited financial means. One downside however, is the reduced investment flexibility. The loan, endowment and life insurance are inseparably linked. Therefore you cannot benefit from either changing to high yield bonds on the investment portion or benefiting from lower interest rates on your borrowing over the period of the loan.

If you have a *spaarhypotheek* when you die, the insurance company will pay the insurance amount. However, not every insurance company deposits the full amount to the next of kin, so there is some risk in this form of insured mortgage.

7. **Depot Hypotheek (Deposit Mortgage)**
   This version gives you the highest amount of available financing coupled with an optimal tax deduction structure. The *depot hypotheek* combines two financial products into a new product; namely the *spaarhypotheek* and the *depot-rekening*. The first part consists of a mix of a loan, savings and insurance. You pay an amount of interest and purchase a life insurance which is coupled with the loan. The deposit portion (*depot*), allows you to withdraw money as needed (usually by submitting the invoices – *notas* – from the construction company (*aanemers*)).
   The *depot hypotheek* can be used for building projects, either new construction or for large renovations (it is sometimes also referred to as a *bouw depot rekening*). The money that is on deposit accrues interest as long as it is not being used. As portions of money are deducted, the amount of interest decreases, until the *depot* is finally empty. Once you have spent it of course, you are subject to repay the agreed upon rate of interest and capital of the outstanding loan. The interest (*depot hypotheekrente*) is also tax-deductible. You may either choose to have the *spaarhypotheek* cover the total amount of the mortgage loan, or, depending on the amount of your loan, using the *spaarhypotheek* to cover only a portion of the mortgage, and to have the second portion *aflossingsvrij* (meaning that you do not repay the outstanding loan, but only the interest on the loan).

8. **Krediethypotheek (Credit Mortgage)**
   If the value of your current house is considerably higher than your mortgage loan, you can use the 'excess value' (*overwaarde*) of your house as collateral and open a credit account (*kredietrekening*). The ceiling for your credit limit will be determined by your income and the current market value (*verkoop-waarde*) of your house. You pay interest only over the outstanding amount that you have borrowed that has been used. This allows you some freedom in determining how you want to allocate funds that have become available thanks to the increased worth of your property. This 'line of credit' also allows you to pay back portions of the loan, and then have more spending room, similar in structure to a continual credit account (*doorlopend krediet*), see further on, under *Additional Finances*.

9. **Effectenhypotheek (Stock Portfolio Mortgage)**
If you want to arrange an *effectenhypotheek*, you increase the amount of your present mortgage and with the extra money purchase a stock portfolio (*effectenportefeuille*). *Effecten* are anything traded on the '*effecten beurs*' or stock market. Your financial or mortgage advisor (*hypotheekadviseur*) will gladly explain the legal and tax implications of this type of mortgage. A word of caution: the stock market is always in a state of flux, and the return on your 'risky' investments may not be adequate to cover the full mortgage loan should you incur too many losses.

10. **Groene Hypotheek (Green Mortgage)**
When you would like to purchase or build an environmentally friendly house (*milieuvriendelijke woning*) or you have a heart for the environment and want to make environmentally efficient changes to your home such as by the use of eco-materials (insulation materials and sound isolation materials) or energy and water savings devices (heating systems, solar energy, heat pumps) then you can make use of a very attractive interest arrangement. This consists of two mortgage parts: the first is a maximum of € 34,000 and is the green portion (*groene deel*) which has an interest (*rente*) that is lower than the current market interest (*marktrente*) for a period of twenty years maximum. The Dutch Agency for Energy and Environment (NOVEM – De Nederlandse Onderneming voor Energie en Milieu) provides you with a green statement (*groenverklaring*), to be used for arranging the 'green portion' of the mortgage. The second portion of the loan is treated as a regular mortgage loan and goes at the normal (current) interest rates, based on the type of financial construction that you have chosen for your mortgage.

This mortgage is available for existing ecological 'eco homes' as well as new construction when the material costs or foundation costs do not exceed a maximum of € 181,500.
See www.novem.org or www.novem.nl for more information.

Second Mortgages

A second mortgage is known as a *tweede hypotheek* – If you are a already a homeowner, or at some point in time require more funds after purchasing the home you are currently about to buy, a *tweede hypotheek* can be used to enable you to secure more capital for renovation projects (or possibly that longed-for trip around the world). The second mortgage has traditionally been a means of providing extra financing by utilizing the increased over value of your property (*overwaarde*) as collateral (*onderpand*) to arrange for a new loan and some financial 'room.' See section E for more information on additional financing.

One word of warning: if you use take out a second mortgage for the purpose of renovating (or otherwise making adjustments to) your home, the interest of this second mortgage will remain tax-deductible. However, if you use it to make that longed-for trip around the world, the interest will *not be tax-deductible*.

C. Interest Rates

Everybody is of course looking for the lowest rate of interest (*rente*) on loans and of course the highest rate of interest on savings. For your convenience there is a list of banks and financial institutions in the Netherlands provided at the end of this chapter. As interest rates do tend to fluctuate, and given the historical context of the impact of world events and economic upheavals on interest rates, we will not go into a discussion on the geo-political aspects of variances affecting your financial situation with regards to purchasing a house here in the Netherlands. Suffice it to say, the best advice, is to secure professional advice from financial experts.

It stands to reason that the lower the interest rate you need to pay, the better it may be for your finances. However, much will depend on whether your fixed term is set for 5 years or 10, or if in fact you choose for a fluctuating interest structure which changes monthly or yearly. Equally important, depending on the type of mortgage you have, your mortgage interest and your savings interest may be inextricably linked, so that the lowest interest rate might not even be the most attractive.

Deducting the Mortgage Interest

Mortgage interest is deductible from your taxable income, so that in effect you only pay a certain percentage of your interest yourself, depending on your tax bracket. The interest that you can deduct from your taxable income is paid back out to you by the tax authorities, either after filing your income tax return, or on a monthly basis – to which purpose you submit a request with the tax authorities.

30%-Facility

Of interest in this context is the fact that, if you benefit from the 30%-facility (which is discussed further on in the chapter in more detail), your net salary is effectively reduced, so that you may end up in a lower tax bracket, as a consequence of which a lower percentage of your mortgage interest is paid back to you.

Stock Market Performance

Mortgages that are dependent upon stock market performance to produce repayment capital may produce poorly in a depressed market. Although yields may be adequate, you carry a higher risk, and no guaranteed end capital, only projected.

Types of Interest

1. **Nominale** (nominal) – This is the interest rate that is advertised, and the rate that will be fixed in your mortgage agreement. However, the time frame in which you will repay the loan, will impact your actual costs. Will you repay per month, yearly, before a period, or afterwards? Above the cost of the actual mortgage loan, the costs of the insurances and closing costs of the loan are also to be considered, as having financed the whole package, you will also be paying interest over these additional costs as well.

2. **Effectieve** (in effect) – After tallying up all of the *bruto* (actual) costs of the mortgage, plus the time and type of the payments, we are referring to the effective interest rate. Money lenders are legally required to post this amount as well. Consumer groups hope this will make it easier to make a comparison of the actual costs.

3. **Netto werkelijke rente** (net real interest) – In this term the interest rate percentage of the mortgage interest, the closing costs, the tax benefits, the premiums on the life insurance and the (eventual) payout of the life insurance are worked together to arrive at the true total 'real' (*werkelijke*) costs that you will actually be paying.

4. **Variable rente** (variable interest) – The rate of interest you pay 'varies' with the market fluctuation of rates, so you do not have a 'fixed' rate of interest.

5. **Projectrente** (project interest) – Often, new housing projects (*nieuwbouw*) will have a very attractive rate of interest tied to the project. However, it is usually for a limited amount of time (perhaps only the first year during project construction) and thereafter your interest rates will be at the going rate. It is often to your advantage to secure a mortgage with attractive terms for a longer period of time, say 5 to 10 years. Likewise, some 'cheap' interest rates have expensive payback terms or other penalties included in their financial construction.

6. **Bouwrente and Depotrente** (building and deposit interest) – A new house may often consist of the purchase of a building plan on paper, perhaps the actual

construction has not yet even begun. You cannot wait until it is finished to pay for the house. First the ground needs to be paid for, and the bank will pay the contractor in set terms as the construction progresses. With the purchase of the house, a full mortgage needs to be in place. You will pay the mortgage interest on this portion of the loan, on the portion that has not as yet been paid out to the builder you will receive deposit interest (*depotrente*). Ideally, the deposit interest is identical to the mortgage interest, whereby you in effect are only paying interest over the mortgage portion that has been paid out to the builder. The mortgage interest that is paid out during the building is referred to as *bouwrente*.

7. **Rentevaste periode** (set interest term / period) – This the specific period of time that the agreed upon interest rate is fixed (*vastzetten*); secured at a fixed rate in your mortgage contract, valid until such time as the period is over, whereby you will then need to negotiate a new term and rates for your (outstanding) mortgage loan. This rate will change to a new rate that will be negotiated. For example, on a 30-year mortgage, you may decide to fix your interest rate for seven years with an option to renegotiate at the 5-year mark and before the 7-year mark for a new rate of interest. This gives you some flexibility in determining your costs as, if interest rates decline considerably, you will be able to fix your rate at a lower rate for the next agreed upon period. A fixed rate for a 30-year mortgage for the full term is generally not done. Interest rates continually fluctuate.

NHG – Nationale Hypotheek Garantie – The National Mortgage Guarantee

The National Mortgage Guarantee (Nationale Hypotheek Garantie, or NHG) is an instrument of the Home Ownership Guarantee Fund Foundation (Stichting Waarborgfonds Eigen Woningen) and is an important incentive for encouraging home ownership and improving the quality of the homes in the Netherlands. Since its establishment in 1995, more than 300,000 guarantees have been granted.

With the NHG you receive a lower rate of interest, and you can safely borrow money as your financial situation will be examined so that you have sufficient funds to live on, and not overextend your self. Furthermore, all the costs incurred are tax-deductible; you can finance the entire amount needed in full (for purchase or improvements), not needing to supply any down payment of your own and, with the purchase of a property in need of repairs, the repair / renovation costs can be financed at the same time with the purchase.

Conditions for Eligibility
Conditions for eligibility are the following:

- you must be at least 23
- you may not have been an owner-occupant during the past three years
- you must live in the dwelling yourself (not rent it out)
- you must be a legal resident of the Netherlands.

You will need to have a steady source of income, though in some instances allowances are made for irregular or seasonal employment such as restaurant or garden work if you have been employed by the same employer for more than two years. Likewise 'flex work' and temporary agency workers may also apply for an NHG mortgage if all criteria are met.

Non-Dutch nationals who are legal residents with a *verblijfsvergunning voor onbepaalde tijd* (permanent resident status) must provide a legitimate proof of identification from their home country along with a copy of their residence status. They may therefore possibly be eligible (if meeting all of the requirements for eligibility) to apply for a National Mortgage Guarantee.

With the NHG, consumers can finance the purchase of their home and the accompanying costs in full with borrowed capital. In addition they get a discount varying from 0.2 to 0.5% on the prevailing market interest rate. It is also possible to use the NHG to finance renovations to an existing home in the case of overdue maintenance.

One-Off Premium
The consumer has to pay a one-off premium for this guarantee. For instance, for 2001, this premium was fixed at 0.3% of the mortgage sum. This premium fee can be included in the financing and is tax-deductible. The cost of the dwelling is defined as ALL the costs involved in acquiring it. There is a ceiling of € 200,000 (April 2002) for all costs incurred, including the transaction costs (*transactiekosten*) such as the *notaris*, estate agent, transfer provisions, taxation and building reports and the costs of improvements, repairs and other additional building costs. When calculating the cost of acquiring an existing structure you may assume your costs to be 12% *transactiekosten* of the purchase price of the dwelling. For new construction home purchases (*nieuwbouw*) the estimated percentage of the transaction costs is 8% of the purchase price. Again, these costs may be financed into the amount of your loan, however, you cannot exceed the € 200,000 maximum allowable NHG mortgage loan.

Risks and Guarantees
In the case of a mortgage loan with the NHG, the financier is not faced with any interest or repayment risks should the borrower be unable to comply with his

interest and repayment obligations. The NHG takes on all of the risk and guarantees that the financier will be paid.
The house will be sold and the *Waarborgfonds* has the responsibility of paying off the mortgage loan, taking on the debt from the house owner.

Target Group NHG
NHG was begun in order to encourage people in the lower and middle income categories to secure a loan for the purchase of a home whereby the costs of repairing neglected properties and making necessary improvements can also be financed at the same time. It is also available to *flexwerkers* and *uitzendkrachten* (people who work flexible jobs or are sent out from employment agencies, in other words, who do not have a steady full time job – *vaste baan*).

It is also possible for existing homeowners to secure a loan through the NHG to finance only improvements and/or major repairs.

Benefits
In summary, the NHG does offer quite a few benefits:
- lower interest rate: thanks to the security offered by the guarantee of NHG the financial lending institution will reward you with a lower rate of interest
- safe and responsible lending: maximum security due to the guarantee that the full amount of the loan will always be repaid in full in the event you are unable to do so. Margin of spending capital (*bestedingsruimte*) is secured
- tax-deductible costs: all the costs for NHG (0.3% security deposit – *borgtochtprovisie*) are tax-deductible
- full 100% financing: you can finance for the full amount needed. You do not need to provide your own money
- co-financing of improvement loans: with the purchase you can at the same time secure the funds needed up to the maximum amount allowed for repairs and improvements.

Website
www.nhg.nl – you can check for participating *gemeentes*, news, press release, etc. All information is in Dutch. The list search for *gemeentes* only requires entering in the name.

D. Purchase Subsidy – Koopsubsidie

The government wants to encourage renters to purchase, thereby giving people with lower incomes the freedom of choice between renting and buying.
Therefore, as of January 2001, anyone who meets the conditions stipulated in the *Huursubsidiewet* (Rental Subsidy Law) can be considered for a purchase subsidy.

The *koopsubsidie* lowers the cost of your mortgage debt (*hypotheeklasten*) and can be used for the purchase of a house or trailer on a registered site (the latter which translates as *woonwagen in combinatie met een standplaats*).

NOTE: In July 2002 a new brochure with figures is published on *Koopsubsidies*.

Maximum

The subsidy is currently possible up to a maximum amount of € 117,892.10, which in total amount may include all of the extra costs for the transfer of the property, the *notaris* fees, the estate agent fees, and property tax. For new housing there is no transfer tax. The amount of the mortgage loan itself may only be to a maximum amount which covers ONLY the purchase price, which may not total more than € 94,295.53. Dependent upon the income of the buyer and the amount of the mortgage loan, the possibility exists of receiving a *koopsubsidie* purchase subsidy up to a maximum of € 152.47 per month. The subsidy payments for the maximum loan are distributed in monthly subsidy allotments; you do not receive a lump sum payment. It is not only your income that determines your purchase subsidy, your capital also counts, such as the amounts in savings accounts, and the sales value of property such as an automobile, caravan or boat.

Please refer to the eight-page folder *Your Own Home? Purchase Subsidy Means Freedom of Choice* available on the www.koopsubsidie.nl website.

Submitting the Application

On the grounds of the Wet Bevordering Eigenwoningbezit (BEW) (determination of homeownership) the application for the *koopsubsidie* has to be submitted by the institution lending the money.

Conditions and Information

The *koopsubsidie* is only given in conjunction with an NHG loan (see explanation above).
For more information contact a financial (mortgage) advisor or *hypotheekadviseur* who can explain in full the benefits and procedures involved in securing a *koopsubsidie* from the NHG. You may also contact the Spatial Planning and Environmental Ministry VROM, tel.: 0800 – 566 77 82, or visit the website: www.koopsubsidie.nl.

For a complete explanation, more information can be found on this website. You can read the information in English, and there are down loadable folders in seven languages. In addition, you may use the site calculation model to determine if you are eligible, and for what monthly amount. You can also ask the staff of the purchase subsidy questions at the help desk.

E. Additional Financing

You may need at some point to secure additional financing in addition to your mortgage. A second mortgage is of course always a possibility. However, with a second mortgage you are carrying a larger financial burden, and given your fixed rate of payment extended over a long period, of 25 or 30 years, you will be paying more in the long run for this type of financing. Some shorter-term options are explained below.

The best form of financing actually depends on the purpose of the loan. Whether the reason is for purchasing furniture or large appliances, installing a new kitchen, decorating the baby room, investments or a vacation trip, there are a number of ways to finance your needs. It is always advisable to orient yourself as much as possible as to what is available, and which form would best suit your needs. Again, the professional advice from your bank or financial advisor is invaluable.

1. Doorlopend Krediet (Continual Credit Account)
   A *doorlopend krediet* or continual credit is a flexible loan whereby you always have money on hand, or as the Dutch say, *geld achter de hand* (behind your hand). The amount of money you 'borrow' decreases as you make your monthly payments. The amount that has been repaid into the account can be borrowed again; you only pay interest over the outstanding debt (*uitstaande saldo*). The monthly payments consist of a portion of payment and a fixed rate of interest. Repayment (*aflossen*) is always free of penalties (*boetevrij*) should you wish to pay back an extra amount to reduce your outstanding debt, or to pay off the entire amount. There is no time limit set, as the loan 'continues throughout' (*loopt door*): you have the continued option of using the money available in your credit limit.

2. Persoonlijke Lening (Personal Loan)
   With a personal loan (*persoonlijke lening* – PL) you can determine the duration of the loan based on the expected lifespan of the item you wish to purchase, for instance a new automobile, furniture or a computer. In this way you can avoid still paying for something long after you no longer are using it. A *persoonlijke lening* has a fixed term (*looptijd*) and a fixed rate of interest. You pay off the amount of the loan plus the amount of the interest owed in identical monthly payments for the full term. Early repayment will be subject to penalty payment.

3. Spaarkrediet (Savings Credit)
By way of payments for a fixed term (*termijnbetalingen*) you save up an amount of money whereby at the end of the term of the loan there will be sufficient funds to repay the loan in full. Since January 1, 2001, there are strict conditions imposed regarding this form of borrowing / saving money.

4. Effectenlening (Stock Portfolio Loan)
Effecten are stocks and bonds, anything traded on the stock market (*effectenbeurs*). It may be that you wish to temporarily have some extra financial liquidity or take advantage of investments in foreign stocks. In this case, a loan to invest in your stock portfolio (*effectenlening*) could be the solution. In this way you need not sell off existing investments to raise the needed capital.

F. Dutch Tax Issues for Expatriates

International tax law is a complicated and complex maze of information, rules and regulations. Seek professional advice, either through your company who may have in-house consultancies or through an external consultant. You will need to have someone who understands both Dutch law and the law of the country you come from – where you may have an additional tax liability. This book is concerned with Housing in Holland and therefore we will not go into great detail here.

Your status, though, with regard to mortgages and financing needs to be considered. A mortgage is a tax-driven product. In the Netherlands as an expat, in order to determine your tax status, the two major tax issues are the 30%-facility and the choice between resident and partial non-resident status.

The 30%-Facility

The 30%-facility allows an employer to grant an employee a tax-free allowance of up to 30% of his total remuneration for so-called extraterritorial expenses, for a maximum period of ten years. If you make use of this facility, this will effectively reduce the effective rate of wage tax, resulting in a higher net salary (*netto salaris*). In the fifth year the tax authorities re-evaluate your situation as to whether or not you still meet the conditions of eligibility for the 30%-facility. As you can read further on, those who opt for the 30%-facility may choose to be treated as so-called partial non-resident taxpayers; as with the 30%-facility, your partial non-resident tax status lasts for a maximum number of years, after which you become a resident taxpayer. Each year you can switch tax status, depending on your personal and financial situation. It is also possible to choose to have a partial foreign tax obligation, thus splitting your tax burden.

(Partial) Non-Resident Tax Status

Expats who have non-resident tax status are taxable on some sources of income stipulated in Dutch tax legislation. This includes immovable property (*onroerend goed*).

There are a couple of points for (partial) non-residents to keep in mind on this matter:

- since this immovable property could be leased out and provide income, the notional income (also known as the 'deemed rental income' – *eigenwoning-forfait*) is assessed on the basis of the WOZ-appraisal value (see chapter 6) and is added to your taxable income
- (partial) non-residents are entitled to tax deductions for specified income sources and alimony
- since your property is taxed, the interest payments on the mortgage are tax-deductible, provided the home is your principle place of residence
- your net wealth is not taxed (however, full resident taxpayers are taxed at a rate of 1.2% over their net assets minus liabilities).

If you own multiple properties or come from a country with common law (U.S.A., Great Britain) versus the civil law here in the Netherlands, taxes on your world-wide income become increasingly complex. Expert advice from a professional in international tax law would be an excellent choice to help clarify the intricacies of international home ownership.

Resident Tax Status

If you do not opt for the (partial) non-resident tax status than you are considered to be a resident taxpayer under the law, the same as any other ordinary Dutch citizen. You are only entitled to mortgage relief for your principle place of residence. Other properties fall subject to taxation under the wealth tax (box III-tax), which is currently taxed at 1.2% over your assets (*vermogen*).

Finding the Right Mortgage

The objective is to find a mortgage which allows you to take the most effective advantage of the tax deductions in your given circumstances, whether with a resident or (partial) non-resident status. Additionally, the type and duration of the mortgage you choose needs to be one you can live with, and with affordable payments. It goes without saying that you must consult with a professional to determine which is the best mortgage in your given (tax) situation.

TIP: an attractive mortgage type for partial non-resident taxpayers is one that is linked to a savings scheme – allowing you to benefit from the tax-deductibility of the mortgage interest, while exempting you from taxation over the investment income from the savings scheme.

Refer again to the list on additional costs and levies in the Netherlands (Chapter 2 section G) and take them into consideration in your calculations. Also calculate the estimated costs of your or monthly required payments (*maandelijkse lasten*) – gas, electric, water, insurances, car payments – as well as your general living expenses such as food clothes, recreation, etc. to give you a total financial picture.

G. Insurances for Houses

When you purchase a house you are required to carry a number of insurances. Some of them are mandatory and required by law and in other cases your mortgage lender will require the insurance to provide security to cover the loan. Other insurances are optional, though generally wise to have.

1. **Opstalverzekering – Homeowners' Insurance**
   This insurance covers all the damage to your house and everything that is built on your land in the event of fire, burglary, storm, lightening, burst water pipes, etc. When you have arranged your mortgage and the paperwork has been signed at the *notaris*' office, this house coverage (*opstalverzekering*) is mandatory (*verplicht*). The reason for this is that the property serves as collateral (*onderpand*) for your loan. The bank wants their investment insured against damage that would depreciate or destroy this collateral.

   It is wise to arrange for a yearly index (*jaarlijkse indexering*) on this policy, which will insure that each year your insured amount is increased, otherwise you could wind up being under-insured. The yearly index reflects the percentage of increase in the cost of living and the increase in property values.

   When you purchase an apartment, ALL of the owners in the building must have an *opstalverzekering*. TIP: if the apartment owners all have their insurance with the same insurance company (one company), they can save a lot of money on the costs of the insurance premiums.

2. **Inboedelverzekering – Personal Property / Household Effects**
   This insurance covers your personal effects (*inboedel*) such as books, television, furniture, dishes, clothes, etc. Damage or theft to personal property insurance is not mandatory, but it is highly recommended. Suppose

your house or apartment burned down and you had the required *opstalverzekering* but no *inboedelverzekering* – you would receive no compensation for the loss of all of your personal belongings, only for the house. The insured amount needs to be sufficient to replace all items lost. The costs of the premiums for this type of insurance are determined by the region where you live. Unfortunately, due to the increased number of burglaries in large cities, many of them now require you to cover the first portion of the damage under your own risk (*eigen risico*) of € 250. Generally this insurance covers the following claims: damages resulting from storm rain (*regen*), snow (*sneeuw*), break-ins (*inbraak*), burglary / theft (*diefstal*), vandalism (*vandalisme*), leaks (*lekkage*), fire damage (*schroeischade* is singed damage or *brandschade* is burn damage). Renters are well advised to secure *inboedel* insurance to cover their belongings. The landlord is only insured for eventual damage to the building.

This insurance will pay out (*vergoeden*) only up to a certain maximum. For Amsterdam, The Hague, Rotterdam and Utrecht there are much stricter requirements. Additionally, you will not receive the new value of many items, as everything in your home is considered used. A sofa you have had for two years, or a stereo you have had for four years will not be reimbursed for the original purchase price. Also, oftentimes items that can be cleaned – for instance from smoke damage after a fire (curtains, furniture) – will be refurbished rather than replaced. Make sure this insurance is indexed yearly as well, to ensure you are not under-insured. Some people make a video recording of their home and the items in it for insurance purposes. In any event, keep an accurate and up-to-date list of your purchases. Most people have many more items of value in their possession than they stop to consider.

3. **Waardegoederen Verzekering – Personal Exceptional Valuables Insurance**
Covers the risk of theft or damage to items of exceptional value, such as jewelry, or expensive computer equipment. Antiques and artwork need to be listed. Coverage will only be accepted upon submitting a purchase note or appraisal report that is not older than one year.

4. **Glasverzekering – Glass Insurance**
Most *opstalverzekeringen* or homeowner's insurances cover damage to glass windows. It is advisable to purchase separate coverage for the replacement or repair of expensive stained glass windows (*glas-in-loodwerk*) and beveled glass (*geslepen glas*).

5. **Wettelijke Aansprakelijkheidsverzekering (WA) – Liability Insurance**
This insurance, also known as the WAP, or *Wettelijke Aansprakelijkheids-*

verzekering voor Particulieren, is a personal liability insurance and is absolutely necessary for homeowners. You are insured for damages occurring from your house, for instance a roof tile falling on someone's head, or someone falling through a rotted floorboard, as well as any damages to another person or their property resulting from actions of you or any of your family members. You may inadvertently cause an accident whereby another person is injured or his property is damaged. In such cases it is an advantage to have an insurance policy that will cover the costs of the financial consequences of your liability. By taking out a liability insurance you can cover most costs for damages caused by accidents, ranging from a scratch to destruction of the property of another, or your child smashing your neighbor's window with a ball to the costs of causing serious bodily injury to someone.

A claim for compensation at the insurance company often implies a lot of tiresome paperwork, but some accidents for which you can be held liable have such high financial consequences that a liability insurance is essential coverage. This policy also covers the costs of legal actions in resolving the claims, whether they have grounds to prosecute or not.

6. **Rechtsbijstandsverzekering – Legal Aid Insurance**
   This insurance is a type of extension of Liability Insurance in as much it covers the cost of any legal assistance you may need, should you be sued by another party. A disputed bill, for example, which you find unacceptable and refuse to settle, may lead to a session in court for which you will need the services of a lawyer. The considerable costs of such aid will be covered by a Legal Aid Insurance.

7. **Overlijdensrisicoverzekering – Death Risk Insurance**
   If you have a mortgage loan for more than 100% of the rebuilding value (*executiewaarde*) – which is 60% of the worth of the building – you must always have a 'death risk insurance' (*overlijdensrisicoverzekering*) to cover the amount of value in excess of this *executiewaarde*. Many mortgages will couple a life insurance (*levensverzekering*) to the financing. Should you die before the loan has been paid off, this insurance will pay off all or part of the mortgage loan. One of the benefits of this is that your heirs need not be confronted with heavy costs.

   Another option is to combine a death risk insurance with a work disability policy (*arbeidsongeschiktheidsverzekering*) to cover payments in the event you become incapacitated.

References

Acquiring Insurance

There are two ways of arranging an insurance policy in the Netherlands. You can either go directly to an insurance company to arrange a policy (direct writer), or you can hire the services of a middleman, someone who will figure out the most appropriate policy at the best price and arrange the insurance for you (by an insurance agent/broker or *assurantiebedrijf*).

We did not discuss health insurance in this chapter, however, in order to make our list complete, we have included the telephone numbers for health insurance in the following list. NOTE: you will notice that we have made a distinction between private health insurance and *Ziekenfonds*-insurance. *Ziekenfonds* is a total medical care package that is offered to all employees with an annual income of no more than € 29,813.36 and is required by law for all employees whose annual income lies below this level.

Contact information for insurance companies:

Gouda International Insurance
Gouda has a unique and complete insurence package for the expatriates
P.O. box 9
2800 MA Gouda
tel: 0182-544916
www.expatriatesinsurance.com

Zilveren Kruis Achmea
Zilveren Kruis is a large, well-run insurance company. You may call them (cost € 0,05 p/m) or visit one of their 'service shops' to get an introduction or further information from one of their representatives, as they all speak English. Some literature is available on private insurance in English, but none for *Ziekenfonds*.

Medical insurance
Ziekenfonds, tel.: 0900 9674
Private insurance, tel.: 0900 8625
www.zilverenkruis.nl
www.achmea.nl

Service shops

Amsterdam	Raamplein 44a 1016 XK Amsterdam
Rotterdam	Westblaak 214 3012 KP Rotterdam
Rotterdam-Zuid	Zuidplein 106 3083 CX Rotterdam

Beverwijk	Meerstraat 68 1941 JD Beverwijk
Utrecht	Radboudkwartier 193 3511 CJ Utrecht
Haarlem	Rijksstraatweg 56 2022 DB Haarlem
Noordwijk	Van de Mortelstraat 4 2203 JD Noordwijk

FBTO

FBTO is a direct writer for insurance, offering a variety of insurances. www.fbto.nl
Damage insurance (for: car, motorcycle, home (rental), travel and camper insurance)
Tel.: 058 234 56 78
Fax: 058 234 54 39

Medical insurance (*ziekenfonds* or private)
Tel.: 058 234 55 55
Fax: 058 234 55 54

Income insurance (liability, disability and mortgage insurance)
Tel.: 058 234 56 56
Fax: 058 234 53 64

Life insurance (death insurance, risk policies and partner policies)
Tel.: 058 234 53 00
Fax: 058 234 53 83

General contact
Tel.: 058 234 53 45

NVS

Offers *ziekenfonds* health coverage, private insurance and most others. They do not have information or brochures in English, however their operators all speak English.
NVS Zorgverzekeringen N.V.
Postbus 1200
7400 CB Deventer

Customer service line
Tel.: 020 555 26 33

OHRA

Ohra is a direct writer for insurance. They have all kinds of insurance policies (for car, house, medical, etc.) and supposedly profitable rates along with good service. Their employees and telephone operators all speak English.

Contact:
Customer service line
Tel.: 026 400 48 48

Offices
Tel.: 026 400 40 40
OHRA B.V.
Visiting address:
Rijksweg West 2
6842 BD Arnhem (Mailing address: Postbus 40000; 6803 GA Arnhem)
www.ohra.nl

ANOZ
The advantage of this company is their services in English, which are extensive (they are currently working on having all of their services available in English).

Ziekenfonds-insured clients:
Tel.: 0900 8685 (10 cent per minute)

Private insured clients:
Tel.: 0900 8494 (10 cent per minute)

Insurance shops:

Almere-Stad	Marktmeesterstraat 87
Apeldoorn	Brinklaan 140
Groningen	Herestraat 92
Heerenveen	Breedpad 15
Hilversum	Groest 31
Leerdam	Nieuwstraat 43
Leeuwarden	Zuiderplein 33
Zutphen	Stationsstraat 6

Request that the insurance companies provide you with quotes so that you may compare the costs. Often it is less expensive to have all of your insurances provided through one insurance provider. Generally a discount is given for 'all-in-one' packages. In case of claims for multiple damages your insurance company representative will be able to insure that all coverage claims are inspected and payments paid out. In the case of litigation, one provider may also be of advantage.

Further Resources
For information on insurances in general in the Netherlands (and comparisons of prices and packages) you can visit a number of independent websites. These are

all in Dutch, however if you can find a Dutch friend or associate to help you translate, these sites are worth looking into. Again, the best advice is to talk to a professional about your financial needs.
www.veh.nl – Vereniging Eigen Huis -Association of (Own) Homeowners.

Websites

Start pages for mortgage advice and financial loans:
www.verzekeringen.pagina.nl – a homepage for all insurance companies and other services.

www.vsv.nl/frameengels.htm – social security and insurance explained in English.
http://verzekeringen.pagina.nl – under startpagina.nl the insurance start page for all types of insurances throughout the entire country.
www.hac.nl – hypotheek advice center (*hypotheekadviescentrum*)
www.hypotheker.nl – mortgages
www.huis-hypotheek.nl – home mortgages
www.hypotheekshop.nl – mortgage shop
www.skhb.nl – certification for mortgages (*stichting keurmerk hypotheek bemiddeling*)
www.fx.nl – various insurances
www.independer.nl – various insurances
www.wellowell.nl – comparative prices of insurance providers
www.eubos.nl – mortgage site
www.europeloan.com – financial assistance
www.hypotheeknu.nl – mortgages site
www.moneyyou.nl – money of course – financial information
www.planhetzelf.nl – financial planning for all your needs

Financial Advice Links

www.nibud.nl – Nationaal Institute voor Budget and Finance Information
www.nirov.nl – Netherlands Institute for Spatial Planning and Public Housing
www.minvrom.nl – Ministerie of VROM (environment and milieu)
www.skhb.nl – Stichting Keurmerk Hypotheekbemiddeling (mortgage approval)
www.svn.nl – Stichting Stimuleringsfonds Volkshuisvesting Nederlandse Gemeenten

Financial Institutions

For a complete listing of the banks and financial institutions in the Netherlands (and Europe) go to the start page: http://banken.pagina.nl

The most well known banks in the Netherlands are:
ABN Amro bank – www.abnamro.nl or www.abnamro.com (international)
Robeco Advies – www.robeco.com

Rabo Bank – www.rabobank.nl or www.rabobank.com (international)
CVB Bank – www.cvbbank.nl
ING Bank – www.ing.nl or www.ingbank.com (international)
FortisBank – www.fortis.com
SNS Bank – www.snsbank.nl
DSB Bank – www.dsbbank.nl
Finasbank – www.finasbank.nl
Postbank – www.postbank.nl
Kempen Merchant Bank – www.kempen.nl
Van Lanschot Bankers – www.vanlanschot.nl
Staal Bankers – www.staalbankiers.nl
Credit Lyonnais Bank – www.creditlyonnais.com

Financial / Insurance
AXA Verzekering – www.axa.nl
Aegon – www.aegon.nl
Amersfoortse – www.amersfoortse.nl
Centraal Beheer Achmea – www.centraalbeheer.nl
Nationale Nederlanden – www.nn.nl
Reaal – www.reaal.nl
Delta Lloyd – www.deltalloyd.nl
Europe Loan – www.europeloan.com
De Hypotheeker – www.hypotheeker.nl
OHRA – www.ohra.nl
FBTO – www.fbto.nl
Aon – www.aon.nl
Unigarant – www.unigarant.nl

www.belastingdienst.nl – Tax Office of the Netherlands.
Also information in english on customs duties and imports to NL
www.volkskrediet.nl -Nederlandse Vereniging voor Volkskrediet (NVVK)
Dutch people's credit association

Interest
www.hypotheekrenteverwachting.nl – for tracking current mortgage interest rate expectations
www.delaagsterente.nl – will give you 'the lowest rate of interest (*rente*)'
Newspapers publish an overview of what rate of interest the banks are offering in the real estate section or housing pages.

International Housing and Finance Links
www.housingfinance.org – International Union for Housing Finance

www.societasinternational.org – International Institute for Real Estate
www.fanniemae.com – Federal National Mortgage Association in the USA
www.hypo.org – European Mortgage Federation
www.euhousing.org – European Commission facts & figures for housing market.
www.nber.org – National Bureau for Economic Research (USA)
www.oecd.org – Organisation for Economic Development and Cooperation
www.worldbank.org – The World Bank
www.ihfp.wharton.upenn.edu – Wharton International Housing Finance Program
www.fha.com – Federal Housing Administration
www.hud.gov – U.S. Department of Housing & Urban Development
www.barra.com – Website of American organisation that builds and offers risk models for professional investers.
www.federalreserve.org – The Federal Reserve – America's national bank
www.housingamerica.org – Research Institute for the American Housing market

Endnote

The Publisher does not subscribe to nor advertise any of the above-mentioned companies or services in particular. This book is meant purely as a reference guide only. No rights can be obtained nor should any person be held accountable for any discrepancies or inconsistencies, which may arise when finding the insurance company or policy of your preference.

8

8 Pests and Problems

As exciting as it may be to go looking for your dream house, don't forget to have a really good look at the condition of the house. Don't be blinded to reality, especially if you've just really fallen in love with a newfound house ...

A. Hidden Defects and Responsibility

If it turns out after you have purchased the house that there are a number of things that are not in order, you will have to ask yourself whether it is a 'hidden defect' – in connection with the question of who will be held responsible for the repairs. For instance, wooden constructions could be infected with wood rot, mould or fungus growth and in the case of pests; there are the costs for extermination. Your realtor has an obligation to inform you of known defects to the house. If it turns out that you were not adequately informed, you may have to go to court and let the judge decide about compensation to repair the damages. (You may find legal information in the *Burgelijk Wetboek* of Dutch Law under BW 7a 1584/1586/1596 and 1619 *onderhoudsartikelen* [the articles on maintenance].)

In either a rental or purchase property, any hidden defect will need to be reported within a reasonable time frame of six months from the date of purchase.

The List for Inspections in chapter 9 may be used as a guideline of where and what you need to look at when checking the premises.

Responsibilities on Rentals

In case of a dispute, who is responsible for what? The chart in Chapter 2 under *Rights and Obligations* shows the maintenance responsibilities of the *lessor* and the *lessee* and will give you some indication as to how these responsibilities are generally handled in a rental property.

A general rule of thumb is, anything that is structural is the responsibility of the party letting out the property (*verhuurder*). The best recourse is to be very clear beforehand as to the division of the responsibilities. If you discover problems after you have moved in, you will need to contact the landlord (and the housing agency) to make your complaint. Hopefully something can be done immediately to solve the problem right away, however, sometimes this is not the case. You may wind up having to pay for the repairman or the exterminator yourself, and then attempt to be reimbursed.

Each situation is looked at on its own merits, on a case-by-case basis. For instance, in a situation where there are pests, the question is raised as to whether this was a pre-existing condition, or if the tenant was responsible, for instance by negligence in leaving food scraps and garbage out, or other unhygienic activities. For building or structural problems such as a leaking roof, (water damage interior vs. exterior building defect) or a ceiling that falls down, it becomes an insurance question for the landlord for the repairs.

Responsibilities on Purchased Property

For a purchased property, you will have to report any defect or problems to the estate agent who sold you the property and he will negotiate on your behalf with the seller. The seller has the duty to report beforehand (*mededelingsplicht*) any hidden defects or problems in the house at the time of the sale. This can be an existing condition or defect that is known, or something that you should reasonably know about, such as contaminated ground in the neighborhood, or problems in the area, such as wood rot of foundation poles under the houses. The buyer has a buyer's responsibility to also check to see if there are problems in the area (*kopers onderzoeksplicht*), or if there are any pre-existing building reports (*bouwkundige keuringen*). As this can be a rather 'gray area' as to proving conclusively whether or not one can presume that the selling party is withholding vital information, you may need the services of a lawyer if a timely agreement to remedy the situation cannot be reached.

B. Pests

When it comes to the infestation of pests, most likely you will need to get rid of them yourself, unless you can prove they were there already in residence when you moved in or that there is an infestation in your apartment building.

1. **Rats and Mice – Ratten en Muizen**
   No, they are not cute, and who wants a mouse in the house? They are carriers of disease to humans as well as pets or livestock and are a threat to the public

health. Homes situated along canals or by the water have more chance of having uninvited four footers. They also can cause damage by chewing on cables, resulting in a short circuit, or cause contamination of food supplies.

2. **Cockroaches – Kakkerlakken**
   These scurrying creatures are carriers of bacteria and salmonellas, and get into everything in your kitchen or bathroom, with a preference for food bits in dark, damp areas, such as under the sink.

3. **Doves (or Pidgeons) – Duiven**
   As beautiful as these birds may be, their nests and roosting can be a problem as can the acidic nature of the bird excrement. They also carry paratyphoid fe-ver and other vermin.

4. **Flies – Vliegen**
   Swatting and shooing aside, flies spread viruses and bacteria and are a real pest, especially when you just want to enjoy sitting in the garden! Use fly tape or aerosol sprays.

5. **Fleas – Vlooien**
   These little bugs cause skin irritation and can be carriers of disease. If house pets are not treated, you could find your self with a manifestation of fleas. Their eggs can live and hatch in carpets for some time, even if the pet has been removed, and yes, they will bite humans. You can purchase flea bombs at pet stores or at the drugstore.

6. **Silver Fish – Zilvervisjes**
   These little silver 'slivers' of creatures cause damage to the paper in old books and can also damage old drawings and paintings.

7. **Wasp Nest – Wespennest**
   Wasps do not carry disease, but they do build nests under the eaves of houses and getting stung hurts! Wasps also attack the wood by boring holes.

C. Wood

In old buildings, new homes or remodeling or renovation projects, wood is a popular and much used building material. It is a natural product (*natuurprodukt*) consisting of fibers and pulp that can be subject to problems, especially in areas where the moisture index (*vochtigheidgraad*) is high. This wet moisture can have a negative impact on the quality and lifespan (*duurzaamheid*) of the construction. The durability of wood can be increased by using the proper chemicals for treating wood substances to combat moisture (*vochtbestrijders*), such as creosote (*carbol (in)eum*) or paint or in some case the use of the proper insecticides.

Wood Pests

All the insects that attack wood, such as the *houtworm, boktor, spinthout and bonteknaagkever* (also known under the collective name of *drooghoutboorders*) weaken the structure of wood, and its ability over the long term to support weight, which can result in severe structural damage to areas of the roof beams or to floor beams.

The woodworm (*houtworm*) can lay between twenty and sixty eggs in the wood. These eggs will hatch when the temperature and moisture levels are ideal. They will then keep chewing away at the wood for a lifespan of up to three years.

The longhorn beetle (*boktor*) lays between one hundred and sixty to two hundred and twenty eggs. The larvae are approximately 3 cm. in size and change into flying insects that can keep on eating and then fly to other places to lay more eggs.

When building upstairs bedrooms under the eaves and insulating rooms it is advisable to first treat the beams with an impregnating chemical, which will protect against all the 'wood attackers'. The chemical soaks into the wood and crystallizes and is effective for many years.

For prevention, it is necessary to hire in a specialist company to take care of these problems.

Moisture, Moulds and Fungus

Known in Dutch as *vocht*, *schimmels* and *zwammen*, having these in the house causes many problems for children, older persons and people with breathing problems such as asthma (also known as CARA), as well as those suffering from rheumatoid arthritis. If you have moisture problems, the damp air that is not properly circulated can give opportunity for moulds to grow which are detrimental to your air passages as well as your house. Studies show that children living in houses where there are places with water under the floor or the presence of moulds or fungus growth are more frequently sick.

Where Do They Occur?

Moulds and fungus in places where it is very damp, the air is still (no movement or poor air circulation) or in an area where wood is stacked or piled up (such as logs for the fireplace) can damage surrounding wood. Mould and fungus growth are generally found under the house but can also occur in other rooms due to a leaking roof, walls that let outside moisture in, if the mortar is missing or if the bricks are so porous and old that they no longer keep the damp out.

Another source of problems is damp that seeps upward (*optrekkend vocht*) from a cellar (*kelder*) into the walls. The groundwater evaporation under a house can go right into the house through cracks in the floor since there is usually only a layer of sand on the ground in the crawl space between ground and floor. The walls will generally feel cold and moist and there is often a musty smell to the air. One solution is to have 25 to 30 centimeters of shells (*schelpen*) placed under the floor as an insulation material. The layer of shells forms a natural barrier between the ground water and the floor and since the moisture cannot get into the house, it will remain warmer.

Costly

Fungus when seen in the forest on trees is quite interesting as to color and shape, but of course the trees eventually die from this. When fungus grows under the floor it attacks the cellulose in the wood of beams and flooring, eventually weakening the floor, resulting in substantial costs to have a floor and beams replaced. Not to mention the risk of sinking through a weak area of the floor and seriously damaging yourself.

Inspection

Clearly, it is advisable to have an inspection take place under the floor in the crawl space. This investigation is known as a *kruipruimteonderzoek* and can be carried out by professionals. They will also check the house for other moisture problems (*vochtproblemen*) and supply you with a report listing the problems and giving a price indication for repairs or for intervention.

The costs are about € 75 and the reports can be used for applying for NHG loans (see chapter 7), and for information to be supplied to estate agents, banks or insurance companies in conjunction with loans or claims. Professionals with an accreditation (*keurmerk*) will provide the most reliable and comprehensive building inspection reports.

Extermination companies services are known as *ongediertebestrijding*.

References

For more information on pests and problems call 0900-2020219 (10 eurocent cost per minute), or visit www.apkvastgoed.nl.

9

9 Housing Inspections

Whether you are renting or purchasing a place to live, a thorough inspection of the property is always advised. Some items of damage or neglect may be immediately obvious, some defects may better be found out by having the property inspected by a professional. An increasing number of homebuyers are wisely choosing to include a professional inspection prior to their real estate purchase. However, many home-buyers are confused about the home inspection services that are performed. When hiring a home inspector, buyers typically believe that stability of the foundation is the main focus of the inspection when, in reality, serious foundation problems are among some of the least common building defects. Here are the 'Top Ten' most common defects found in residential real estate.

Additional damages information is discussed in chapter 8 Pests and Problems. Make sure you take notes when inspecting the premises. It may be helpful to use the checklist included at the end of this chapter, or the Apartment Hunting checklist in chapter 2.

A. Defects

1. **Roofing defects**: Problems with roofing material, due to aging, wear, or improper installation, are likely to be found in the majority of homes. This does not mean that most roofs require replacement, but rather that most could use some type of maintenance or repair.

2. **Ceiling stains, indicating past or current roof leaks**: Unfortunately, you often can't tell if the roof still leaks unless you inspect on a rainy day. Some stains are merely the residual effects of roof problems that have been repaired, while others may be related to leaky plumbing.

3. **Water intrusion into basements or crawlspaces due to ground water conditions**: Faulty drainage can be pervasive, difficult to resolve, and sometimes very damaging to buildings. Correction can be as simple as re-grading the exterior grounds or adding roof gutters. Unfortunately, major drainage improvements are often warranted, requiring costly ground water systems such as French drains designed by geotechnical engineers.

4. **Electrical safety hazards, especially (but not always) in older homes**: Examples are ungrounded outlets, lack of ground fault interrupters (shock protection devices), faulty wiring conditions in electrical panels or elsewhere in a building, etc. Such problems may result from errors at the time of construction but often are due to wiring that was added or altered by persons other than qualified electricians.

5. **Rotted wood at building exteriors and at various plumbing fixtures**: In areas where wood remains wet for long periods, e.g. roof eaves, exterior trim, decks, around tubs and showers, or below loose toilets, fungus infection is likely to attack, resulting in a condition commonly known as dry rot. If left unchecked, damage can be quite extensive.

6. **Building violations where additions and alterations were constructed without permits**: Home owners will often tell a home inspector, 'We added the shed without a permit, but it was all done to code'. This is a red flag to most inspectors, because no one could possibly know the entire building code, let alone the average person without construction knowledge. Whenever an owner offers code assurance, problems are likely to be found. Always ask if a permit is needed. Approved drawings should be provided.

7. **Unsafe fireplace and chimney conditions**: Problems with wood burning fixtures can range from lack of maintenance to faulty installation. Most common are missing spark arrestors and faulty placement of freestanding fireplaces. Wood-burning stoves are typically installed by homeowners and handymen, persons without adequate knowledge of fire safety requirements. Common violations involve insufficient clearance between hot metal surfaces and combustible materials within the building. Fire hazards of this kind are often concealed in attics, where they remain undiscovered until a roof fire occurs.

8. **Faulty installation of water heaters**: Not all water heaters are installed in full compliance with plumbing code requirements. Common violations include inadequate strapping, improperly installed overflow piping, unsafe flue conditions, or faulty gas piping. Leaks can develop in units that are only five years old. Ask what year the water heater (*cv ketel*) was installed. Most cv systems

have a life span of no longer than 15 years. High efficiency heaters (*hoge rendement ketels*) are the most efficient central heating systems. If you purchase a house with a *ketel* that is older than ten years, expect to be confronted with repairs and replacement costs within the coming years.

9. **Hazardous conditions involving gas heaters**: Most gas-fueled heaters are in need of some maintenance, if only the changing of an air filter or a long-overdue review by the gas company. In some cases, however, gas heaters contain life-threatening defects that can remain undiscovered until too late. These can range from fire safety violations to the venting of carbon monoxide into the building. A cracked firebox, for example, can remain undiscovered unless found by an expert or until tragic consequences occur. In some older Dutch homes the only source of heating is *kachels* or gas heaters. In rural areas people may also heat with oil or kerosene heaters, which tend to be less safe.

10. **Firewall violations in garages**: Special fire-resistant construction is required for walls (*brandmuur*) and doors (*branddeuren*) that separate a garage from a dwelling. Violations are common, due to faulty construction, damage or alterations to the garage interior, or changes in code requirements since the home was built. In older homes, where firewalls are not installed, sellers and agents will often suggest that the building predates the code. Approved doors and walls need a fire retardation rating of one hour before fire breakthrough.

B. Checklist for Inspection

Before you take possession of the house, there are a number of items that should be checked and some actions to be undertaken. The maintenance (*onderhoud*) of your house begins on the very first day! Checking for damages and taking action to repair or replace defects will save you money in the long run. Good maintenance will keep your house in good condition and save you from further costs from increased damage through neglect.

We include some of the Dutch wording as well, just in case you need to explain the specific problem to repair or service people.

What You Will Be Checking for What

Inside the house you will need to check the following:

Doors, ceilings and walls – deuren, plafonds, muren

- Hanging of doors – straight or crooked (*hangwerk, recht of krom*)
- Door handles – closures (*sluitwerk*)

- Doors general – tighten loose screws in doors and tap down the pins in hinges that have popped up
- Fitting of doors to door jamb encasement – does it close properly
- Condition and finishing of paint work (*conditie schilderwerk*)
- Condition and finishing of ceiling including electrical connection
- Condition and finishing of wall treatments – wall paper
- Condition and finishing of trim paintwork

Kitchen – Keuken

- Closure of cupboard doors and drawers
- Putty sealing between the counter and tiles the connection with damage or leakage
- Wall tile (lose or damaged)
- Ventilator above the stove (filter) – does it need to be cleaned

Bathroom – Badkamer

- Putty sealing (*kitvoegen*) along the shower / tub (*douchebak / bad*)
- Grouting between the tiles
- Wall tiles (loose or damaged)
- Floor tiles connection with the wall (*vloertegels en aansluiting op muren*)
- Water spots on the ceiling

Toilet

- Wall tiles – loose or damaged
- Floor tiles connection with the wall (*vloertegels en aansluiting op muren*)
- Connection of the toilet pot
- Functionality of the water closet (*stortbak*)

Interior Plumbing – Binnenriolering

- With the exception of the toilet, flush (*spoel*) hot caustic soda (*caustisch soda*) through drains to make sure they are clear of any blockage
- Make sure the drain (*afvoerputje*) in the shower or bath is clear of obstructions
- Loosen swan necks (*siphons*) behind the sink plumbing and clean
- Smear all threaded fixtures with Vaseline (*schroefdraad met vaseline insmeren*)
- Check pipes (*leidingen*) for leaks in the crawl space (*kruipruimte*)
- Check copper pipes for green spots

Water Installation – Waterinstallatie

- Make sure all of the main and secondary faucets open fully and close and make sure there is no dripping

- Smear all threaded fixtures with Vaseline
- Soak the little screen filters from the faucets in *anti-kalk middel* (vinegar will do) to remove calcium deposits from hard water

Heating Installation – Verwarmingsinstallatie

- Check the water pressure on the heating kettle unit
- Check all fittings for leakage
- Clean drainage collector (*convectorputten*)
- Check gas pipes for rust spots (*roestplekken*)
- Clean chimneys (also for heaters (*kachels*))

Electrical Installations – Elektrische Installatie

- Check switches and contact boxes (*schakelaars & wandcontactdozen*)
- Check working of earth grounding cable and switch (*aardkabel*)

Mechanical Ventilators – Mechanische Ventilatie

- Clean the ventilator

Outside the House – Buiten Woning Terrein

- Stone, brick or tile work (*bestrating*)
- Check for sinking, low areas (*verzakkingen*)
- Check for growth of algae and moss (*alg- en mosgroei*)

Dividing Fences – Erfafscheiding

- Wood rot (*houtrot*)
- Growth of algae and moss (*alg- en mosgroei*)
- Warping of the wood (*verwering van het hout*)
- Condition of paint (*conditie afwerklaag*)

Garage or Shed – Garage / Schuur

- Check condition of the roofing
- Inspect the mortar and brickwork (*voegen metselwerk*)
- Check the working of the garage door – smear the tracking rails
- Check the condition of the paint on doors and windows
- Check for rust spots and wood rot
- Check rain gutters /runoff and clean out debris

House Roof – Dak Woning

- Check if roof tiles (*pannen*) are lying properly – with no space in between (*liggen niet goed aaneengesloten*)
- Check if there are damaged or missing tiles (*pannen beschadigd of weg*)
- Check for growth of algae and moss (*alg- en mosgroei*)

- Check for birds' nests under the eaves or roof ridge (*vogelnesten onder de onderste pannenrij / nok*)
- Check rain gutters / runoff and clean out debris

Chimney – Schoorsteen

- Check the lead connection and sealing at the chimney base (*loodloketten bij dakaansluiting*)
- Check for damaged or missing bricks
- Check for birds' nests in chimney (*vogelnest in schoorsteen*)
- Have chimneys swept by a professional chimney sweep (*schoorsteenveger*)

Ventilation Pipe Heating System – Ventilatie cv *Ketel / Rookgasafvoer*

- Check if lead or other connecting material that has separated by the wind / storm or is cracked (*lood of andere aansluiting opgewaaid, gescheurd*)
- Check if there are pipes that are damaged or crooked (*pijpen scheef, beschadigd*)
- Check anchoring of chimney pipe (*verankering*)

Roof Windows – Dakramen

- Clean and wash (*schoonmaken/wassen*)
- Check for leaks (*lekkages*)
- Determine functionality of roof window (*werking dakraam*)
- Clean rain gutters under windows (*gootstukken rondom dakraam schoonmaken*)
- Check connection of roof tiles and gutters (*aansluiting pannen op gootstukken*)
- Check condition of sealing rubber and draft strips (*conditie raamrubbers en tochtstrips*)

Roof Gutters – Dakgoten

- Remove debris in the gutters (*vuil in de goten*)
- Check for leaks and damage (*lekkages, beschadiging*)
- Check drainage (*afwatering*)

Roof – Dak

- Check inside of house for leaks (*controleren binnenzijde dakbeschot op lekkage*)
- Check wooden roof for insects or wood worm (*houten daken op boktor en/of houtworm*)

Rain Pipes – Regenpijpen / Hemelwaterafvoer

- Check for cracks and damage (*barsten en beschadigingen*)
- Check connection to gutter (*aansluiting op dakgoot*)
- See if connecting brackets are loose, rusty or broken (*bevestigingen los, geroest of kapot*)

Facade of House – Gevelbekleding / Hout

- Clean paintwork (*schilderwerk schoonmaken*)
- Check for wood rot (*houtrot*)
- Look for cracks and warping (*scheurvorming / kromtrekken*)
- Check space between wood elements (*openstaande verbindingen*)
- Check condition of the paint – is there peeling, algae growth, cracking, loss of color or shine, bubbling (*afwerklaag afschilferen, algaanslag, barsten, glansverlies, blaasvorming, beschadiging*)

Masonry – Metselwerk

- Check for cracks (*scheurvorming*)
- Check for damp spots (*vochtplekken*)
- Check for white spots (*witte plekken*)
- Check for growth of algae and moss (*alg- en mosgroei*)
- Check for loose or missing mortar (*voegwerk los, uitgevallen*)
- Check for debris in ventilation grate or crawl space (*vuil in ventilatierooster van de kruipruimte*)

Exterior Window Frames and Doors – Buitenkozijnen Ramen en Deuren

- Clean and wash (*schoonmaken / wassen*)
- Check for wood rot (*houtrot*)
- Check open spaces at connection points (*openstaande houtverbindingen*)
- Check the wood strips holding in the glass, also horizontal strips for cracks or warping (*glaslatten gescheurd / krom*)
- Window sill bricks loose or damaged (*raamdorpelstenen beschadigd*)
- Check for loose screws, hinges, or locks (*loszittende schroeven hang- en sluitwerk*)
- Check for damaged weather stripping (*tochtafdichtingen beschadigd*)
- Check for moisture or condensation between the thermal glass (*vocht/condens tussen dubbelglas*)
- Check condition of putty (*conditie kitranden/stopverf van de beglazing*)
- Clean window ventilation grates (*schoonmaken ventilatieroosters*)
- Check condition of paintwork (*conditie schilderwerk*)

Sliding Doors – Schuifpui

- Lubricate rails (*geleiderails smeren*)
- Lubricate locks (*slot / vergrendeling smeren*)

Guttertrim – Gootomtimmering

- Clean/wash off paintwork (*schilderwerk schoonmaken / wassen*)
- Check for woodrot (*houtrot*)
- Check for moisture spots, leakage (*vochtplekken, lekkage*)
- Check for cracks and warping (*scheurvorming, kromtrekken*)

C. Ready-Made Housing – Kant & Klaar Kopen

If you are planning to purchase a newly built house (*nieuwbouwhuis*) there are a number of steps to be taken.

A checklist follows, just so you won't forget anything.

1. You see the advertisement for housing project or property
2. Request brochure with details of proposed project
3. Go to the bank and see if your finances are sufficient, or see what your limit is
4. Register your name for the drawing
5. Once accepted, arrange for the mortgage
6. Make definite decisions about extra work or things you can leave undone (*meer- of minderwerk*)
7. Go to the notary to sign the purchase agreement (*koopovereenkomst*)
8. Count on double costs (*dubbele lasten*) from this point, such as your rent or mortgage from your old house and the *bouwrente* of the new house
9. Save up some money (for the interior decorating)
10. Order new furniture well in advance (it can take up to 3 months!)
11. Make appointments with family, friends and trades people to help or to hire for assistance with projects in the house
12. Give notice on your rental of intention to vacate or sell your old house
13. Arrange the moving service of the PTT Post office
14. Let everyone know you are moving by sending cards
15. Have yourself and your family written out of the population register (*uitschrijven in het bevolkingsregister*)
16. Hire a moving company or hire a moving van or truck
17. Arrange for insurances on the new house and cancel insurances on the old
18. Receive the key (*eerste oplevering*)
19. Check the house for defects / problems
20. Introduce yourself to the neighbors
21. Give the builder a maximum of 30 days for repair work (*herstelwerk*)

22. Place your signature for the second conveyance (*tweede oplevering*) – if everything is in order
23. Register in the population registry (*bevolkingsregister*) at the town hall in your new place of residence (must be done within three days of the move)

10

10 Tradesmen – Vakmensen: Getting the Help You Need

Whether you have a rental property or are a happy home owner, chances are at some point you may need to hire help (hopefully professional!) to assist you in installing a new kitchen or bathroom, adding on a conservatory or sunroom (*serre*), repairing the roof, building an extension, or perhaps general carpentry, plumbing or electrical repairs. Perhaps you will need a new garden put in or brickwork done, or a new floor laid or even have a fireplace built. Who do you contact? *Vakmensen*.

Vakmensen – Trades People

Vakmensen are professionals (men or women) in a *vak* or trade. An A to Z list using the Dutch term with an explanation follows. A list of national organizations with contact information and websites is included at the end of the chapter. Although they are of course all in Dutch, (we are in Holland!) most will be able to provide you with information in English if you telephone them or e-mail them.

Working 'Black'

In order to have a guarantee on your work it is best to work *wit met een bonnetje* or 'white with a receipt'. Some tradesmen will work *zwart* or 'black'; that is, without a receipt, whereby you do not pay the 19% VAT (BTW) (nor does the tradesperson declare this work) and thus may receive a discount on the rates – however, this is illegal and constitutes tax fraud. In addition, you forfeit your right to any claims due to shoddy workmanship or the incompletion of the project. Nor will insurance companies cover claims resulting from damages incurred by leaking pipes, electrical fires and the likes. Furthermore, you have no receipt of proof regarding the services rendered and materials used.

Sometimes people will hire in a handyman (*klusjesman*) who works at the going rate of around € 15, however, if he works 'black' (*zwartwerken*), the handyman will not be insured, and any liability claims that would arise from accidents (like the handyman falling off your roof while working) will not be covered and a settlement will not be possible.

The best course of action, as the saying goes: it is better to be safe rather than sorry.

A List of Vakmensen

Aannemer – Contractor

The *aannemer* could be a one-man operation or a company (*bouwbedrijf*) ranging in size from two people to several hundred skilled employees. The *aannemer* will purchase all the necessary supplies (*bouwmaterialen*) and oversee the installation of the project, making sure that all of the skilled personnel (*vakmannen*) complete their portions of the project at the right moment in the process. Planning, coordination and quality control is key to the success of the work completion. A contractor will also make sure that the materials used are up to code and meet current safety requirements.

All necessary paperwork can also be handled by your *aannemer*. It is best to leave the requesting of building permits and the execution of building plans and blueprints in the hands of the contractor. Not only do they have ample experience in dealing with the bureaucracy inherent in securing permission, it tends to go much faster than if you attempt to do it your self. (This is of course an option for the ultimate DIY-hobbyist or '*doe-het-zelfer*' – though not recommended for the uninitiated and non-Dutch speaking resident, especially for large projects, unless you have time to spare and don't mind loads of frustration or are a glutton for punishment perhaps....)

The beauty of leaving it all in the hands of a good contractor is efficiency and talent. A contractor has qualified plumbers, electricians, carpenters, etc. on his payroll and this central coordination of talent saves you having to contract each skill individually, not to mention the headache of timing when and where everyone needs to show up, if the materials have been delivered and is the cement is dry! Orchestrating all the details on your own would be quite an accomplishment, and quite a headache!

Architect / Interieurarchitect – Architect or Interior Architect

The architect or interior architect will make a design proposal taking into consideration your requests and desires surrounding an exterior or interior project. Based on your demands (*programma van eisen*) drawings will be executed conforming to national building standards. An architect can:

- advise you on the optimal use of your available space and the effect of using certain colors as well as help you optimize the use of daylight
- give advice on the choice of central heating installation, energy saving equipment and materials and the types of construction possibilities
- request building permits based on the drawings and technical specifications completed by the architect
- take charge of the execution of drawings and technical specifications whereby the contractor can make a cost analysis quote (*offerte*) of the expected budget of the project
- check the quality and progress of the contractor's work
- keep track of extra work or less expensive work (*meer-en-minder werk*) that is carried out and the actual costs of certain work (*stelposten*) whereby an estimate (*stelsel*) is given and the exact cost calculated after the fact. Used for variables such as when a choice is left open for example: a type of tiles to be used, or more expensive wood sort.

An *interieur architect* may also assist you in your shopping with the choice and purchase of carpeting, flooring, furniture, lighting, home furnishing accessories, etc. They will control delivery and installation dates and monitor the execution of the time frame necessary to complete the renovations. Professional advice can be invaluable for creating just the 'right look' you wish to achieve. Some interior architects may also advise you on the purchase of antiques or works of art.

Badkamer Specialist – Bathroom Specialist

The *badkamerspecialist* can supply you with sinks (*wastafels*), bathtubs (*badkuipen*), showers (*douches*), tiles (*tegels*), and faucets (*kranen*) as well as advise you on the technical installation of the diverse elements composing your new bathroom. Whether you need a complete new bathroom or just remodeling, a bathroom specialist can provide you with working drawings (*werktekening*) and arrange for the contractor for installation.

cv-Installateur – Central Heating Installer

The central heating installer (cv = *centrale verwarming*) advises you on the best method to warm your home and which type of central heating kettle or heater (cv *ketel*) is needed and which type of systems are available and the different

price classes. He or she can give advice on energy efficient systems and assist in requesting available subsidies (if applicable) for the installation of energy saving equipment.
He will deliver the material and carry out the technical installations. A certified installer will ensure that everything is safely installed in compliance with current safety codes.

Dakdekker – Roofer

The roofing specialist (*dakdekker*) will take care of your roofing needs. In Holland you will find a variety of roofing. There are houses with a reed or straw roof (*riet of stro dak*), orange, black or gray roof tiles (*dakpannen*), slate (*leien*), black tar (*teer*) roof (generally used on a flat roof and also referred to as *bitumineuze asfalthoudende dakbedekking*), or metal plates (*metalen beplating*).

Elektrotechnisch installateur – Electrician

The electrician (*elektrotechnisch installateur*) will install a cable (*kabel*) network; wall outlets (*wand contactdozen*), light switches (*lichtschakelaars*) or extra capacity (*een extra groep in de groepen kast*) for instance for large energy items such as washing machines, dryers and ovens. In addition, he can also run extra telephone lines with outlets (*telefoonlijnen*) throughout the house and install security systems (*beveligingsapparatuur*) and domotica.

Domotica is 'domestic / domicile informatica' or the collection of intelligent applications for a 'smart house' such as the automatic sensors for lighting (*verlichting*) by electronic eye or movement indicators, or a central vacuum cleaning system (*centraal stofzuigersysteem*) to increase the efficiency of communication in your house. The houses of the future are expected to have even more domotica applications such as telephoning your microwave to start cooking or having a refrigerator that knows when to order items you are out of, and placing the order for you!

Important Note: For the installation of ISDN or ADSL Internet lines and cable connections we recommend reading the booklet **Getting Connected** (ISBN 9055942537) for more detailed information.

Haardenbouwer – Hearth or Fireplace Installation

The fireplace specialist (*haardbouwer*) may build a brick or stone fireplace (*gemetselde open haard*) or install a classic marble mantle (*klassieke schouwen*) or a freestanding metal fireplace (*kachel*) with or without a chimney (*rookkanaal*).

You are well advised to have these installations done by a professional to ensure that safety requirements are met.

It is customary to have your chimneys swept once a year, preferably before the winter sets in. Chimney sweeps (*schoorsteenvegers*) often leave a card in your mailbox indicating when they are working in your area of town, or you can ask your neighbors who they use. Chimney fires can cause structural damage to the chimney and a lot of smoke damage in the house from burning bird nests and creosote build up. Nonetheless, an open hearth or fireplace certainly gives a cozy feel to your home.

A word of caution: Make sure you agree on the price before he goes up on the roof, or you may find he has installed a new *windkap* to protect against birds and downdraft winds without your requesting it and at a special price! It is a good idea also to know beforehand how many chimneys (*rookkanalen*) you have on your roof and if they already have *windkappen* installed.

Hovenier – Garden Architect

The Dutch love their gardens almost as much as their homes and often arrange for the services of a garden architect (*hovenier*) who will design the garden (*tuinontwerp*) and arrange for the layout of stone or brickwork (*sierbestrating*), using brick (*stenen* or *klinkers*) or garden tiles (*grindtegels*). As for the green elements; all of the plants (*planten*), shrubs (*heesters*) and trees (*bomen*) can be chosen with your hovenier who will deliver and plant them. Your hovenier can also install dividing fencing (*schutting*), lighting (*tuinverlichting*), ornamental items (*tuinornamenten*), statues (*beelden*) and installation of and items for your small pond (*vijver*). A maintenance contract will provide you with upkeep, pruning and replacement of plants as well as gardening advice.

A garden architect (*tuinarchitect*) may sometimes only do the design work on paper, and then hire in a qualified *hovenier* for the actual execution and installation of the garden. All *hoveniers* have garden plans and stone patterns on hand as well as their experience in all facets of creating your dream garden. The talents of a specialty garden architect may be requested for unique spaces or office grounds or public areas. (See also chapter 12 – *The Garden*)

Keukenspecialist – Kitchen Specialist

The kitchen is one of the most highly trafficked areas of the home, and with good reason. Next to shelter, food is the most important daily need. Dutch kitchens are notoriously small and kitchen remodeling is very popular. (Also, some of us spend a lot of time there!). A kitchen specialist (k*eukenspecialist*) can advise you on the layout of the kitchen, making the most of your available space and allowing you to work efficiently. Cupboards (*keukenmeubelen*) and counters (*aanrechten*) can be made to your height to make work more comfortable. The keukenspecialist can advise you on the various types of materials used, and the brands and ratings of appliances (*apparatuur*) such as the refrigerator (*koelkast*), electric stove (*fornuis*), gas stove (*gasfornuis*), microwave (*magnetron*), combi-oven (*combi-magnetron*) or dishwasher (*vaatwasmachine*).

Loodgieter – Plumber

A plumber (*loodgieter*) is a multi-talented *vakman* who can deliver and install water pipes (*waterleidingen*), sewage system (*rioleringen*), faucets (*kranen*) and bathroom fixtures as well as fix or clean roof gutters (*dakgoten*) and repair and install leading work on roofs. He can give you advice on reducing your water usage (*waterbesparing*) and on fire prevention sprinkler systems (*brandpreventiesystemen*).

NOTE: Fire protection is usually not installed in rental properties – for your own safety look into installing smoke detectors (*rookmelders*).

Metselaar – Mason

Turning a pile of stones or bricks into a wall (*muur*), garage (*garage*), fireplace (*schouw*) or shed (*schuur*) takes the talent of a bricklayer or stone mason (*metselaar*) – a *vakman* who can called upon not only for *metselwerk* but who generally can also do plasterwork (*stucwerk*), pour cement (*beton storten*), and/or set tiles (*tegelzetten*).

Meubelmaker – Furniture / Cabinet Maker

Handcrafted furniture or restorations of antique furniture can be made by a furniture maker (*meubelmaker*). For restoration work they often use the services of an upholsterer (*meubeldecorateur*) for upholstering or re-upholstering (*herstofferen*) furniture. A *meubelmaker* can also produce original custom design pieces based on your specifications or make furniture reproductions (*namaak stukken*).

Parketlegger – Wooden Floor Specialist

The *parketlegger* can deliver (*leveren*), lay (*leggen*), and finish (*afwerken*) wooden floors in every possible pattern (*patroon*) and color combination (*kleurcombinatie*). Possibilities include: massive wood floor (*massief strokenparket*), mosaic (*mosaïek parket*), bamboo (*bamboe*) as well as laminate (*laminaat*) and cork (*kurk*) floors.

Schilder – Painter

Often referred to as 'the best friend for your house' the painter (*schilder*) can take care of your interior (*binnen*) en exterior (*buiten*) paintwork (*schilderwerk*). Hanging wallpaper (*behangen*), setting glass (*glaszetten*) and advice on protecting the wood in your house (*bescherming van houtwerk*) can often be taken care of by your painter.

Stoffeerder / Woninginrichter – Carpet and Curtain Installation

The delivery and installation of carpet (*tapijt*) or other floor coverings (*vloerbedekking*) and the measuring, making and delivery of custom-sized curtains (*gordijnen*) is the job of the *stoffeerder / woninginrichter*. He will install (*hang*) everything including the rails. Hallways (*gang*) and the covering of the stairs (*trap*) are also part of his services.

Stucadoor – Plasterer

For professional plasterwork (*stucwerk*) on walls (*wanden*) or ceiling (*plafond*) the stucadoor can give your home a new look using a patterned plastering (*schuurwerk*), sprayed plaster (*spuitpleister*), or framed panels (*lijstwerk*). In addition, wall and ceiling ornaments often used in older homes (*sierpleister*) can be restored or replaced. There are *sierpleister* specialists who make models / molds of old ornaments and then pour plaster to make new ones, or if possible use existing centuries-old pattern molds.

Tegelzetter – Tile Specialist

The *tegelzetter* will install tile work according to the building plans (*bouwtekening*) on floors (*vloeren*) and walls (*muren*) The tiles will then be grouted (*ingewassen*) and, where the tile and wall meet, sealed (*ingekit*). Many *tegelzetters* also install natural stone (*natuursteen*) such as marble (*marmer*), granite (*granite*), and slate (*leisteen*).

Timmerman – Carpenter

The carpenter (*timmerman*) can do just about anything with wood (*hout*) – from making beams (*balklagen*), finishing walls (*wanden aftimmeren*), making and placement of window sills (*kozijnen maken en plaatsen*), hanging doors (*deuren afhangen*) to some furniture construction (*meubelwerk vervaardigen*). Most carpenters will also do small repairs (*kleine reparaties*), build closets (*kasten*), construct bookshelves (*boekenkasten*) and create banisters (*trapleuning*).

Vloerenlegger – Flooring Specialist

The *vloerenlegger* is specialized in leveling floor surfaces of cement or poured flooring material on the surface in order to level or equalize (*egaliseren*) the floor before further work is done. Thereafter, a floor consisting of small stones (*woon-grindvloer*), natural stone (*natuursteen*), or wood (*parketvloer*) are some of the possibilities.

Zonweringsbedrijf – Sun Screen Awnings

The *zonweringbedrijf* manufactures (*maken*) and delivers (*afleveren*) sun screen awnings (*zonneschermen*); namely framed awnings (*markiezen*), roll-out screens (*uitvalschermen*) or pull-down sun screens (*rolluik zonneschermen*). They can arrange for a permit if necessary, and can remove, clean and store the awnings over the winter period for a yearly maintenance fee. Many *zonweringsbedrijven* also sell vertical blinds (*verticale lamellen*) and jalousie blinds (*jaloezieën*).

A Word About 'Doe-Het-Zelf'

Many people who are a bit handy themselves may decide to tackle some smaller projects on their own. Doe-het-zelf or do-it-yourself projects have become increasingly more popular over the past years. There have been a number of programs on TV showing how to do some projects and some of the building markets (*bouwmarkten*) also supply handy take along sheets with step-by-step instructions.

By doing the project yourself, you will be saving money, reducing all or a portion of your costs and of course will have the satisfaction of completing something for your home just because you love working with your hands and creating a new look in remodeling projects.

We would however strongly caution against doing your own work with gas lines (you would not be the first person to cause an explosion) as well as major water and electrical revisions. Again, if you do it and something goes wrong your insurance will not cover the damages.

If you wish to sew your own curtains (*gordijnen*) you will need to purchase fabric (*stof*) at a fabric store, or for very good deals, try visiting the local market on the day they sell fabrics. You can also have curtains made up for you rather reasonably at department stores such as Vroom & Dreesman and the Hema, or at fabric shop

such as Leen Bakker by using their *opmaak service*. Curtains will be made to measure. You may choose fabric from the samples.
If you are looking to hang wallpaper (*behang*) you can purchase this at a *décor-winkel*, a local paint and wallpaper shop, or at a large building supply depot (*bouwmarkt*).

References

Household projects (klussen)
See the start page: http://klus.pagina.nl

For household disasters
www.watnu.nl (what now?) for requesting help from repairmen in Amsterdam, The Hague and Rotterdam.

Building markets – Bouwmarkten
When you need supplies for your building projects look under the yellow pages for *Doe-het-zelf winkels* or *bouwmarkten*. Hardware stores are known as *IJzerwinkels* or *ijzerhandel* .

The largest chain stores in the building market are:

www.praxis.nl
www.gamma.com
www.karwei.nl
www.fixit.nl

11

11 Making a House into a Home

After having found a place to live in the Netherlands come the concerns of how to fill your new lodgings with the comforts of living in order to make it a home. Not everyone who relocates to the Netherlands brings his or her own furniture. Considering that the employment period that one stays can often be of short duration, not everyone is interested in the work and expense of shipping their furniture to the Netherlands. Some of the Dutch houses and apartments may be too small to fit all of your furniture, and if you have large pieces of furniture they will often not fit here as well. Make sure you have a list of the measurements of your present furniture, and take accurate measurements here in your new location. It will save you the expense of having shipped pieces you can't use, or in having to rent storage.

Buying

One option is buying furniture here, to use during your stay. Of course that involves expense and again the added work of re-selling it when you leave. If you decide to go this route, we give some suggestions at the end of the chapter. You can always resell your furniture to other expatriates through the news magazines from social clubs or Internet postings. Additionally you can contact an auction house (*veiling-huis*) who will pick up and sell the items for you, minus of course their commission and handling fee.

Renting

Perhaps renting furniture is a more suitable option. Styles vary and there are ranges of possibilities to choose from. There are a number of furniture rental companies who rent out complete household furnishings, sofas, chairs, lamps, tables, carpets, including, if you so desire, linens, pots and pans, dishes, glasses and cutlery.

There are also electronics stores that rent televisions and stereos, and even computers, scanners and printers.

VAT / BTW

Note: On any furniture, art or antiques you purchase that you are planning to have move with you when you leave, make sure you keep the sales receipt with the BTW tax of 19%.

You may claim this back again when you leave. Manifests or certificates of authenticity for antiques or artworks should be kept in a safe place. You will need them for shipping, insurance and customs declarations. Most people wind up collecting quite a few items more than they started out with. Especially if you are renting furniture, all those lovely mementos and souvenirs are adding just the right touch to your home. These will probably be some of the special things that you move with you, any perhaps for many moves after, to remind you of the good memories of living in Holland.

One Man's Trash ...

Some people post items for sale on the bulletin boards of the supermarkets. And, believe it or not, you would be surprised what people set out on the street on large item collection days. As the saying goes 'one man's trash is another man's treasure'. You never know what treasures may be yours for the taking! (Especially in suburban residential areas.)

Although anything by the curbside is free for the taking, often people will ring the bell and ask if the person minds if they cart it away. They usually say, 'Yes, please, take it!'

Auction Houses

If you are interested in antiques, furniture, art, second hand items, books, etc. perhaps an auction house is the place for you to have a look. All auction houses (*veilinghuizen*) have open days (*kijkdagen*) where you can have a look at the items being offered for sale. You may place a sealed bid with your instructions if you cannot attend the actual auction. If no one bids higher, than you get the item. International auction houses such as Sotheby's and Christie's have the prestige of their name and reputation, they are known for dealing in exclusive, up scale and expensive items and artworks.

Many Dutch auction houses are also being checked over by international antique dealers who are looking for good buys. It is quite possible for you to find some unusual and unique items at an auction (*veiling*) and even get a good deal for a reasonable price, a *koopje*.

'Black Market'

Another option is of course second hand stores or flea markets. The 'Black Market' (*Zwarte Markt*) in Beverwijk and the 'Darling Market' in Rijswijk near The Hague are two large flea markets. The Black Market in Beverwijk has an international section with items from around the world. Contact your municipality (*gemeente*) for the calendar of when the local community flea markets are scheduled.

Local Shops

Additional items of furniture can be found in large department stores such as Vroom & Dreesman, or the Hema, and in the many local furniture shops in the town where you will live. Often when you are taking the time to explore the shops, you will be surprised at the unique, charming or unusual pieces you may find. If you want furniture that is custom designed and made by hand, reproductions of antique furniture, or you are in need of furniture restoration or repairs you need to contact a *meubelmaker*, or furniture maker.

For reupholstering of furniture you will need a *stoffeerder*. Read chapter 10 for additional information.

Where to Go

Holland has great shopping, lots of stores and shopping centers (*winkelcentrums*) so you should be able to find what you need. There are many options available to an expatriate in acquiring the necessities to furnish their new home. Below you will find information for companies and shops where home furnishings can be purchased or leased.

We include places to buy, rent, lease, antiques, and auction houses or shops that buy second-hand furniture.

References

Amsterdam (and surroundings)

Mega stores

IKEA
Hullenbergweg 2
1101 BL Amsterdam z.o.
Tel.: 0900 235 45 32 (22 ct/min)
For other IKEA stores see: www.ikea.nl

Villa Arena

Located right next to the Amsterdam Arena (right off the A2 follow signs P4) this is shopping mall (with more the 100 stores) dedicated to everything that has to do with living and home furnishings. Tel.: 0800 845 52 27 Website: www.villaarena.nl

Het Arsenaal Jan des Bouvries

Founded by Holland's most famous interior designer, this villa is filled with many kinds of furniture and decorative home furnishings.
Kooltjesbuurt 1
1411 RZ Naarden-Vesting
Website: www.hetarsenaal.nl

Budget Stores

Leen Bakker

Klimopweg 17
1032 HZ Amsterdam
Tel.: 020 636-0873
Website: www.leenbakker.nl

Molukkenstraat 192
1098 TW Amsterdam
Tel.: 020 663-0016
Website: www.leenbakker.nl

Anthony Fokkerweg 45
1059 CP Amsterdam
Tel.: 020 615 6570
Website: www.leenbakker.nl

Kwantum
Plein 40 – 45 No. 12
1063 KR Amsterdam
Tel.: 020 613-9248
Website: www.kwantum.nl

Both Leen Bakker en the Kwantum are a chain of stores and can be found in many towns and cities throughout the country.

Antiques

Belgium and Holland Antiques Online
This is the portal site for Belgian and Dutch Antique shops, dealers, wholesalers, exporters, auctioneers, fairs and flea markets.
Website: www.belgiumantiques.com

Europe Antiques Network
This site provides not only links to sites concerning antique furniture, but also direct contact with shops and stores all across Holland.
Website: www.europeantiques.net

Rental Furniture

Furniture Lease
This company is especially for expats in that they rent out complete furniture packages (including kitchenware and linens) on a lease basis.
St. Walburg 10
6671 AS Zetten
(Showroom) Julianaplein 9
6671 CA Zetten
Tel.: 048 845-2586
Fax: 048 845-2369

Interior Rent
Just as above, this company provides complete home furnishings in varying styles, including kitchen appliances.
Oude Baan 69
B-2610 Wilrijk, Belgium
Tel.: +32 (0)3 825-3654
Fax: +32 (0)3 825-2124
E-mail: interiorrent@skynet.be
Website www.interiorrent.com

Television, Stereo & Computer Rentals

Skala Electronics Stores
The Skala chain of electronics stores has a 'virtual winkel' on line with pictures, so you can easily shop and check products and prices for home or business rentals. www.skala.nl

Second-Hand

Second Hand Specialist
Kinkerstraat 382-388
1053 GJ Amsterdam
Tel.: 06 53 25 14 15

Second Best
Wolvenstraat 18
1016 EP Amsterdam
Tel.: 020 422 02 74

Further Resources

www.interieur.pagina.nl & www.meubel.pagina.nl: These are starting pages for websites listing numerous shops and companies that deal with home furnishings (and specifically furniture). Most of the sites listed are in Dutch, however, with a little help it is an excellent way to acquire contact information on shops and companies.

If you are looking for galleries, artists and paintings or information on the art world try the following resources:
www.kunst.pagina.nl – Dutch 'art' start page, also art history
www.galerie.pagina.nl – galleries of Dutch and other artists work
www.kunstenaars.pagina.nl – artists and their work
www.schilderijen.pagina.nl – paintings and artwork
www.kunstactief.pagina.nl – active art including art auctions and exhibitions

Auction Houses

Christies' Amsterdam
Tel: 020 575 52 54, Website: www.christies.com

Sotheby's Amsterdam
Tel: 020 550 22 00, Website: www.sothebys.com

De Eland, De Zon & Loth Gijselman (Amsterdam)
Elandsgracht 68
Tel: 020 623 03 43 Website: www.veilinghuis-de-eland.nl

Leidsegracht Auctioneers (Amsterdam)
Leidsegracht 76
Tel.: 020 627 26 77

Oprechte Veiling (Haarlem)
Tel: 023 531 94 08
Website: www.oprechteveiling.nl

Van Zadelhoff (Hilversum)
Tel: 035 624 71 70
Website: www.vanzadelhoff.nl

Van Stockum Den Haag (Den Haag)
Tel: 070 364 98 40

Venduhuis Den Haag (Den Haag)
Tel: 070 365 88 57
Website: www.venduehuis.com

Van Spengen Auctioneers (Hilversum)
Tel: 035 640 09 89
Website: www.vanspengen.com

Vendu Notarishuis Rotterdam (Rotterdam)
Tel: 010 412 85 44
Website: www.notarishuis.nl

Venduhuis Utrecht (Utrecht)
Tel: 030 231 01 90
Website: www.veiling-utrecht.nl

Black Market / Darling Market
www.zwartemarkt.nl
www.darlingmarkt.nl

Events – Art / Furnishings / Antiques

www.huishoudbeurs.nl – The Household Fair or 'Huishoudbeurs' is held at the RAI (Convention Center) in Amsterdam in March and features the latest trends in furniture, accessories, kitchens, bathrooms, food kitchen gadgets, cosmetics and fashion.

At the same time you can visit the 'Negenmaanden Beurs' or '9 months exposition' which showcases new products and services for those planning or expecting a baby. Entrance fee to the 'huishoudbeurs' also gives you access to the 'negenmaanden beurs' Both events are very popular with the Dutch, and certainly of interest to foreign residents as well. www.babybox.nl/negenmaandenbeurs
www.tfo.nl – Home and Lifestyle Fair – exclusive fair with inspirational and new decorating ideas.
www.hollandartfair.nl – Holland Art Fair in The Hague featuring old and modern art.
www.tefaf.com – The prestigious European Fine Art Fair in Maastricht.
www.artrotterdam.com – Art & Antiques fair in Rotterdam.

Free Gifts

When you are moving, or for certain special occasions, be sure to contact the following organizations for free gifts.

www.felicitas.nl – Felicitas means, 'congratulate' – Order online the new house package for 'newly moved. Felicitas also has 'congratulations' packages for babies & newly-weds.
www.rejoice.nl – Rejoice company – order online – free box of gift products from a Christian organization for 'nieuwe woning' also for newly-weds, anniversaries, and babies.
www.vt-wonen.nl – Nieuwe Huisplan – book full of ideas in Dutch for moving and one for remodeling. Order online under 'verhuizen'

Glossary

The amount of websites and listings in the Netherlands dedicated to home furnishings is quite large, however, for the non-Dutch speaker, most of these require a basic knowledge of Dutch in order to find what one is looking for. This glossary aims to provide you with a general indication (and pronunciation) to the meaning of some of the most frequently mentioned words.

Bathroom	*bat-kahmer*	*badkamer*
Bedroom	*slop-kahmer*	*slaapkamer*
Blinds	*lah-mel-len*	*lamellen*
Bunk beds	*stah-pel-bed*	*stapelbed*

Chair	*stool*	*stoel*
Child- (products)	*kender*	*kinder-*
Closet	*kahst*	*kast*
Couch	*bonk*	*bank*
Curtains	*gor-dine-nen*	*gordijnen*
Desk	*boo-row*	*buro*
Dishwasher	*off-voz-mah-sheen*	*afwasmachine*
Do it yourself	*do het zel-uf*	*doe het zelf*
Dresser drawer	*lah-den kahst*	*ladenkast*
Dryer	*drow-ger*	*droger*
Duvet	*deck-bed*	*dekbed*
Freezer	*freece-er*	*vriezer*
Furniture	*mu-bull*	*meubel*
Garden/yard	*teun*	*tuin*
Kitchen	*ku-ken*	*keuken*
Ladder	*trop*	*trap*
Lighting	*fer-lig-ting*	*verlichting*
Living (as in house)	*vone*	*woon*
Living room	*vone-kahmer*	*woonkamer*
Mattress	*mah-tros*	*matras*
Mega store	*vone-vinkel*	*woonwinkels*
Microwave	*mag-ne-tron*	*magnetron*
Office	*kahn-toor*	*kantoor*
Pillow	*cus-sen*	*kussen*
Pull-out couch	*slop-bahnk*	*slaapbank*
Refrigerator	*cool-kahst*	*koelkast*
Second hand	*tway-de-honce*	*tweedehands*
Sheet	*lah-ken*	*laken*
Stovetop	*for-neus*	*fornuis*
Table	*tah-full*	*tafel*
Vacuum cleaner	*stof-zeu-ger*	*stofzuiger*
Window	*rrr-aam*	*raam*

12

12 The Garden

The Dutch LOVE flowers and plants and many are avid gardeners. Flowers and plants are for sale everywhere, at local kiosks, in florist shops, on the street, on the market, at the grocery stores, even at the gas stations! Even if you don't have a green thumb, there are a great variety of potted plants available in all price ranges to give your house that decorating accent of 'instant green'. Popular plants and flowers are reasonably priced and exotic or very large plants are of course more expensive.

Florist Shop / Garden Center

You may want to visit a florist shop (*bloemenwinkel*) for purchasing flowers or plants for gifts. Or you may want to go to a garden center (*tuincentrum*) where there is a large selection. In addition to flowers and plants they also sell gardening supplies, ground, compost, fertilizer, pots, baskets, everything you might need. There are a number of garden centers you can visit to get ideas, and there are special ornamental gardens on display and garden shows.

Local Sources

If you are looking for flowers and plants on the market – try purchasing at the end of the day, in the late afternoon, say 3:30 or 4:00 P.M. or so. The vendors want to get rid of their stock of plants and flowers and rather than take it back with them again – and offer their goods at greatly reduced prices. Often you can get really 'give away' prices, or *twee halen één betalen*, which translates into 'take two – pay for one.' Pots are less expensive on the market as well.

Town and Country Fair

Sometimes you will see signs or ads for a 'town and country fair'; these are (outdoor) lifestyle events that are often held on the grounds of a castle or country estate. Vendors set up inspiring displays, and many unusual items are offered for sale.

Design

If you are choosing to completely renovate your existing garden, you will need to hire a *tuinarchitect* who can design the garden for you drawing up a *tuinontwerp*, or you can design it yourself and hire a *hovenier* to take care of the physical work of laying out the stones and delivering and planting trees, shrubs and plants. A maintenance contract will provide you with upkeep, pruning and replacement of plants as well as gardening advice.

Courtyards & Roof Terraces

Some city homes are fortunate enough to have gardens but this is often the exception rather than the rule. Many homes in the cities either have only a *binnenplaatsje* (very small courtyard) or they have no garden at all. If possible, with permission of the landlord, and a building inspection that the roof can support the weight, many people are fond of installing roof top gardens (*dakterras*), for the enjoyment of a garden on their roof terrace.

City Gardens

Even in small spaces you will see great utilization of space to beautify the towns and cities. Pots filled with plants, benches filled with potted plants, flowers in old wooden shoes, street tiles removed and flowers planted next to buildings, even neighborhoods working together to place plants around the bases of trees in residential areas, or to plant flowers around local playgrounds.

You will also see flowers planted in the parks, in the median strips of some of the highways, in decorative pots from the municipality, or along the street you live in. The municipality is responsible for the design and upkeep of these areas, and even though you might have one right in front of your house, you are not allowed to 'mess with it' – even if it has a tree that takes away the lovely afternoon sun from your favorite corner in the garden (or sun room!). If you do, you run the risk of a visit from a local civil servant, who will tell you (sometimes rather sadly) that what you have done is quite illegal.

As for removing a tree in your own garden, here too you may not just chop it down. You will need to ask for permission to remove trees larger than 10 centimeters in diameter. Request a *kapvergunning* from your local *gemeente*. This is to ensure that Holland stays green, protects its remaining trees, and that people don't decide to play lumberjack in their backyard! If in doubt, check it out before hacking away.

Beautification Committees

In some areas there are 'beautification committees' (*schoonheidscommissies*) who will inform you if your garden is not being well maintained. You are expected to keep your hedges trimmed, grass mowed, and take care that the plants in areas visible to your neighbors or passers by give a good, well-kept impression. If you do not want to do all this gardening maintenance in the weekends you can hire a gardener (*tuinman*) who will come as often as you specify and trim plants, maintain the property and clear debris. You can find someone through a garden center, or through the local newspaper. Occasionally in contracts for rental houses the landlord will insist on having the services of the gardener included as part of the agreement. This will ensure that everything in the garden is well tended.

Volkstuin

For people who live in apartments and have no access to gardens at all, the local government rents out 'people's gardens' (*volkstuinen*), also known as victory gardens.

Many people enjoy growing their own vegetables and flowers in these little plots. Often small garden houses will be constructed and these *volkstuinen* serve as a green oasis away from home. Some elementary schools also maintain these gardens in order to teach children about the care of growing plants and your own food. See also: www.volkstuin.pagina.nl.

References

Whether you are intending to bring the green inside and decorate with plants, or work on making your garden a little paradise for your enjoyment and relaxation, you certainly have enough resources here in the Netherlands. There are a multitude of plants, products and services available. Take the time to enjoy your garden on the days that it does not rain... the climate here makes that a luxury at times!

Garden Design

Intratuin is a well-known chain of gardening centers where you can purchase just about everything you may need for your house plants as well as all your garden needs. They will give you advice, and can design and execute new garden plans for you. Periodically, and especially around the holidays different types of demonstrations are given on making decorations with plants and natural materials.
Visit: www.intratuin.nl

Another group of garden centers for supplying all your 'green wealth' is Groenrijk. Visit: www.groenrijk.nl
The best starting page for gardeners is www.tuin.pagina.nl
Here you will find sub headings on the following suggestions and much more:
Garden Clubs – *Tuinvereniging*
Gardening events and fairs – *Tuinevenementen*
Garden Furniture – *Tuin meubilair*
Garden houses – *Tuinhuis*
Botanical gardens – *Botanische tuinen*

For a complete listing of gardening centers and supplies also flower or bulb sites, see:
www.tuinbouw.pagina.nl – gardening start page listing relevant sites
www.bloembollen.pagina.nl – flowering bulbs

Gardening

To locate help there is a national listing of *hoveniers* and *tuinman* see: www.uwtuinman.nl

They also have a professional organization called *Vereniging hoveniers en groenvoorzieners* which lists some 1200 certified *hoveniers* per region: www.vhg.org

For the amateur gardener there is www.avvn.nl, which is the Dutch chapter of the international garden hobbyists organization, which counts some 3 million gardening members worldwide

The Netherlands Flower bulb Information Center has a beautiful website: www.bulbsonline.org

Gardening enthusiasts will also enjoy www.tuinweb.nl

To get some new ideas from the photos and illustrations as well as useful addresses, you may like to have a look at some Dutch gardening publications:
De Watertuin for water gardens – www.watertuin.nl
Bloemen en Planten, a magazine over flowers and plants – www.bloemenenplanten.nl
Groei & Bloei, lit. Growing and Blooming – www.groei.nl
Mijn Tuin – lit. My Garden will be entitled 'Home and Garden' www.mijntuin.nl
The best starting page is www.tuin.pagina.nl. Of course there are more starting pages such as www.bloemen.pagina.nl for flowers and www.planten.pagina.nl, as well as the same for fruits and vegetables, respectively www.fruit.pagina.nl and www.groenten.pagina.nl

Glossary

stone or brickwork	(*sierbestrating*)
brick	(*stenen or klinkers*)
garden tiles	(*grindtegels*)
plants	(*planten*)
shrubs	(*heesters*)
trees	(*bomen*)
dividing fencing	(*schutting*)
lighting	(*tuinverlichting*)
ornamental items	(*tuin ornamenten*)
statues	(*beelden*)
small pond	(*vijver*)

Special Events

Special events are held whereby you can admire Dutch flowers and horticulture at their very finest. Check with the vvv for details. www.vvv.nl

www.floriade.nl – mega manifestation flower garden show held once every ten years. This year 2002 it will be held in Hoofddorp, near Amsterdam and Haarlem. The terrain took ten years to build and showcases plants from Holland and around the world.

www.keukenhof.nl – The 'kitchen gardens' have visitors from just about everywhere on the planet, it is THE place to go to see spring bulbs. The Keukenhof also hosts a 'Zomerhof' in the summer months featuring dahlias, roses and other summer flowers.

To have a look around and visit some Dutch people's gardens, a number of 'open garden days' are organized each year. For details see: www.opentuindagen.nl

For inspiration and a look at the millions of flowers and plants that are bought, sold and exported from the Netherlands, an early morning visit to the Aalsmeer Flower auction will leave a lasting memory. See www.bloemenveilingaalsmeer.nl for directions and opening times.

For general gardening information in English see:
www.yourgarden.com
www.gardenweb.com
www.uk.gardenweb.com – gardening info from the UK
www.dutchflowers.com – a Dutch bulb site in English

13

13 Safety – Veilig Wonen – Protection of Property and Goods

Along with the concept of *gezellig* or the feeling of cozy living, you will also want to be sure that you have taken adequate measures, and all necessary precautions for your safety (*veiligheid*). *Veilig wonen* is living safely. Though Holland does not have a particularly high rate of crime, those living in cities are at greater risk proportionately than those in smaller communities, though any house could be a potential target for thieves. A free-standing house that is unlit and vacant could be an open invitation to *inbrekers* – or the thieves who 'break in'.

Open Curtains

Although it is customary for the Dutch to leave their curtains open so that you can see into their homes, it is generally not a good idea to show off too many possessions. Though this may seem like a contradiction, you should understand that the Dutch in their openness want to show they have nothing to hide, and that there is nothing un-towards going on in the home (they *do* frown on ostentatious displays of wealth, so a moderately low profile is advised). However, having expensive television, stereo and computer equipment out in full view might prove to be too tempting. Likewise leaving a pocketbook or wallet on the table, or jewelry you have removed from your person could peak the interest of a potential thief.

Security Situation

Most local police departments have a program called *Veilig Wonen* and will send an expert to come to your house and do a thorough check of your current security situation. This service is free of charge as the intention is of course to prevent burglaries. The police expert will provide you with advice and suggestions for improving your security measures.

Going on Vacation

When you go on vacation or are traveling for an extended period of time, you may fill in a card for the police to let them know the house is vacant. They will then alert the officers to keep an eye open for any unusual activity. A good electronic security system is also advised (see next paragraph).

Some tips:

either use house sitters during an extended absence, or have neighbors come and go so that the illusion of activity is given. Have them open and close curtains

- leave books and magazines lying about, old wash on the line, even dishes in the sink; give a 'lived in' appearance
- have the neighbors park their car in your driveway
- always leave your vacation address and contact number with someone here
- make sure newspapers have been stopped, and have your mail picked up
- be cautious about address labels being too visible on your suitcases at the airport
- let the police know the house will be vacant for a week or longer, also let them know who will have a key and access to the house (for plants or house pets).

Security Companies

There are security systems companies (*beveiligingsbedrijven*) with security specialists who can install security systems for you. They can help you with alarm systems, video cameras, security fences, electronic eyes, movement detectors, security lighting, etc.

In order to ascertain that you are dealing with a reputable agency for your security needs, look for the BORG *Certificaat* registration. Not only does this guarantee the reliability of their personnel and the quality of the work, it also is recognized by insurance companies, whereby you may be entitled to discounts on your personal property (*inboedel*) and homeowners' insurance (*opstal verzekering*). The National Centrum voor Preventie publishes a list on their website. See www.ncpreventie.nl under NCP *erkend* BORG *bedrijf* for a listing of those security companies who have this accreditation. Always ask if a company has this certification before doing business with them.

A house that is properly secured reduces the risk of theft by 80% to 95% you pay a small price for your piece of mind by having taken adequate security measures.

Locks

Make sure you have good locks on doors and windows. Double locks on doors, or dead bolts can offer additional protection. A *dievenklauw* is a special lock that prevents entry.
A locksmith can install these for you, or you can purchase locks your self at a hardware store or building market.

Emergency!

Should you have an emergency and need the police, the fire department or an ambulance, the national number for all services in Holland is: 1-1-2. You should have a 1-1-2 sticker on your phone, and let all family members know this is the number to call if a serious emergency arises. The operator will send the services you need, or all three if required.

Fire Protection

All homes should have smoke alarms, and they are easily installed. If you are renting, ask your landlord to do it. If he is unwilling to do so, do it your self. The life you save could be your own. If a fire breaks out, you generally have less than three minutes to vacate the premises before it is too late! Don't worry about trying to carry out belongings, get yourself and your family to safety. Property can be replaced, people cannot.

You should also plan an escape route in the event of a fire, and make sure each family is aware of the emergency plan. A practice run with children is a good idea. If you live in an apartment building, or occupy upper bedrooms in a house, an escape ladder could save lives. There are not always fire escapes on buildings, and central stairwells could be blocked by flame or smoke. Small fire extinguishers can also be purchased at hardware stores and building markets, and one should always be available in the kitchen. Fire blankets for kitchens and powder extinguishers are also available.

Occupant Identification Card – Meterkast Identificatie Kaart

You can fill out a special red, white and blue identification card, whereby you will list the names of all of the occupants of the house (including pets) which is then to be hung in your meter closet (*meterkast*) in the hallway. In the event of an emergency, or a fire, the police and fire department will first look here for any information on the inhabitants of the house. You may have received a card from your relocation company, if not, they are available at your local police bureau.

Lighting

When it comes to lighting, here are a few suggestions:

- make sure there is good exterior and interior lighting. Use a timer for the lights
- multiple timers with movement detectors on exterior lighting offer sequenced lighting and can detect movement of thieves in the garden
- interior lighting using energy saving lamps and a timer will give the appearance of occupancy
- make sure you keep your hedges and bushes trimmed, don't provide a hiding place for thieves.

Documents

Taking the necessary precautions will help to put your mind at ease, knowing that you have done everything possible to make your home a safe place to live. In addition to taking care for the fire and theft protection of your home, it is also recommended that you have multiple copies of essential documents, and the following original documents kept in a safe place:

- a copy of each family member's passport showing pages with photo and personal information
- birth certificates for all family members
- marriage certificate
- divorce and child custody papers
- home country driver's license
- passport-size photographs for all family members
- certificates of citizenship for naturalized individuals
- adoption papers
- medical insurance coverage
- medical records from home country and last posting if possible
- dental records (also from last posting if possible)
- property records for real estate abroad
- motor vehicle registration and auto insurance records
- income tax records for several previous years, covering your world income
- last will and testament
- power of attorney for designated individual
- lease or rental agreement for housing in your new country
- employment contract and benefits coverage review
- donor codicil or living will
- list of all credit cards and expiration dates with the telephone numbers needed to block their use in the case of theft
- list of all bank accounts, investments and other financial information
- insurance policies and bank account statements

- diplomas
- school records for children
- household inventory list with photographs (and receipts if purchased here).

In the event of an emergency evacuation having access to these documents is essential. Should you have to report stolen property, file a police report, submit insurance claims, block credit cards, or replace damaged or missing items, you will have all the information you need in your possession. As the saying goes 'forewarned is forearmed' so do be conscientious and have your affairs in order. It pays to be prepared.

A Few Extra Security Tips

Here are a few extra good ideas:

- mark, register and photograph your valuable belongings
- keep an updated inventory list
- always lock doors and windows when you leave the house
- use good quality locks and bolts
- small windows can also be a point of attempted entry
- make sure the quality of the door and window frames is strong; a lock will do no good if the construction is weak
- be careful where you hide extra keys, and to whom you give keys to, as well as where you keep them in the house, including the reserve set. Do not just keep keys lying about or in a kitchen drawer, keep all keys in a safe place, or in a locked (key) cupboard
- do not leave ladders, garden furniture and trash containers easily accessible for burglars to use them to climb into your house
- do not leave tools lying about that could be used by a thief to gain forced entry.

References

For additional information, and companies that can help you be more safe and secure, check the pink or yellow pages of your phone directory under:

Beveiliging (Inbraak preventie)	security systems, in break prevention
Brandbeveiliging	fire protection
Sloten	locks
Slotenmakers	locksmiths
Slotenservice dag en nacht	locksmith service around the clock
Sleutels	keys

Starting Pages

www.veiligheid.pagina.nl – everything having to do with safety or being *veilig*.

Some suggestions on agencies in the Netherlands:
www.ncpreventie.nl – National Center for Prevention
www.politie.nl – police website
www.brandweer.nl – fire departments in the Netherlands
www.minjust.nl – Ministry of Justice
www.asisonline.org – American society of industrial security (see Benelux division)
www.minbzk.nl – disasters (*rampen*) prevention and plan
www.vpb.nl – safety (*veiligheid*) organization

Home Safety

www.ecosa.org
www.safewithin.com
www.cdc.gov/niosh/nasd/menus/tophome.htm
www.rospa.org.uk
www.babyproof.com
www.babysafe.com/tips.htm
www.safekids.org

14

14 Recycling

In general the Netherlands is considered to be a very 'green' country; not just for its wide-open fields, but also for the mentality of the Dutch in protecting their environment. A vast majority of the population takes part in various recycling efforts. From the organic waste, which is collected separately, compost is made which is then reused in gardens and agriculture. Of the more than two million tons of paper collected, close to 90% is recycled and used for new products. More than 85% of all glass is recycled. There are many organizations working to maintain the welfare of the people and monitor issues such as living space, respect for nature, space and raw materials.

Environmental Ministry

The Dutch Environmental Ministry VROM (Ministerie van Volkshuisvesting Ruimtelijk Ordening en Miliuebeheer) works in close cooperation with international and domestic partners on improving the living environment of this country. Over 4,000 people are concerned with issues of living space, housing and environment. An additional task is to plan, conduct and supervise the building of projects in government housing, and to develop a sustainable environmental policy. There are numerous programs and activities for getting involved in helping to preserve and improve the environment.

Rules and Regulations

To foreigners coming to live in the Netherlands, the rules and regulations may seem to be bewildering in their detail, so here is a basic guideline to the most common recycling practices.

1. **Recycling tax**: upon purchasing new electronic and household equipment, you will automatically be charged a recycling tax or removal tax known as

verwijderingsbijdrage. Regardless of whether you are handing in an old appliance or not. The assumption is that, for each new appliance purchased, the old one will have to be environmentally disposed of or recycled at some point in time. A list of tariffs is available from the store.

2. **Household waste**: outside of Amsterdam, households are usually furnished with two separate waste containers (green *groenbak* for garden, fruit and vegetable waste and gray *grijs container* for all remaining waste). These containers are emptied on alternating weeks. Pay attention – if you place the wrong container at the curbside it will not be emptied. In some cities the city provides a multi-purpose waste container, a so-called *duobak*. This is one container with a separation inside. The smaller part in the back is intended for 'green' waste, the larger part in the front for all other waste. If you feel the container(s) provided is/are not sufficient, you can always contact the city council for an additional one. This will entail an additional yearly contribution, as the additional waste also needs to be disposed of. Make sure you do not leave your containers on the street at the end of the day. You can be fined for not returning them to your home. There are also towns where glass and paper are also collected curbside, usually in wealthier suburban areas.

3. **Groenbak**: cat litter and used baby diapers are not considered organic waste for the *groenbak* and should be placed in the gray container. Milk packages, plastic bags, large pieces of wood and thick tree branches, the ashes from your fireplace, sand, dog and cat hair and the contents of your vacuum cleaner are also NOT to be placed in the green container. 'Green waste' is vegetable, fruit, and potato peels, leftover cooked food, fish and meat leftovers with bones (wrap in newspaper in the summer months) nut shells and eggshells, hardened cooking fat, tea bags, coffee filters with coffee grains, small garden trimmings, mowed grass and leaves, weeds, flowers and houseplants, straw and *mest* from small animals such as hamsters and rabbits.
   In some cities, due to the lack of space, there unfortunately is no separation of waste, other than what a private individual brings to the separate waste disposal stations and/or containers. Most towns publish a calendar, distributed in January to each household, of contact addresses for properly disposing of all types of wastes, as well as pick-up dates and locations for chemical cars (*chemokars*). Request one from your sanitation department (*gemeentereinigingsdienst*).

4. **Refunds on bottles**: most glass soft drink bottles, the large acrylic plastic *euroflessen* and some small glass bottles or jars have a deposit that is paid upon buying them. The word *statiegeld* (deposit) and an amount will be listed on the label. Once you return these to the store for recycling (there are special

bottle stations for these at most supermarkets), the deposit is returned to you by way of a paper receipt (*bonnetje*) after you have placed the bottles into the bottle return machine. This receipt can be redeemed when you pay for your groceries or at the customer service (*klantenservice*).

5. **Glass**: all glass that does not have a deposit can be dropped in special containers which are usually placed at convenient locations throughout the town. There is often a symbol on the label showing a hand with a bottle and the word *glasbak*. These 'glass collectors' (*glasbakken*) are often, but not always, yellow. Some cities allow for the separation of white, green and brown glass. The containers will stipulate *bont* (white) *groen* (green) or *bruin* (brown). Since this effort was started, the Dutch have come to recycle more than 89% of their glass.

6. **Paper**: often placed near to the glass recycling containers you will find the blue paper collectors (*papierbakken*). Again, most of the paper in the Netherlands is recycled. You may recycle newspapers, magazines, junk mail, envelopes, paper packaging, wrappers. No plastic please.

7. **Batteries**: most supermarkets and some stores and schools have special containers for collecting old batteries. Often these are located by the bottle recycling station at the grocery store or at the checkout counter of stores; the *batterijenbak* is usually red or blue. If none are available close by, you can ask at the supermarket or inquire with the city council on the nearest collection points (batteries can also be handed in with other chemical waste – see next point).

8. **Chemical waste** (paint and painting materials, oil, turpentine, nail polish and caustic cleaning agents, etc.): many cities have a special car (*chemokar*) that comes by every three months to collect chemical waste. You can check with the city council on collection dates and times or request the calendar listing all relevant contact information for the year. Alternatively you can dispose of these materials, as other large pieces of rubbish (construction waste, car tires, etc.) with the waste separation and recycling station that is available in nearly every city.

9. **Medicines:** outdated prescriptions and any overdue non-prescription medicine can be handed in at most pharmacies for proper disposal. Pills, cough syrup, suppositories, antibiotic crèmes, etc. should all be disposed of via the pharmacy.

10. **Clothing:** some cities have a large container for clothes and shoes, generally by local organizations, and most often located close to a shopping area.

During the year there are often also special initiatives by schools or churches to collect clothes for specific charities. Apart from the Salvation Army (Leger des Heils) you can contact the following toll free number to get information on addresses to hand in clothes: Stichting Kleding Inzameling Charitatieve Instellingen (KICI), tel.: 0800 022 80 90 or www.kici.nl

11. **Large waste** (*grof vuil*): any furniture (if not recycled through second hand shops) and large household debris can be collected by special appointment through the city's waste collection department. Within certain volume limitations, this waste will be collected free of charge, but it has to comply with certain regulations, e.g. wooden parts have to be gathered and tied with rope. Anything outside city regulations is best brought to the municipal waste separation and recycling station (*afvalscheidingsstation*) or, alternatively, one could order a private container to collect and dispose of all waste. This waste container (*puinbak* – generally used during construction for large amounts of debris) can be ordered for a fee covering the delivery and removal. Contact your town hall and ask for *gemeentereiniging grof vuil*.

12. **Small litter**: every citizen is expected to keep the streets clean and there are trash cans everywhere. As there is a fine on littering, it is advisable to put your trash in the bins. More and more, on large highway exits, there are 'can collectors' (*blikvangers*); large nets where you can dispose of the remainders of food and drink from in your car.

13. **Second hand shops** (*Kringloopwinkels* or *Tweedehandswinkel*) (also Salvation Army): anything that you no longer need is by no definition a throwaway item. Many people can be made very happy with furniture, toys, clothes and other household goods that you no longer need. Clothes in good condition can be brought to special second-hand clothing shops and left under your name for resale. If the items are sold you will receive a small payment. If you do not collect the unsold garments after three months the clothes will be donated to charity. Second hand stores specializing only in children's clothes, shoes and toys have become increasingly more popular. For household goods, appliances that still work, paintings, books, tools, etc. it is always worthwhile to check with a *Kringloopwinkel* or the Salvation Army; they will often come to collect your things for free. You may of course also drop them off there yourself.

14. **Shoes**: some shoe stores have a recycle bin where you can deposit your old shoes. These are either donated to charity or properly recycled.

15. **Eyeglasses**: many eyeglasses can be reused for others. Ask your optician about recycling.

16. **Books**: there are also bookstores dealing in used books (*tweedehands-boekwinkels*). Many will take English or other-language books. Old and antique books may go to an *antiquariaat*. In addition, many expatriate clubs and international schools have book drives to raise money for charities or to send the books to schools in developing countries.

17. **Afvalscheidingsstation** (waste separation and recycling station): anything that is too large or specific (e.g. chemical waste) to be put in your regular waste container can be taken to a waste disposal station. For private individuals the rules here are pretty lax, as opposed to business disposal of waste, which usually comes at a price. You will usually be questioned upon entering the station as to what kind of waste you want to discard and will be directed to the right locations. There are, for instance, separate containers for wood, cardboard, tires, stones and construction rubbish and chemical waste. It bears to be kept in mind that any soil and earth removed when redoing a garden is generally not accepted unless a special government inspection (at a price) has taken place to ensure that it is not polluted by contaminants such as oil, lead or chemicals.

18. **Toner and Printer Cartridges**: these can be recycled and sometimes can be refilled and reused. You can check to see if your municipality (*gemeente*) has a program for collection (often, they are collected together with other chemical waste), or possibly the company you work for. See www.empties.nl for more information on disposal and reuse.

19. **Computers, Printers and Scanners**: if you need to dispose of ICT equipment in working order you can contact ICT Netherlands, tel.: 0348 493 636, and ask about *grijsgoed* (gray goods) recycling. Another option is to donate your old computer equipment to Stichting Computer Bemiddeling Onderwijs, www.scbo.nl, where it will be used for educational purposes in schools. Another benefit: your contribution is tax-deductible.

20. **Flea markets and Fancy Fairs**: many towns have flea markets, vlooienmarkt, where you can rent a table and sell your goods. Churches and schools also organize fancy fairs or a rommelmarkt, where they will be happy to have your contributions. The biggest rommelmarkt of course takes place on Koninginne-dag, April 30th, the Queen's mother's birthday, when the whole country turns into one huge flea market. On this day, it is a free market, and you can sell your goods on the street. Two of the best-known flea markets are the Zwarte Markt or 'black market' in Beverwijk and the Darling Market in Rijs-wijk near The Hague. See www.zwartemarkt.nl or www.darlingmarkt.nl or con-tact your municipality (*gemeente*) for a listing of local community flea markets.

21. **Dogs**: you are required to have your dog make his deposits in the street at the side of the curb (*goot*) and not on the pavement where pedestrians may carry it off upon their shoes. The best course of action is to take along a bag or shovel to remove the waste and dispose of it properly. Many cities have special dog toilet areas (*hondenuitlaatplaatsen*) where your dog can go to do his duty. There you will also find special plastic containers where you can deposit the waste material. There are handy 'pooperscooper' bags available from pet shops.

22. **Christmas trees**: after the New Year celebrations, on around the 3rd or 4th of January, there are used Christmas tree collections. Children will often haul away your tree for you if you put it on the street, whereby they will receive 20 eurocents per tree and a *lootje* for a chance in a prize drawing. All the collected trees are either put through the wood chipper or burned.

Becoming Involved Yourself

If you wish to become involved in a local environmental group you may check with your *gemeente*. There are 'eco-teams' in many neighborhoods who work to increase awareness of the necessity to recycle and to protect our milieu or environment. Some local projects are carried out.
For additional information on environmental policy and recycling contact VROM, the Ministerie van Volkshuisvesting Ruimtelijk Ordening en Miliuebeheer.

We all have the responsibility to help to keep the environment that we live, work, and recreate in livable – not only for ourselves but for future generations as well.

References

www.vrom.nl – VROM – The Ministry of Housing, Spatial Planning and Environment
www.snm.nl – Stichting Natuur en Milieu – The Foundation for Nature and Environment
www.milieucentraal.nl – Center for the Environment
www.foei.org – Friends of the Earth Netherlands chapter
www.greenpeace.nl – Dutch activities for Greenpeace

For all relevant resources concerning all aspects of the environment use the start page: http://milieu.pagina.nl

15

15 Recommended Reading

We are fortunate in the Netherlands to have a large expatriate community and therefore a number of excellent support resources by the way of magazines, books and the Internet, especially for the foreign resident. As the saying goes, 'why re-invent the wheel?' Many expatriates and other experts have written a variety of helpful information:

Our recommended reading list:

Books

The Holland Handbook – the most comprehensive guide to living in the Netherlands featuring expert advice, beautiful photography and a multitude of excellent resources. Chapters well indexed. Annual updates. www.hollandhandbook.com

At Home in Holland – a practical and informative guide to all aspects of living in Holland, written by expatriate women, based on real life experiences! Excellent index for searching for particular items or interests. A best seller, now in its 9th printing.
Available form The American Women's Club of the Hague www.awcthehague.org

Dealing with the Dutch – written by the KIT from an expert on cross-cultural issues, an engaging and humorous overview to understanding the Dutch in order to deal with them in the workplace as well as socially

Minding your Manners – a guide to Dutch social and business etiquette takes a look at some of the usual and perhaps unusual Dutch customs where you will need to mind your cultural manners, on any number of occasions

Getting Connected – A guide to (Tele)communications in the Netherlands – a summary of options for connecting telephone, internet, cable for your communication needs. www.xpat.nl

Here's Holland – the ultimate guide for traveling in and around Holland, offering many tips and suggestions for seeing the country and its attractions. www.heresholland.nl

The Low Sky – delves into details historically as well as socially, of the Dutch character, giving the reader a better appreciation of what makes the Dutch so singularly unique

The Low Sky in Pictures – outstanding photo documentary of the Netherlands enhanced with excerpts from The Low Sky textbook edition. www.xpat.nl

Holland – Living with Water – a fascinating look at the centuries-old fight of the Dutch to control the water that surrounds them. www.xpat.nl

Handling Holland – A manual for international women. A book of ideas and how-to-do-it details for expatriate women wanting to make the most of their time handling life in Holland. www.xpat.nl

Food Shoppers' Guide to Holland – this book will whet your appetite while learning to food shop with mouthwatering explanations and details of where to find whatever ingredients you're looking for

Alphabet Soup – decoding terms in Dutch business, politics and society

Magazines

The *XPat Journal* – This excellent expatriate magazine is published quarterly, and offers informative articles on life in the Netherlands and highlights special events/activities. Well-researched contributions by professionals offer great resources. www.xpat.nl

Roundabout Magazine – monthly magazine which gives you access to all the 'goings-on' for cultural, social, and practical information. www.roundabout.nl

Expats Magazine – Publication with light articles of interest to expatriates, restaurant & film reviews, cultural events and editorial views. www.expatsonline.nl

Holland Horizon – is published every three months by the Dutch Ministry of Foreign Affairs and reports on economic, cultural, historical, social and political developments. www.minbuza.nl (see international site).
Each issue of the Holland Horizon is available online in six languages.

Websites

Although there are numerous websites for expatriates, www.expatica.com is geared to reporting Dutch news in English, and featuring articles about living in Holland.

www.xpat.nl –XPat Media publishers has archived articles from The XPat Journal quarterly magazine, book reviews , and a great events calendar

Other expatriate sites where the suggestions come from those who have been here awhile and already figured out a lot of do's and don'ts are:

www.awca.org – The American Women's Club of Amsterdam – see section 'Life in Holland' and the Resources links pages

www.outpostexpat.nl – website developed by Shell families with extensive information on living in Holland under the 'Europe' section.

16

16 Important Addresses

Architects

Architects (register)
Bureau Architectenregister
Nassauplein 24
Postbus 85506
2508 CE Den Haag
tel.: 070 346 70 20
fax: 070 360 30 28
e-mail: sba@wirehub.nl

Architects (research)
Stichting Architectenonderzoek
Wonen en Woonomgeving (STAWON)
Keizersgracht 321
1016 EE Amsterdam
tel.: 020 555 36 66
fax: 020 555 36 99

Architecture (biological)
Vereniging Integrale Biologische
Architectuur
Veemarktkade 8
Gebouw B
5222 AE Den Bosch
tel.: 073 621 69 43

Architects (general)
Bond van Nederlandse
Architecten (BNA)
www.bna.nl
Keizersgracht 321
Postbus 19606
1000 GP Amsterdam
tel.: 020 555 36 66
fax: 020 555 36 99
e-mail: bna@bna.nl

Architects (interior decorators)
Beroepsvereniging van
Nederlandse Interieurarchitecten
(BNI)
Postbus 19126
1000 GC Amsterdam
Falckstraat 53
1017 VV Amsterdam
tel.: 020 423 32 33

Building

Housing
Stichting Woningborg
Boelekade 3
2806 AS Gouda
tel.: 0182 58 00 04

Heating (fireplaces)
Vereniging Haard en Rookkanaal
(VHR) www.fme.nl
Boerhavelaan 40
Postbus 190
2700 AD Zoetermeer
tel.: 079 353 12 70
infolijn: 010 243 36 12
e-mail: vhr@fme.nl

Outer walls/facades (synthetic):
Vereniging van Kunststof
Gevelementenfabrikanten (VKG)
www.nrk.nl
Vlietweg 16
Postbus 420
2260 AK Leidschendam
tel.: 070 317 54 80
fax: 070 317 74 08
e-mail: kunst@xs4all.nl

Building contractors
Nederlands Verbond van
Ondernemers in de
Bouwnijverheid (NVOB)
Postbus 320
3740 AH Baarn
tel.: 035 542 79 11

Fitters/Installation
Vereniging Nederlandse
Installatiebedrijven(VNI)
Postbus 7272
2701 AG Zoetermeer
tel.: 079 321 44 02

Builders (quality control)
Buro Kwaliteitsverklaringen
Bouw (BKB)
Veerhaven 7
3016 CJ Rotterdam
tel.: 010 436 22 00

Kitchens
Algemene Nederlandse
Vereniging van
Keukenspecialisten
Postbus 762
3700 AT Zeist
tel.: 030 697 31 05

Floors (wooden/parquet)
Vereniging van Parketvloeren
Leveranciers
Westeinde 8
1334 BK Almere
tel.: 036 537 16 42

Building (environmental)
VIBA Milieuvriendelijk
Bouwcentrum
Postbus 772
5201 AT Den Bosch
tel.: 073 621 69 43

Building (wood skeletons)
Vereniging van
Houtskeletbouwers
G. Sondermanstraat 2
Postbus 647
9200 AP Drachten
tel.: 0512 52 40 60
fax: 0512 52 52 96

Handyman

Vereniging van Klussenbedrijven (VLOK)
www.vlok.nl
Postbus 582
2700 AN Zoetermeer
secretariat: 023 551 06 71
fax: 079 343 62 14
e-mail: info@vlok.nl

Building society (city)

NV Bouwfonds Nederlandse Gemeenten (BNG)
Westendorpstraat 66
Postbus 15
3870 DA Hoevelaken
tel.: 033 253 91 11

Building (national guarantee fund)

Stichting Landelijk Garantiefonds Woningbouw (LGW)
Printerweg 10
3821 AD Amersfoort
tel.: 033 455 87 90

Building (guarantee fund owner-occupied properties)

Stichting Waarborgfonds Koopwoningen (SBK)
Westblaak 32
Postbus 29160
3001 GD Rotterdam
tel.: 010 411 16 74

DIY *(periodical, helpdesk)*
Advieslijn maandblad Doe-het-zelf

Tel.: 023 556 45 00
Mon. 9.30 – 17.30

Masonry (natural stones)

Bedrijfschap Natuursteenbedrijf
Burg. Elsenlaan 321
Postbus 377
2280 MA Rijswijk
tel.: 070 336 65 55
fax: 070 319 11 79

Painters

Bedrijfschap Schildersbedrijf
Burg. Elsenlaan 321
Postbus 377
2280 MA Rijswijk
tel.: 070 336 65 00
fax: 070 319 27 37

Plasterers

Bedrijfschap Stukadoors, Terrasso- en Steengaasstellersbedrijf (BSTS)
www.bsts.nl
Blekerijlaan 1
Postbus 375
3440 AJ Woerden
tel.: 0348 42 08 44
fax: 0348 43 01 23
e-mail: post@bsts.nl

Building (general)

Bouwcentrum
www.bouwcentrum-rotterdam.nl
Schiekade 830
3032 AL Rotterdam
Postbus 299
3000 AG Rotterdam
tel.: 010 243 36 00
fax: 010 243 09 17

Roofing

Bureau Dakadvies
(bureau for Roofing advice)
Avelingen-West 33
Postbus 389
4200 AJ Gorinchem
tel.: 0183 69 96 90
fax: 0183 63 06 30
e-mail: bda@euronet.nl

Housing (public)

Centraal Fonds Volkshuisvesting
Huizerstraatweg 117a
Postbus 5075
1410 AB Naarden
tel.: 035 695 40 70
fax: 035 695 40 80

Isolation (mineral)

Centrum Minerale Isolatiestoffen
De Woerd 8
5397 AK Lith
tel.: 0412 48 15 46

Technical (advice/information)

Centrum Onderzoek en Technisch
Advies (COT)
Zijlweg 340-342
2015 CP Haarlem
Postbus 98
2050 AB Overveen
tel.: 023 531 95 44
fax: 023 527 72 29
e-mail: cothaarlem@hetnet.nl

Roofing

Dak Informatie- en Adviescentrum
www.dakinfo.nl
Randstad 20-02
1314 BA Almere Stad
tel.: 036 530 49 50
fax: 036 530 42 72
e-mail: dakinfo@tip.nl

Isolation

Stichting Dak & Wandfolie
www.nrk.nl
Vlietweg 16
2266 KA Leischendam
Postbus 420
2260 AK Leischendam
tel.: 070 317 54 90
fax: 070 317 74 08
e-mail: stidawa@nrk.nl

Isolation (glass)

Fabrikanten Isolerend Glas
Nederland (FIGN)
Gentseweg 13
Postbus 2803
2800 BE Gouda
tel.: 0182 53 78 77
fax: 0182 57 21 66
e-mail: gwo@glasnet.nl

Painters (&window fitters)

Federatie Ondernemers Schilders-
Afwerkings en Glaszetbedrijf
(FOSAG)
www.fosag.nl
Hanzeweg 17
Postbus 651
2800 AR Gouda
tel.: 0182 57 14 44
fax: 0182 57 20 83
e-mail: algemeen@fosag.nl

Floors (environmental wood)

Hart-voor-Hout-lijn (informatie
over milieuvriendelijk hout)
Tel.: 020 636 91 61
Mon-Fri 09.00 – 12.00

Isolation (outer wall)

Landelijke Specialisten Gevel
Isolatie (LSGI)
www.lsgi.nl
Zuid Willemsvaart 119
Postbus 1243
5200 BG Den Bosch
tel.: 073 613 00 03
fax: 073 613 00 41
e-mail: info@isgi.nl

Restoration Fund

Nationaal Restauratiefonds
Westendorpstraat 68
Postbus 15
3870 DA Hoevelaken
tel.: 033 253 94 39

Roofing (thatched)

Bureau Vakfederatie Rietdekkers
www.riet.com
Van Oldebarneveldstraat 69
3862 SG Nijkerk
tel.: 033 245 49 00
fax: 033 245 39 66
e-mail: henkhor@worldonline.nl

Engineers (advisory)

Orde van Nederlandse
Raadgevende Ingenieurs (ONRI)
Koninginnegracht 22
Postbus 30442
2500 GK Den Haag
tel.: 070 363 07 56
fax: 070 360 06 61

Blinds & Shutters

Rolluiken-, Markiezen- en
Zonweringbedrijven (ROMAZO)
www.romazo.nl
Einsteinbaan 1
Postbus 2600
3430 GA Nieuwegein
tel.: 030 605 64 48
fax: 030 605 32 08
e-mail: branches@metaalunie.nl

Building (woman's advisory board)

Stichting Vrouwen Advies
Commissies Woningbouw (VAC)
Faustdreef 187
3561 LG Utrecht
tel.: 030 261 04 75
fax: 030 266 10 01
e-mail: icvac@nowhere.nl

Building (quality control)

Stichting Bouwkwaliteit (SKB)
Treubstraat 1
Postbus 1201
2280 CE Rijswijk
tel.: 070 399 84 67
fax: 070 390 29 47
e-mail:
sbk.bouwkwaliteit@pobox.com

Building (ecological)

Stichting Ekologisch Bouwen
Liezeweg 29
2851 ED Haastrecht
tel.: 0182 50 30 68
fax: 0182 50 11 40

Quality Control (building, housing, etc)

SKW Certificatie BV
Markenlaan 2
1355 BA Almere-Haven
Postbus 50231
1305 AE Almere
tel.: 036 539 19 66
fax: 036 539 19 98
e-mail: skw@skw-certificatie.nl

Glass & Glazing

Stichting Veiligheidsbeglazing +
Glas Branche Organisatie
www.glasnet.nl
Genseweg 13
Postbus 2075
2800 BE Gouda
tel.: 0182 53 71 21
fax: 0182 53 12 39
e-mail: gbo@glasnet.nl

Building (subsidies)

Subsidie Afhandeling
Woningbouw
Postbus 30934
2500 GX Den Haag
tel.: 070 339 11 00

Technical (damage prevention)

Technisch Bureau Bevordering
Schadepreventie
www.ncpreventie.nl
Rembrandtlaan 31
Postbus 61
3720 AB Bilthoven
tel.: 030 229 60 00
fax: 030 229 60 10
e-mail: info@ncpreventie.nl

Building (general)

(Ver. van Certificatie Instellingen
in de Bouw,aangesloten:
BDA,BKB,KIWA,BMC,IKOB,SKG,SKH,
INTRON En Gastec NV)
Postbus 229
3000 AG Rotterdam
tel.: 010 217 14 13

Roofing (thatched)

Vereniging Dakbedekkers-
branche Nederland
www.vebidak.nl
Groningenhaven 4
Postbus 1248
3430 BE Nieuwegein
tel.: 030 606 32 38
fax: 030 606 15 69
e-mail: info@vebidak.nl

Roofing (tiles)

Vereniging
Dakpannenfabrikanten Nedaco
Postbus 473
6800 AL Arnhem
tel.: 026 442 82 22

Roofing (foils & coating)

Vereniging Nederlands
Dakrolfabrikanten
Utrechtseweg 93a
3702 AA Zeist
tel.: 030 691 86 44

Fitters/Installation
Vereniging Nederlandse Installatiebedrijven (VNI)
www.vni.org
Ierlandlaan 45
Postbus 7272
2701 AG Zoetermeer
tel.: 079 321 44 02
fax: 079 321 07 02
e-mail: wagter@vni.org

Building (private land owners)
Federatie Particulier Grondbezit (FPG)
Postbus 645
3700 AP Zeist
tel.: 030 693 45 55
fax: 030 693 37 94
e-mail: fpg@grondbezit.nl

Building (guarantee/quality control)
Stichting Garantie Instituut Woningbouw (GIW)
www.giw.nl
Kruisplein 25
Postbus 1857
3000 BW Rotterdam
tel.: 010 433 22 44
fax: 010 433 25 72
e-mail: giw@giw.nl

Building (general)
PRC Bouwcentrum
www.prcbc.nl
Goudseweg 181
Postbus 1051
2410 CB Bodegraven
tel.: 0172 61 93 44
fax: 0172 61 19 02
e-mail: p&o@prcbc.nl

Carpentry (general)
Nederlandse Bond van Timmerfabrieken (VBVT)
Postbus 24
1400 AB Bussum
tel.: 035 694 70 14

Building (claims & mediation)
Raad van Arbitrage voor de Bouwbedrijven in Nederland (RVA)
Stationsplein 29
Postbus 19290
3501 DG Utrecht
tel.: 030 234 32 22

Carpentry (quality control)
Stichting Keuringsbureau Hout (SKH)
Postbus 50
1270 AB Huizen
tel.: 035 526 87 37

Outer Walls/Facades (quality control)
Stichting Kwaliteitscentrum Gevelementen (SKG)
Veldzigt 26
Postbus 212
3454 ZL De Meern
tel.: 030 662 16 33
fax: 030 662 16 77
e-mail: skg.cert@wxs.nl

Outer walls/Facades & window frames

Vereniging van Metalen Ramen en Gevelbranche (VMRG)
www.vmrg.nl
Einsteinbaan 1
Postbus 1496
3430 BL Nieuwegein
tel.: 030 605 36 44
fax: 030 605 32 60
e-mail: info@vmrg.nl

Consumers

Consumer Interests (safety & security)

Stichting Consument en Veiligheid
Rijswijkstraat 2
Postbus 75169
1070 AD Amsterdam
tel.: 020 511 45 11
fax: 020 669 28 31
e-mail: infodesk@consafe.nl

Consumer Interests

Consumentenbond
www.consumentenbond.nl
Enthovenplein 1
Postbus 1000
2500 BA Den Haag
tel.: 070 445 45 45
redaktie@consumentenbond.nl

Consumer Interests (mediators)

Stichting Geschillencommissies voor Consumentenzaken
Surinamestraat 24
2585 GJ Den Haag
tel.: 070 310 53 10

Consumer Interests (finances)

Vereniging Consument & Geldzaken
ABC gebouw Unit 13
Donker Curtiusstraat 7
1051 JL Amsterdam
tel.: 020 684 90 55
fax: 020 686 37 19

Energy

Energy (information on subsidies)

Centraal Informatiepunt Subsidie Energiebesparing (CIP)
tel.: 010 404 66 11
Mon – Fri 9:30 – 12:30; 13:00 – 15:00

Energy (information on clean energy)

Centrum Energiebesparing en Schone Technologie
Oude Delft 180
2611 HH Delft
tel.: 015 215 01 50
fax: 015 215 01 51

Water (installation supplies)

Keuringsinstituut voor Waterleidingartikelen (KIWA)
www.kiwa.nl
Sir Winston Churchilllaan 273
Postbus 70
2880 AB Rijswijk
tel.: 070 414 44 00
fax: 070 414 44 20
e-mail: certif@kiwa.nl

Energy (wind)

Nederlandse Windenergie Vereniging
Westerduinweg 3
Posbus 1
1755 ZG Petten
tel.: 0224 56 42 78

Electro-Technical

Unie Electrotechnische Ondernemers (UNETO)
www.uneto.nl
Bredewater 20
Postbus 188
2700 AD Zoetermeer
tel.: 079 325 06 50
fax: 079 325 06 66
e-mail: uneto@wxs.nl
Geschillencommissie Electra:
tel.: 070 310 53 10

Energy (solar)

Zonne-energie Nederland BV
p.a. KEMA
Postbus 9035
6800 ET Arnhem
tel.: 026 356 24 52
fax: 026 445 82 79
e-mail: j.h.c.vanderveer@kema.nl

Energy (& environment)

Nederlandse Maatschappij voor Energie en Milieu(NOVEM)
www.novem.nl
Catherijnesingel 59
3511 GG Utrecht
tel.: 030 239 34 93
e-mail: info@novem.nl

Energy (solar)

Nederlandse Vereniging Toepassing Zonne-energiesystemen Holland (SOLAR)
Korte Elisabethstraat 6
3511 JG Utrecht
tel.: 030 232 80 08

Gardening

Garden (design/implementation)

Hoveniers Informatiecentrum
Postbus 85
3980 CB Bunnik
tel.: 030 659 55 50

Environment (general information)

Milieu Informatiecentrum
tel.: 0800 022 67 60

Environment

Stichting Milieukeur
Eisenhowerlaan 150
Postbus 17186
2502 KD Den Haag
tel.: 070 358 63 00
fax: 070 350 25 17
e-mail: milieukeur@milieukeur.nl

Environment (natural monuments)

Vereniging Bescherming Natuurmonumenten Heemschut
Nieuwezijds Kolk 28
1012 PV Amsterdam
tel.: 020 622 52 92

Environment

Vereniging Open Monumenten
Prinsenhofsteeg 10
1012 EE Amsterdam
tel.: 020 420 55 57

Gardening

Vereniging van Hoveniers en Groenvoorzienigen(VHG)
www.vhg.org
John F. Kennedylaan 99 Gebouw Rhijnhaeghe 2
Postbus 85
3980 CB Bunnik
tel.: 030 659 56 50
fax: 030 659 56 55
e-mail: info@vhg.org

Gardening

Nederlandse Vereniging voor Tuin- en Landschaparchitectuur (NVTL)
Oudebrugsteen 11-2
1012 JN Amsterdam
tel.: 020 427 55 90

Insurance

Insurances (brokers)

Nederlandse Vereniging van Makelaars in Assurantiën en Assurantieadviseurs (NVA)
www.nva.nl
Postbus 235
3800 AE Amersfoort
tel.: 033 463 14 14

Insurances (information)

Bureau Voorlichting Verzekeringen
Groot Hertoginnenlaan 8
Postbus 93450
2509 AL Den Haag
tel.: 070 333 85 00

Insurance Brokers

Nederlandse Bond van Assurantiebemiddelaars
Kersenboogerd 13
Postbus 6152
4000 HD Tiel
tel.: 0344 62 02 00
fax: 0344 61 79 28
e-mail: nbva@atriserv.nl

Insurance - Life (ombudsman)

Ombudsman Levensverzekering
Groot Hertoginnelaan 8
Postbus 990
2501 CZ Den Haag
tel.: 070 360 82 61

Insurances (helpdesk)

Verzekeringshelpdesk
tel.: 030 228 08 14

Insurance – Damages (ombudsman)

Ombudsman Schadeverzekering
Groot Hertoginnelaan 8
Postbus 990
2501 CZ Den Haag
tel.: 070 365 25 06

Insurance – Damages (supervisory board)

Raad van Toezicht Schadeverzekeringsbedrijf
Groot Hertoginnelaan 8
Postbus 990
2501 CZ Den Haag
tel.: 070 333 85 00

Insurances

Verzekeraarsinstituut voor
Preventie
Postbus 61
3720 AB Bilthoven
tel.: 030 228 08 14

Insurances (general)

Verbond van Verzekeraars
www.verzekeraars.org
Bordewijklaan 2
Postbus 93450
2509 AL Den Haag
tel.: 070 333 85 00
fax: 070 333 85 10
e-mail: info@verzekeraars.org

Insurances

Verzekeraars Instituut voor
Preventie (VIP)
Rembrandtlaan 31
Postbus 61
3720 AB Bilthoven
tel.: 030 228 08 14

Finance

Mortgage (national guarantee)

Nationale Hypotheek Garantie
(NHG)
www.nhg.nl
Paletsingel 28
Postbus 309
2700 AH Zoetermeer
infolijn: 0900 112 23 93
fax: 079 361 07 83

Taxes (office for monuments)

Belastingdienst Bureau
Monumentenpanden
Postbus 4050
3800 EB Amersfoort
tel.: 033 450 52 22
fax: 033 456 08 70

Taxes (info/advice, toll-free number)

Belastingtelefoon
tel.: 0800 0543 (free)

Ministry of Finance

Ministerie van Financiën
Postbus 20201
2500 EE Den Haag
tel.: 070 342 80 00
fax: 070 342 79 05

Taxes (registration & death duties)

Inspectie der Registratie en
Successie Rijswijk
Steenvoordelaan 370 Gebouw M
Postbus 5404
2280 HK Rijswijk
tel.: 070 372 59 11
fax: 070 396 41 25

Finance (budget information)

Nationaal Instituut voor
Budgetvoorlichting (NIBUD)
www.nibud.nl
Postbus 19250
3501 DG Utrecht
tel.: 030 2306706

Legal

Land Register
Kadaster
Hofstraat 110
7311 KZ Apeldoorn
tel.: 055 528 51 11

Government (advisory council)
Raad van State
Binnenhof 1/ Kneuterdijk 22
Postbus 20019
2500 EA Den Haag
tel.: 070 362 48 71
fax: 070 365 13 80

Adminstration (financial & land register)
Stichting Kadastrale en Financiële Administratie
Lovinklaan 1
Postbus 139
6800 AC Arnhem
tel.: 026 377 82 72

Ministry of Economic Affairs
Ministerie van Economische Zaken
www.minez.nl
Postbus 20101
2500 EC Den Haag
tel.: 070 379 89 11
fax: 070 379 72 87
e-mail: internetaanvragen@minez.nl

Notary Publics
Koninklijke Notariële Beroepsorganisatie
Spui 184
Postbus 160200
2500 BA Den Haag
notaristelefoon: 0900 346 93 93 (50 ct pm)
Mon – Fri 9:00 – 14:00

Makelaars/housing

Real Estate (intermediaries)
Vereniging Bemiddeling in Onroerend Goed (VBO)
Eerste Sweelinckstraat 25
2517 GA Den Haag
tel.: 070 345 87 03

Housing
Nationaal Woninginstituut (NWI)
www.woningcourant.com
Groenekanseweg 70
Postbus 81
3730 AB De Bilt
tel.: 030 300 22 88
fax: 030 300 22 23
e-mail: info@nwiwoning.net

Housing (general)
Stadswonen
Postbus 4057
3006 AB Rotterdam
tel.: 010 402 82 00
fax: 010 414 50 86
e-mail: info@stadswonen.nl

Housing (general)

Landelijke Vereniging Centraal Wonen (LVCW)
Grenadadreef 1J
3563 HE Utrecht
tel.: 030 261 25 85
Fri 11.00 – 12:30
and 13:30 – 16:30

Housing Corporations

Aedes Vereniging van Woningcorporaties
www.aedeswcp.nl
Olympia 1
Postbus 611
1200 AP Hilversum
tel.: 035 626 82 00
fax: 035 626 82 11
e-mail: aedes@aedeswcp.nl

Housing (general)

Nederlandse Woonbond
www.woonbond.nl
Nieuwe Achtergracht 17
1018 XV Amsterdam
tel.: 020 551 77 00
fax: 020 551 77 99
e-mail: info@woonbond.nl

Housing (general)

Woonzorg Nederland
www.woonzorg.nl
Overschiestraat 57
Postbus 90118
1006 BC Amsterdam
tel.: 020 408 66 66
fax: 020 408 65 00
e-mail:
communicatie@woonzorg.nl

Housing (general)

Stichting Stuurgroep Experimenten Volkshuisvesting (SEV)
Kruisplein 25
Postbus 1878
3000 BW Rotterdam
tel.: 010 413 09 35
fax: 010 411 42 11

Housing (real estate owners)

Huis en Eigendom, Vereniging van Eigenaren van Vastgoed
Laan van Meerdervoort 2
2517 AJ Den Haag
tel.: 070 302 80 80
fax: 070 302 80 81

W. de Withstraat 45
3012 BM Rotterdam
tel.: 010 413 75 08
fax: 010 213 37 19

Rijswijkstraat 175
1062 EV Amsterdam
tel.: 020 346 31 23
fax: 020 346 31 10
St. Annastraat 171
6524 ET Nijmegen
tel.: 024 323 75 25
(only the fist and third wednesday of the month between 14.00 and 16.00)

Housing (real estate agents)

Koophuisnet Nederland
Postbus 7001
6800 Arnhem
tel.: 026 445 22 22

Ministry of Public Housing & Environmental Planning
Ministerie van VROM
Bureau persoonlijke voorlichting
Rijnstraat 8
Postbus 30944
2500 GX Den Haag
tel.: 070 339 50 50

Housing (home owners association)
Vereniging Eigen Huis
www.eigenhuis.nl
Displayweg 1
Postbus 735
3800 AS Amersfoort
tel.: 033 450 77 50

Housing (real estate agents)
Landelijke Makelaars Vereniging (LMV)
Raadhuisplein 2d
Postbus 2541
2940 AA Lekkerkerk
tel.: 0180 66 40 99

Housing (real estate agents):
Nederlandse Vereniging van makelaars in onroerende goederen (NVM)
Fakkelstede 1
Postbus 2222
3420 DC Nieuwegein
tel.: 030 608 51 85

Housing (real estate appraisers)
Vereniging van Register Vastgoed Taxateurs (RVT)
www.rvt.nl
De Doom 23
Postbus 8025
6401 VA Heerlen
tel.: 045 560 05 82
fax: 045 560 05 85
e-mail: rvt@cuci.nl

Environment (planning & public housing)
Nederlands Instituut voor Ruimtelijke Ordening en Volkshuisvesting (NIROV)
Mauritskade 21-23
Postbus 30833
2500 GV Den Haag
tel.: 070 302 84 84
fax: 070 361 74 22

Safety

Locks & keys/security
Sloten en Beveiliging Expert (SBE)
Geestweg 3
1861 TL Bergen
tel.: 072 589 74 01
fax: 072 589 73 01
e-mail: sbe@multiweb.nl

Locks & keys/security
Stichting Slotencertificaat
Postbus 61
3720 AB Bilthoven
tel.: 030 228 08 14

Security
Vereniging Europese Beveiligingsbedrijven (VEB)
www.veb.nl
Energieweg 63
Postbus 1001
2400 BA Alphen a/d Rijn
tel.: 0172 43 72 82
fax: 0172 43 20 65
e-mail: info@veb.nl

Miscellaneous

Noise abatement
Nederlandse Stichting
Geluidshinder(NSG)
www.nsg.nl
Stieltjesweg 1
Postbus 381
2600 AJ Delft
tel.: 015 256 27 23
fax: 015 257 86 63
e-mail: info@nsg.nl

National Support of independent living for Handicapped persons
Stichting FOKUS
Van Iddekingeweg 33
Postbus 6124
9702 HC Groningen
tel.: 050 527 83 57
fax: 050 527 62 24

Disablement (advisory board)
Stichting Nederlandse
Gehandicaptenraad
www.gehandicaptenraad.nl
Sint Jacobstraat 13
Postbus 169
3500 AD Utrecht
tel.: 030 291 66 66
fax: 030 297 01 11
e-mail:
bureau@gehandicaptenraad.nl

Monuments (government)
Rijksdienst voor de
Monumentenzorg
www.monumentenzorg.nl
Broederplein 41
3703 CD Zeist
tel.: 030 698 32 11
e-mail: info@monumentenzorg.nl

Moving (general)
Savam (Brancheorganisatie
Erkende Verhuizers)
Plein van de Verenigde Naties 15
Postbus 3008
2700 KS Zoetermeer
tel.: 079 363 62 28

City councils (association)
Vereniging van Nederlandse
Gemeenten (VNG)
www.vng.nl
Nassaulaan 12
Postbus 30435
2500 GK Den Haag
tel.: 070 373 83 93
fax: 070 363 56 82

17

17 Utilities – Gas, Water & Electric

Utilities – we just can't live without them! Getting connected, plugged in, e-mailing the world, cooking with gas, snuggling in warm as toast, bubble baths, delicious meals, TV shows and video films, music and lights, it's all a part of making your house a very comfortable and functional home.

Before you move into your new home, your estate agent or housing agency will assist you in securing your utilities, and should inform you as to which service providers supply utilities to the area where you will be living. In this chapter, a few words about appliances, electricity, gas and water.

For more information on connecting you, by telephone, fax, cable and Internet services, refer to our special guide *Getting Connected*, which covers these subjects in detail.

A. Appliances

In the Netherlands, electrical power is 50-cycle frequency with a voltage of 220 VAC (voltage alternating current). If you bring appliances from overseas, such as North America, they operate at 60 cycles – 110 V, which means you will need a transformer to convert the current. Some machines can be converted, though this is expensive.
Frequency can be a problem, though newer computers, stereos and vcr equipment may have a built in frequency converter.

A large variety of excellent quality small appliances are readily available in all types and price ranges. You are well advised to purchase items here for optimal performance.

Converters

Converters (*omzetters / omvormers*) up to 1600-watt size are available in electronic shops, luggage shops and airport duty-free areas. They are useful for small appliances.

Adaptors

Adaptors (*tussenstukken*) using a plug adaptor or the universal adapter kits are quite handy and may also be used throughout your travels, as plug types vary throughout Europe.

Transformers

Transformers reduce the voltage from 220 v to 110 v, also known as 'step down' transformers. They are much heavier than converters, and quite expensive. You will need more than one if you plan on using a number of foreign appliances. Continued use of a transformer may cause premature failure of the appliance.

Large Appliances

All large appliance items such as a washer, dryer, stove, microwave and refrigerator you are better off purchasing here. Washing machines in Holland heat the water inside the machine, not using outside hot water sources as in other countries. Also, dryers from North America have too high a wattage to use in Holland. American electric stoves will require rewiring, and the power load may be too great, causing problems. Although microwaves will work with a 2000+ watt transformer, you risk damaging the internal chips with regard to the electronic programming and clock. Pre-converted appliance designed for European use can be purchased beforehand in specialty shops, though more expensive, and you have the shipping costs.

Videos

European dual-system Video machines offering NTSC/PAL playback machines will allow you to watch both North American (NTSC) and PAL (European) tapes on your European bought television set. North American televisions will not work in Holland.

Used Items

It is often possible to purchase used transformers, converters and used appliances through sales in the expatriate clubs via their magazines or website bulletin boards.

At Home

Plugs and Electrical Outlets

Plugs on appliances are two prong round pins in Holland, and should be grounded. Lamps can easily have a Dutch plug affixed; the wiring is sufficient to handle European current.

No electrical outlets are permitted in bathrooms in homes or hotels in Holland as a safety precaution. However, some hotels have special low wattage plugs for using a razor. For hairdryer use, there is always an outlet close by in the adjoining room.

Fuses

Overloading your circuit will result in tripped circuit breakers or blown fuses. Many older Dutch homes are not wired to handle today's demand for powering a multitude of appliances. Make sure that more than one or two large appliances are not operating simultaneously on a given circuit, and never plug an 110v device in a 220v outlet. You will ruin the appliance and may harm yourself.

Power Outage (Storing)

New homes have circuit breakers, so if tripped you can just put it back into position. Older homes have fuses. Familiarize yourself with them, and always have spare fuses on hand. If the power does not return, or if you do blow the main fuse, the local electric emergency service man will have to come. The main fuse is sealed with a lead locked clip, so you cannot replace it yourself.

The national emergency number is 06 – 00 13. You should post this number inside your fuse box for easy reference. They will connect you with the proper local agency.

B. Electric

Local Energy Company

A local energy company known as a GEB (*Gemeentelijk Energie Bedrijf*) supplies your electricity, of which there are many throughout the country, and they supply power through different networks. They offer a variety of services such as:

Reduced Rates

Nachttarief or daluren tarief – Energy that is used in lower usage periods (*daluren*) after 11 P.M. until 7:00 A.M. and weekends from Friday 11 P.M. until Monday morning 7:00 A.M. and all public holiday is registered through a second meter. It is almost half as expensive as the high period demand hours (*piekuren*). You can save money by planning washing, drying, dishwasher use, ironing, baking, etc. in the low rate nights and weekends.

Ecological Power

Eco stroom, also known as 'green energy' or *natuurstroom* – This electricity is created through environmentally friendly means, such as a wind turbine or solar power. You need to request this type of service separately. Proceeds go in part to finance creating even more renewable energy services. The Dutch are very keen on developing sustainable eco-energy sources.

Energy Premium

Energie premie – An energy premium that is refunded back to you when you purchase energy savings appliance (*energie zuinige apparaten*). There are also energy premiums available when you make home improvements such as special floor or wall -warming elements, a new energy-efficient central heating system, or a sun boiler.

Solar Energy

Zonne-energie by means of *zonboilers* – 'Sunshine energy'. Your GEB can also provide advice on utilizing solar energy for your home, types of equipment, subsidies available, etc.

Energy Services

Energiediensten – The GEB can inspect your home and offer tips and advice on saving energy as well as provide an approval report (*keuring*) on the electric situation in your home. They also offer *energie lease* where by you may lease an energy-saving boiler (cv ketel) for your heating needs.

Meters

Reading the meter(s) is done in most municipalities (*gemeentes*) in December or January. In some areas a representative will come read your electric, gas and water meters, in other places a card will arrive in the post and you may fill the numbers in yourself. It is also possible nowadays to send your meter reading (*meterstand*) via the Internet.

Prices and Billing

Obviously energy prices (*tarieven*) vary and energy rates generally go up and down (more up than ...) – in other words, the rates are subject to change. You are billed at a monthly rate (*maandelijks termijn*) based on your estimated use. This rate is derived in part from the past amounts used in prior years combined with the number of persons currently living in the house. If you use less energy over the course of the year, the excess paid out will not be refunded directly; this amount will be credited towards your future billing. Likewise if you have used more energy, which exceeds the amounts of your monthly payments, you will have to pay the excess, and ... your rates will go up, the excess neatly split up into 12 portions and added in for the new year.

In addition to your use, you also pay a portion for *Netbeheer* (maintaining the network) which is over kilowatt hours kWh based on the low and high and continual usage tariffs, and a *vastrecht netbeheer* which is your set rate contribution for your use of the electricity network and the meter equipment, regardless of your power consumption.

C. Gas

Seeing as we have such generous supplies of natural gas (*aardgas*), most homes are heated with gas, and many people prefer gas cooking to electric. In rural areas where gas lines have not been installed to all homes, heating may be done by way of an oil furnace fueled by an oil tank that is refilled periodically. Electric heat is also an option, though less popular than gas due to the lower price.

The Gasunie is concerned with gas as a commodity, supplying and transporting it. Its website (see the end of the chapter) provides English-language general information on natural gas and specific information on pricing as well as the liberalization of the gas market in western Europe, which may have an impact on who will supply your gas.

Your local gas service supplier can assist you with questions regarding installations and energy saving units as well as inspections (*keuring*) of existing heating or cooking equipment.

D. Water

Water management is one of the things the Dutch are very good at, and with water everywhere, manage it they do. Dating back to the olden days of *waterlandschappen*, where each town area maintained their own portion of protecting the dikes, the Water Boards (*waterschappen*) are all responsible for regulating different portions of Holland's complex water management system. From pumping the polders to keep us dry, to supplying fresh drinking water, maintaining waterways and rivers, canals, water treatment and purification facilities, water plays an important role. We turn on the tap and don't think too much about the water, we are just glad it's there!

Simply put there are three main water organizations affecting you as a consumer:

Waterschappen
The Water Boards (*waterschappen*) maintain the polders and make sure that neither too little water nor too much water is in the polder land, thus maintaining safe and healthy groundwater (*grondwater*) levels. They work with the windmills and pumping stations. Recreation water and nature areas (such as the water winning from the dunes along the coast) are also managed and maintained.

Waterleidingmaatschappijen
This is the Dutch name for water service delivery companies. These companies are responsible for providing clean and safe drinking water. There are numerous *waterleidingmaatschappijen* throughout each region of the country. They work with the local municipalities (*gemeentes*) with regard to pipelines for delivery.

Hoogheemraadschappen
The *hoogheemraadschappen* are responsible for maintaining clean surface water (*oppervlaktewater*) such as rivers, lakes, canals and delta works as well as providing safe dikes and maintaining the proper water levels (*waterpeil*).

E. Billing

Piggyback Services

In many municipalities (*gemeentes*) the billing for all of your utilities is done on one invoice collectively. It may include your electricity, water and gas as well as the local cable service provider. In other areas cable is separate, and in some places water is billed apart. The fees and/or taxes that you will have to pay for the water management of the *hoogheemraadschappen* and *waterschappen* are billed separately.

Telephone subscription and Internet service providers or ISPs are always billed separately, based on your service contract amount of use.

References

Energy

Folders and information on premiums, subsidies and service are available from your supplier. Your municipality (*gemeente*) can give you more information as to which company supplies electrical power in your area, which gas company and which water service, as well as cable for your TV.
For help with conversions in Holland or electrical problems with you will need to contact an *Elektrotechnische Installatieburo*.

Eneco energie– www.eneco.nl
Nuon energylevering – www.nuon.nl
Customer Care Center 0900 – 0808 (€ 0,10/min)

Gas

www.gasunie.nl

Water

www.water.pagina.nl – If you go onto the Internet, you will find hundreds of Dutch sites having something to do with water in every conceivable use and control.
www.waterbeheer.pagina.nl – sites concerned with water management or *beheer*.

For more insight to living with water, read the book *Living with Water*, which looks at the relationship between the Dutch and the water that surrounds them.
Scriptum Publishers ISBN 90 5594 220 0

Websites

For information and websites per region see: www.regio.pagina.nl

www.milieu.pagina.nl – For all environmental concerns, projects, groups, subsidies, energy, ministries, sewage and wastewater treatment (*afvalwater / riolering*) science and technology.

www.verwarming.pagina.nl – Sites for heating, warmth and energy concerns.

www.facilitair.pagina.nl – Facility services – numerous sites to 'facilitate' your living in Holland, service organizations, etc.

www.watersport.pagina.nl – Starting point for water sports and water recreation.

18

18 Conversions

LENGTH	
AMERICAN	METRIC
0.03937 in	1 millimeter (mm)
0.3937 in	1 centimeter (cm)
39.37 in / 1.094 yard	1 meter (m)
0.621 mi / 3281.5 ft	1 kilometer (km)

AMERICAN	METRIC
1 inch	2.54 cm
1 foot	0.3048 m
1 yard	0.9144 m
1 mile	1609 km

DRY MEASURES	
AMERICAN/BRITISH	METRIC
1 ounce	30 grams
1/2 pound	225 grams
1 pound	450 grams
2.2 pounds	1 kilogram

AMERICAN	DUTCH
3 1/2 ounces	1 ons = 100 grams
1.1 pounds	5 ons = 500 gram = 1 pond 2.2
pounds	10 ons = 2 pond = 1 kg
1/2 cup + 1 T	1 kopje
1 T	1 eetlepel (el) = 15 gram
1/2 t	1 theelepel (tl) = een lepeltje

LIQUID MEASURES	
AMERICAN	DUTCH
1 quart + 3 T	1 liter
3 T + 1 t	1/2 deciliter (dl)
6 T + 1 t	1 deciliter = 1/10 liter
1/2 c + 1 1/2 T	1 1/2 deciliter
3/4 c + 2 t	2 deciliter
1 c	2 1/2 deciliter
1 1/3 c	3 deciliter

Temperature

Fahrenheit to Celsius

- Subtract 32 and multiply by 5, then divide by 9
- Example: 68oF: 68-32=36, 36*5=180, 180/9=20oC

Celsius to Fahrenheit

- Multiply by 9, divide by 5 and add 32
- Example: 20oC: 20*9=180, 180/5=36, 36+32=68oF

OVEN TEMPERATURES	
FAHRENHEIT	CELSIUS
300	150
325	165
350	180
375	190
400	205
425	220
450	230
475	245
500	260

Disclaimer on information – Publication Housing in Holland

Prices
At the time of printing this publication all prices listed in this book were considered correct based on available information. All prices are subject to change. No rights or obligations may be derived from any published monetary amounts. All prices are given for reference purposes as an indication only.

Information
The information included in this publication has been collected from a variety of sources. Every effort has been made to ensure that the information in this publication was correct at the time of going to press. However the publishers and writers cannot accept any responsibility for the accuracy of the information included.

COLOPHON

TEXT
RMS Relocation Management Services b.v., Haarlem
EDITING
Connie Moser
FINAL EDITING
Stephanie Dijkstra
GRAPHIC DESIGN
Marlies Bredie (Manifesta), Rotterdam
PHOTOGRAPHY
Coverphoto: Marco de Nood
Additional photography: Peter de Ruig (page 136/woonark), Rob Niemantsverdriet, Ad van der Kouwe
PRINTING
Snoeck-Ducaju & Zoon, Gent
PUBLISHER
XPAT MEDIA, Van Boetzelaerlaan 153, 2581 AR, The Hague, The Netherlands

ISBN 90 5594 252 9 / NUGI 661